BREAKING GLASS BALLOONS

Short Stories of Sheer Embarrassment

SCOTT McGLOTHLEN

ISBN 978-1-7330420-0-0

For my Family...
who helped me create the earlier stories.

For Luke...
who rescued me from the latter stories.

CONTENTS

WHAT RHYMES WITH PONIES?

Contrary to popular belief, I wasn't always an adult. Long before I sported beards and tattoos, I actually lived as a full-on, literal child - void of facial hair and skin alterations. So, to start, I would like to clear up any misconceptions: I didn't hop out of the womb looking like this. I was yanked out during a C-section looking like a newborn baby.

My parents didn't intend to have another kid. However, to this day, my mother refuses to call me an accident. She labeled me as a "surprise." Except during my conception, they had already technically separated. Dad moved out of the house and the divorce papers were getting drawn up.

One night, Dad dropped by while my oldest sister, who had recently turned twelve, was having a sleepover with her friends. Once the kids were in bed, somehow my parents thought it'd be a good idea to open a bottle of wine. They got to reminiscing, which must have turned into reminiscing a little *too* much, and then BAM, my X and Y chromosomes united in some weird, dysfunctional yet perfect harmony.[1]

A couple of weeks later, my sisters found mom hovering over the toilet, crying her eyes out after having barfed. She knew what it meant. And she can call it a "surprise" all she wants, but this was the epitome of

---

1. I hope my parents don't mind me starting off this book by talking about their sex lives.

a full-scale accident. Though, if I've learned one thing, it's that accidents aren't always (if ever) a bad thing.

Because of my mom's pregnancy, these parents decided to give their marriage another go. They remain together to this day. The thing about accidents is that they can change the path you're on and make it a bit more interesting.

My folks gave me a ridiculous amount of freedom as a kid. As long as I told them where I intended to go, they'd simply tell me what time to come back. This also seemed insane seeing as how I thought time was metric all the way until age six. I didn't know what metric meant, but to me, there were a hundred seconds in every minute and a hundred minutes in every hour. That just made sense.

The one freedom I loved most was the freedom to sing. A child who loves to sing doesn't sound all that unusual. One visit to an elementary school talent show and you'll see kid after kid desperately trying to conquer the most popular song from any current Disney movie.

I, on the other hand, struggled *not* to sing. From the moment I learned to put words together, I slapped little melodies all over them. Sometimes I sang so much that it would be hard to focus on any actual task at hand. I now dub this "Attention Deficit D-Minor."

I'd sit at the kitchen table floundering to eat my breakfast before pre-school because I couldn't stop singing. I could potentially get in like two bites of my waffle (which would be slathered in peanut butter and syrup) before my eyes would glaze over and I would start crooning to the orange juice.

"Deeear miiister oraaange juice, you looook like sunshiiiine and taaaaste like a rainbooooow."

"Scottie, eat your breakfast," my mother would say to snap me out of it.

Fortunately, I didn't sing to human beings, telling them they looked like sunshine or tasted like rainbows - just my breakfast. Otherwise, I would have clearly endured bullying far earlier than I actually did. My singing didn't limit itself to food though.

"Deeear miiister Sesame Street booook, I want to take you hoooome with meeee, so my mom can read you to meeee."

"Scott, come lay down. It's nap time," my preschool teacher would say to snap me out of it. Either that or little Sally would come rip the *Sesame Street* book right out of my hands. I didn't *really* want the book. But without it, I'd have to figure out something else to sing to.

Once, a kid found a small gardener snake during recess and all the other kids ran away screaming. I overheard the teachers giggling over the fact that gardener snakes were harmless. Upon learning this information, I ran up to the snake and squatted down for a closer look.

"Deeear miiister gardener snake, please don't touch meeee. You are grooooss. Okay, byyyye." At least Sally wouldn't try to steal *that* from me.

For the most part, my family found my singing to be endearing. It occasionally got on their nerves, even if they pretended it didn't. I could sense it. A child always senses it. In any case, this certainly didn't stop me from doing it. Especially when it came to my sister Sara - the ever-so-tortured middle child.

Sara received just as much love from the family. But it wasn't the same kind of attentive love given to the first child. And it wasn't the same kind of babying love given to me (not just for being the youngest, but also for being the only boy). Therefore, by age ten, she became filled with a resentful yet colorful rage. A lot of it got directed at me but, in all fairness, I delighted in annoying the hell out of her.

If I found out Sara was having a nice time watching cartoons by herself, I would break from singing to my stuffed animals to come pay her a visit. I didn't want to watch cartoons. I wanted to show Sara how much I cared for her by disrupting her.

I hopped on the couch and wallowed all over her. "Deeear miiister television, I don't want to watch youuuuu. I'm going to turn you offfff."

"Get off of me, Scottie. Your breath stinks," she'd yell while shoving me off the couch.

The older I grew (by older I mean like five or six months), the more sophisticated my songs became. I still didn't want to sing Disney songs like the other kids. But I at least stopped singing as if I was writing letters to animals, foods, or inanimate objects, describing how I felt about them.

My lyrics became more factual *and* I made some seriously major attempts at rhyming. Naturally, these extraordinarily clever tunes would leave me as quickly as they came. Except for one. I called it "Chinese Ponies."

It seemed so random, but the inspiration obviously came from the *My Little Pony* toy collection. Like most normal boys, they were one of my favorite toys. I especially loved the sea horse pony because my mother allowed me to take it in the bath. As to why I couldn't take the other ponies in the bath, I never figured out. They were all made of the same thing - plastic and more plastic.

As to why I made the ponies Chinese in this song, I have no clue where that came from. I'd like to think that, at such a young age, I was already a liberal floating among a sea of conservatives. Thus, I always made sure to go above and beyond to include ethnic diversity in my original musical creations.

The lyrics went something like: "Chineeeese ponieeees, yappa nappa nonies."

Okay fine, the lyrics weren't quite factual. They weren't even real words with the exception of "Chinese" and "ponies." But making things rhyme was freaking hard for a five-year-old.

Deep in my heart, I wanted to use real words. I just couldn't think of anything that rhymed with "ponies." There could have been "phonies."

But children don't usually know that word or how to use it. Even if I had sung "Chinese ponies, what a bunch of phonies," that would have sounded borderline racist.

Then there is the word "alimony." Children *definitely* don't know this word, or at least they shouldn't. It'd be disturbing if they did. "Chinese ponies, I gotta pay up some alimonies."

Kids do know the word bologna (pronounced "bah-lone-ee," in case you didn't know) only because we ask for the multi-animal-meat slab on our sandwiches all the damn time. That said, the disgustingly tasty, all-American lunch meat doesn't really have a proper plural term. Bolognies? "Chinese ponies, they love to eat bolognies?" THAT WOULD HAVE BEEN PERFECT! Seriously, how could this have not occurred to me? Ugh, years of my childhood work... wasted.

Regardless of my inability to rhyme anything with "ponies," the gibberish version was a good song and a family favorite. The verse changed pretty much every time I sang it. But the chorus (as noted in the lyrics above) stayed the same. This is still true of when I start making up songs in my head today. Yes, I never fully broke myself of this stupid habit. Although my lyrics are much better now. I think.

With most children's movies being cartoon musicals, it isn't any wonder why kids love to sing so much. Be that as it may, I got much more excited when I saw real people sing and dance on screen. My mind had first been blown away by this with the 1978 movie, *Grease*, starring John Travolta and Olivia Newton-John.

I got sucked into this film with the intro credits having animation. Something like that immediately demanded my attention. The catchy songs kept the momentum going for me. Then there was Rizzo. What little boy could resist the sassy magic of Rizzo? Or was that just me?

The more I watched movies like this, the more confusing things got in the real world. At first, I thought, *Wow, I can sing anywhere in public and it will be amazing!* But then once, while walking to the park (alone), I saw a grown-up couple walking towards me. I had already been belting out my tunes and didn't want to stop.

Since they did it in *Grease,* I figured I didn't need to stop. As we approached each other, I sang louder waiting for it all to turn into some magical moment. Things got incredibly awkward. I could tell they were looking at me like I was a weirdo. Their stares gave me an odd sensation in the pit of my stomach. I didn't know what it was, but it didn't feel great.

This happened a few times and I didn't get it. Why weren't any of these onlookers jumping in to sing this totally random, made-up song with me? Why, when I sang in public, did musical instruments not start playing a fantastic melody out of nowhere to perfectly match my lyrical structure? And where in the hell were the backup dancers? I couldn't dance unless I had a minimum of at least four people behind me doing the same.

I started to get self-conscious. If people didn't sing and dance with me in public like they did in *Grease,* then undoubtedly, I was doing something wrong. I made the decision to no longer sing anywhere and everywhere like before, and not in front of anyone and everyone. I opted for safer, more private spaces. This included (but was not limited to) my bedroom with my stuffed animals, in the hot tub with some floaty toys on our back deck, or on the swing set with a squirrel in the backyard.

My favorite place for private singing was in the bathroom, particularly while sitting on the toilet. You couldn't beat those acoustics and let's face it, sitting on the toilet is boring. We all need some form of entertainment to pass the time, which is why most dads bring newspapers with them. My sisters always asked why it took men so long.

My ADD gave me the special talent of intensive daydreaming, and something about the toilet kicked my imagination into high gear. The moment I dropped trou and sat down, I took a deep breath to let the songs burst forth from my tiny lungs. Sometimes I would get so caught up in my restroom serenading that I would completely lose track of time.

"Scottie," my mom would shout from the other side of the door. "You have been in there for thirty minutes. We need to leave or you will be late for your friend's birthday party!"

Usually, I would comply, as the only thing more important than singing was birthday cake.

One summer, my grandparents (from my father's side) wanted to host a family reunion at their home in Kansas City to celebrate their long, long, *long* marriage. When you have successfully been with someone for five decades, you deserve to have a giant party so that everyone can come look at you.

I had turned six by this time, and it was the perfect opportunity to show all our relatives what a fine young man I was turning out to be. This *had* to include absolutely no singing. Even though adults sang in the movies, I officially knew that they didn't do this in real life. If I was going to be a real-life adult at six years old, I needed to zip up the old song and dance.

On the road trip out to Kansas City, I heavily practiced not singing and had become fairly good at it. It wasn't until we got to the hotel in my grandparents' retirement community that I broke. Once I put my swim trunks on and hit the pool, I just swam and sang and swam and sang. The hotel also housed some residents, so my risks of someone hearing was mostly limited to elderly people, and they salivate at any chance to give young children candy anyway.

By the main day of the reunion, I had succeeded in making sure not one single non-elderly adult heard me sing (aside from my immediate family). Surely, our relatives must have been impressed by what a mature man I had become. But because I was trying so hard to be a different kind of kid, I ended up feeling more awkward than anything. I stuck mostly by my mom's side instead of going off to play with the other kids.

Growing up, my mother was everything to me. She was (and still is) a lovely woman - tall with short brown hair that she curling-ironed every morning. Somehow that hair never came out like a bad perm, and even her slight overbite made her more pretty.[2]

"Mom," I tugged at her belt loops. "I have to go to the bathroom."

She looked down at me. "Okay. You can go to the bathroom," she said. "It's right over there," pointing about 20-feet away.

"But mom, I need you," I whined. "I neeeed you."

"Sugarfoot, you know how to go to the bathroom by yourself now. You don't need me for that anymore."

Whenever she called me Sugarfoot, my mom could practically get me to do anything. But now, she didn't seem to understand the gravity of the situation. Maybe I had been acting a little too grown-up for my own good. I didn't need her to wipe my butt. I had learned to do that a few weeks prior to this trip.

More so I needed her as a chaperone. If I went to the bathroom without her, we would get separated. I'd be all alone when I got out. What if I couldn't find her? I'd have a six-year-old anxiety attack. I kept begging her and she kept denying my requests. I had to eventually give up.

"Fine," I said, slightly defeated.

"Just knock on the door to make sure no one else is in there first," she reminded me as I headed that way. This made me more nervous.

I tapped on the door, dreading that some adult would be angry at me for disturbing their business, but luckily no one answered. I slowly peaked in to make sure it really wasn't already occupied. The coast was clear. My pants went down and I hopped up on the toilet.

I was relieved that the banquet hall had individual bathrooms rather than ones with multiple stalls. It gave me that sense of safety and comfort of being in the bathroom at home. My mom was right. I didn't need her

---

2. I know the proper term is "prettier," but when you are a kid talking about your mother, it is most definitely "more pretty."

to chaperone me. Things were going perfectly fine on my own.

I realized that, since I was in the safety of my own private bathroom, I could perhaps do some singing. I decided it best to keep working on "Chinese Ponies." It appeared to be the perfect time to fine-tune the lyrics and figure out what in the heck rhymed with ponies.

Konies. Tronies. Lonies. Gonies. Bronies. God, I wish I had been clever enough to coin the term "bronies," the modern-day word to describe manly men who like *My Little Ponies*. All the rest of these words still sounded like gibberish. It didn't matter. It just felt amazing to be singing again. And the longer I got to sing, the louder I got.

"Scottie, is everything okay in there?" Mom knocked on the door.

Uh oh. I must have gone overtime again. Thank goodness it was my mom who knocked and not some other disgruntled restroom-needer who could've heard me. I confirmed that everything had gone swell and that I would be out in a jiffy. I rushed to get myself cleaned up and situated so that I could exit and return back to my more mature self.

When I opened the door to walk out, every single person at the reunion stood there... staring straight at me. All of them, every single one, had stopped talking and remained quiet so that they could hear me singing. They heard me singing... on the toilet... the entire time... all of them. Did I mention it was all of them? They began clapping and laughing hysterically. I didn't know what to do.

I stood there frozen. That odd sensation in the pit of my stomach returned faster and harder and banged at my insides. EVERYONE HEARD ME SINGING! I was mortified. Tears climbed up my throat and shoved themselves out my eyeballs. I couldn't let them all see me cry. I did the only thing a smart, sensible, young man could do: I bolted for the door and ran away.

I ran out the door past the yards where the other kids played. I ran as fast as I could, as far as I could, like a whole hundred feet. When I reached a little creek, I threw myself down in the most dramatic fashion. I supposed I could've bounced over the creek, but it seemed like a good spot to let my incessant sobbing continue. A babbling brook would understand my sorrows.

Moments later, mom came up behind me. "Sugarfoot, why are you so upset?"

I tried catching my breath. "Everyone heard me singing and they all laughed at me."

"They weren't laughing at you," she sat down beside me. "They were laughing *with* you. They were cheering for you. They loved your singing, and they loved the Chinese Ponies song."

She pulled me into her lap as if I were some sort of *Care Bear*. I'd like to think I was a total Funshine Bear. But really, I was acting like that pissy one with the rain cloud on his belly. Behind his big grumpy exterior sat a sensitive softie.

I wanted to act so grown-up and here we were, my mom rocking me back-and-forth. I didn't want to be treated like a baby. That was the opposite of everything I worked for on this trip. Still though, it was exactly what I needed. Life became one notch less horrible being in my mom's arms. I felt safe from all of the laughter.

"But no one was supposed to hear me sing. And then everybody heard me sing… WHEN I WAS POOPING!"

Mom tried not to laugh, acting like my concerns were valid. "Yeah, that's pretty embarrassing," she said. "But you know what? This isn't the first time you've been embarrassed. And I hate to tell you this, but it certainly won't be your last either."

"What do you mean?" I asked.

"Well, we all accidentally do something silly, from time-to-time, that makes people laugh. I do it. Your dad does it. And sometimes people laugh at us and sometimes people laugh with us. The people who laugh with us are the ones that truly love us, and everyone back there at the reunion loves you a whole lot."

"But what do I do when people laugh *at* me?"

"Hmm. What you shouldn't do is run away. You should laugh too. When we do silly things, that's all it is: silly things. They aren't important. If you can laugh too, it shows everyone that you don't let silly things bother you. We can all laugh together and that makes it fun."

This made me feel more ridiculous for having run away. "How do I go back in there and face everyone?"

"I promise you... everyone thought it was cute," she said. "They liked your singing, and they liked Chinese Ponies. No one will be mean to you. If they say anything, it's because they want to compliment you. And after this, they're all going to forget about it anyway."

She did make me feel better about all of it. Although I needed approximately seven more minutes of rocking before I could go back in and make a grand re-entrance.

As we walked back up to the building, I dreaded seeing everyone turn their eyes on me again. Yet, when we walked in the door, barely a single person looked over at us. It was as if they didn't care that I had made a fool of myself. They just carried on with their adult conversations.

I continued to cling to my mother even tighter than before in fear that some random person might come up and ridicule me. Of course, no one did such a thing. As she predicted, someone would occasionally come up to give me a compliment. Their flatteries helped my embarrassment start to slip away.

Once it stopped plaguing my every brain cell, I felt free to be a kid again, which was way better than trying to be a respectable young man for all of my relatives. And with that, I stopped trying to be amongst the adults and ran back outside to go play with the rest of the children.

As it would turn out, mom was right. This was only the beginning. I had so many far more embarrassing moments that lied ahead. Granted, she was wrong about one thing: no one in my family *ever* forgot about this. Oh, and laughing at myself would be far easier said than ever done.

HIGHER FIRE

When my parents decided to give their marriage another try due to having a baby boy on the way, my dad (also named Scott) felt particularly excited. He loved having two girls, but a boy could usher in a whole new set of gender-oriented activities.

He could take his son to sporting events and play one of those ball games with him in the backyard. He could teach him to go fishing or work on the car without the boy complaining it was "icky." He could guide him on how to have a good marriage and children to carry on the family name.

Considering that everyone's first names started with the letter "S," my parents decided to name me Stephen. Then, once I was airlifted out of my mother's body, my dad, in all of his enthusiasm, suggested they name me Scott. Although technically I could not be a true "junior" with his real name being John. Scott was his middle name.

Too bad that, by the time I reached childhood, I had entirely crushed all my Dad's father/son fantasies one-by-one. Sports ball bored me to tears. Fishing and working on cars were, in fact, super icky. And I preferred playing with Barbies over GI Joes (I blame my sisters for that one).

Back then, my dad looked like an older version of me, but instead of a beard, he sported some major sideburns and a pair of coke-bottle glasses. Scott Senior was a great dad. He didn't care that he had a little boy who sometimes acted like a little girl. Well, perhaps he cared a tad, but he treated me the same nonetheless.

If my mother was the loving, nurturing one, my father was the entertaining one who caused all the fun shenanigans. He was a bit like Curious George while Mom was like The Man in the Yellow Hat. Having a boy, if nothing else, meant he could at least have a partner-in-crime. And, for this, he was also my world (just like my mother).

When we would go on shopping trips to Target, he would turn it into a game of tag. Or, better yet, we would hide-and-go-seek the hell out of each other. This mostly involved me sitting in the middle of clothing racks until he could figure out the correct one. He had crazy energy that would easily outlast mine. At some point, I would tire out and lay on the floor in some random spot. Mom prayed that no one from church would see us.

When people would ask, "What does your father do?" I would say, "He's a Nurse Anesthetist." Pretty much no one ever knew what that meant, so I learned to say "He's the nurse version of an Anesthesiologist." This drew some blank stares as well. Finally, I settled on the more ambiguous, "He does anesthesia." If they assumed this meant he was an anesthesiologist, that was their deal.

Because people often acted impressed when I said this, I learned that working in the medical field comes off as fairly glamorous, mostly due to the high income it can rake in. But the good pay came with some other kinds of price tags, one of which includes working long hours. Dad worked *a lot*.

This was absolutely okay. I never felt like I was raised in any kind of "cat's in the cradle" situation. When dad was home, he didn't sit in his recliner with a glass of scotch, watching more sports ball. He was always fully present with us.

My mom did a great job of covering Cub Scouts for him. This probably bummed my dad out more than it did me. I would not classify Cub Scouts as high on my priority list. I hated camping, and every time I couldn't tie a knot, I would cry.

Dad had a love of weird gadgets - a love which he acquired from his father (the one in Kansas City). Granddad had all sorts of crazy things that I could get my grubby hands on when we visited, like 3D mazes and 3D puzzles. If I got bored with those, I could watch *The Sound of Music* five times in a row. My favorite part was when Liesl was totally sixteen going on seventeen.

Dad brought home different kinds of gadgets than my grandfather's (mostly ones from his work). One of my favorites included the cautery, which I had trouble saying, so I just called it "the burny thing."

"Want to see something neat?" Dad asked one night before bedtime.

"Yeah!" My eyes got wide and excited for the next medical device I would get to play with.

Mom was in the bathroom removing her makeup. This always made for perfect timing so that she couldn't yell at us.

"What is it?" I asked him.

"It is a cautery," he said letting me hold it.

"It looks like a tampon!"

My life as a child was filled with SO MANY TAMPONS! When you are the only boy that lives in a house full of older women, you become far too familiar with the horrors of the female monthly visitor. I knew all about periods before the elementary school girls did.

"You're going to bleed one day," I'd tell them.

They either didn't believe me or would run away screaming. It didn't help my first-grade popularity. Seriously though, how did I end up telling them this before their own parents?

Dad laughed. "Yeah, it kinda does look like that."

"What does it do?"

He popped the cap off, which no longer gave it the appearance of a feminine plumbing product. It had a narrow white wand with a tiny looped wire at the end of it. I couldn't wait to see what kind of weird thing it did.

"Do you remember in those old western movies when the cowboy gets injured?"

I nodded, hoping there would be an injured cowboy in the backyard that my dad could demonstrate on.

"You know how his cowboy friends would help by putting a rod iron in the fire until it was so hot it glowed and they pressed it on his wound? Well, what that does is melt the flesh together so that it stops the bleeding."

"Coooool!" I was majorly impressed. "That thing can fix a whole cowboy wound?"

"No," dad laughed. "This is a small one to fix little wounds, like on a blood vessel."

I didn't know what a blood vessel was, but it sounded awesome too. I actually did like icky things as a kid. I just didn't like getting dirty.

"So you're *not* gonna fix any wounded cowboys?" I asked, slightly disappointed.

"No, Scottie, this would be too small for that." Apparently, operating rooms had different-sized instruments for different kinds of flesh-sizzling needs. "But, I will show you another fun thing you can do with it."

Dad got out a white sheet of paper and held it up with his hand. Then he held down the button on the burny thing and the wire came to a bright orange glow. As tiny as it was, I could genuinely feel the heat coming from it. He tapped it lightly against the paper. In a flash, the burny thing seared a hole into it.

"Oh my god!" I gasped. "Do it again!"

He bounced the cautery against the page a few more times and made a few more holes. I noticed that the longer he held it against the page, the bigger a hole would burn into it.

"Do you want to try?"

I nodded with excitement. He handed off the cautery and the paper.

"Don't you dare!" My mom screamed from behind us. We had been caught. "Scott, you shouldn't show that to your son."

This made me want to see it more.

"He is fine," he protested.

"He is too young. He could hurt himself."

"I'll only let him do this when I am with him. I'll make sure he is safe."

The Mom in the Yellow Hat rarely won these arguments. She'd just give up and babble to herself about how nobody listened to her while she continued to get ready for bed.

Dad taught me how to hold the cautery securely in my hand so I could push the button at the same time and not drop it. I tapped it against the paper. It burned a hole. A little smoke puffed out. I liked it. I did it again. And again. And again. Each time, I wanted to hold it against the paper just a tad longer so it would burn a bigger hole.

"Okay, that's enough now," Dad said. "We need to get you to bed."

"Can I keep this?" I pointed to the paper.

"Ummm, sure." He was a little confused.

I wanted to show all my friends at school what I did. My hole-filled paper earned me some bragging rights. Since the kids mostly made fun of me, it was one of the few things I had that made me feel better than them.

I loved having a dad who would more likely get into trouble *with* me. It made everything more interesting. Plus, if he was my accomplice, he wouldn't be the one punishing me. When other kid's dads punished them, it always sounded way worse than when their moms did it.

One time, while sitting through my sister Sara's billionth fifth-grade band recital, Dad and I both got antsy. Of course, this wasn't *our* fault. There were only so many times guys like us could withstand listening to other children play lousy renditions of "Frosty the Snowman" or "Jingle Bell Rock." We were bound to get a bit restless and lose our innocence.

Dad crinkled up his program into a ball and handed it over. "Here, throw this at your sister."

"No way! Mom will yell at me!" I whispered back.

"I'll give you one hundred dollars if you do it," he said.

I held the wad of paper in my hand debating on what I should do. Since I never played sports, I hardly had any throwing power. And Sara sat too far away for me to ever hit her. The chances of humiliating her would be slim (thankfully). It was the audience ahead of us that I worried about. Nevertheless, it would be one hundred freaking dollars! I would be rich!

There comes a time in a young man's life where he must learn to stoop to the lowest common denominator for some cold hard cash. I clutched the wadded-up program in my fist, took a deep breath, and hurled it as far as I could, straight ahead, hoping it would at least make it past the front row. It successfully sailed through without hitting any poor bystanders. But the moment it hit the ground, those bystanders turned to glare at me, and I knew I made a huge mistake.

All the disapproving scowls didn't keep my dad from laughing. He tried his best to keep it under wraps, but everyone could hear him.

"What in heaven's name was that?!" Mother tried quietly jumping down my throat.

I defended myself. "Daddy told me to!"

"You weren't *really* supposed to do that!" He said, throwing me under the bus.

There comes a time in a young man's life where he learns that stooping to the lowest common denominator for some cold hard cash doesn't pay off. I got grounded. Dad's punishment was that he indeed had to pay me the one hundred dollars.

Since this would have rewarded my bad behavior, they tortured me by putting it in a savings bond. Come to think of it… I don't know if I ever got that money or not. (Note to self: ask them to give me my savings bond.)

When it came to our tomfoolery, we knew not to mess with church. Mom put the fear of God (ironic choice of words) into Dad when it came to church. It meant a lot to her that we looked like normal human beings, especially in this place. Dressing up in our Sunday best was less about impressing God and more about impressing the other families.

Mom tried to make church as engaging as possible so that I could sit still and not misbehave. She signed me up for the children's choir. Not only would I get to do *more* singing, but I also got to stand up in front of the entire congregation while wearing a fancy robe. I never got to do a solo. Still, I'd like to imagine that I was the star of the show.

Sunday school provided some entertainment. We did things like stick a bunch of dry macaroni between two paper plates. With their raised edges facing each other, we would staple the rims, and voila! We all had our very own homemade tambourines. I had no idea what that had to do with Jesus, but I had a new tambourine!

When the opportunities to make macaroni instruments didn't exist, I basically felt screwed. Church seemed so incredibly boring. Even singing the hymns bored me. Nobody was looking at me and I only liked singing my own songs. Remember?

The moment my family stood up for the hymns, I opted out and sprawled out across their seats hoping to get in a quick nap. Right when I got comfortable, they would wrap up the song and try to sit on me.

If I had to sit up, I would immediately start to squirm around. In order to offset this, Mom would bribe me with food. If I behaved, we could all have Subway after church. I didn't like the notion of the family's lunch resting entirely on my shoulders. But I did freaking love that meatball sub. I swear they must have put heroin in it. What soul could say "no" to it?

On the days that I *did* have to pay attention in church, I couldn't wait to get home. I was practically twitching in anticipation for some trouble. It didn't matter if I got me that heroin sandwich.[3]

I'd run into my room, unzipping my khakis in such a hurry that I'd accidentally forget to take off my shoes first. I wouldn't bother to try to fix my mistake. There wasn't any time! I'd just roll around on the floor for like ten minutes, ironically wasting more time.

One day, after church, my parents had to run off and do some adult things. I don't remember what exactly. All I knew was that I behaved swimmingly in church, even when we had to sing some atrocious song about Jesus "taking us higher."

"Hiiiigher, hiiiigher," the whole congregation sang together. My sisters loved it. They wouldn't stop singing it during the car ride home. But not one objecting peep came out of my mouth. I wanted to be a good little boy for that heroin sandwich. And yet, on this particular day, I didn't get to have one.

Given that she was so much older than us, Mom and Dad left Stacey in charge. This meant that she had to cook our post-church lunch. Instead of my Sunday meatball sub, I would have to eat mac-n-cheese with cut-up hot dogs. Sara joined her in the kitchen to cook up this exquisite cuisine and it didn't take long for them get back to singing "Higher, Higher" again.

I decided to get away from their dumb song by sneaking into my

---

3. The nice folks over at Subway have asked me to clarify that they do not put heroin in their meatball sub and would like me to stop calling it that.

parent's bedroom to find some good stuff that I shouldn't be touching. After failing to find anything interesting under their bed, I turned to my father's desk. The sharp letter-opener could provide some fun. Surely something around the house needed some good lacerations.

As I was about to run off to innocently puncture things, I noticed a familiar tampon object sitting amongst my dad's pens. There it was: the burny thing. I dropped the letter-opener as my heart pounded in favor of this more disastrous tool.

After pulling the cap off, I pressed the button to make sure the wire at the end came to that good, searing hot, orange glow. To my delight, it worked. As soon as I could find some white sheets of paper, we were ready to roll.

I did exactly what my dad showed me, tapping the cautery lightly against the paper to burn those small holes. I could even make shapes like a smiley face and stuff. *Wait until the kids at school see this!*

When Dad originally showed me all of this, I asked him what would happen if you held the cautery against the paper (rather than tapping it). He said we couldn't do that, and didn't quite explain why. But I wanted to see if it would make a really, really big hole. Since he wouldn't demonstrate it, I figured I could at least now find out for myself.

As I held a few pages in my hand, I placed the cautery against the corner of the first one. A hole burned like normal, and the longer I held it there, the bigger the hole got - exactly as I suspected. I decided to do another one and hold it longer to get an even bigger hole.

When the next hole grew larger than before, a weird thing happened. The hole's sizzling edges continued to grow despite the fact that they weren't touching the cautery anymore. I took the cautery away so it would stop. However, it didn't stop. The hole got bigger and, suddenly, the paper burst into flames.

OH MY GOD! The paper's on fire! What do I do?! What do I do?! I panicked. *Stop, drop, and roll? No! That's if I'm on fire, which I might be in a second!*

The fire started spreading to the other pages and this made the flames grow larger. I had to get it out of the house immediately. But where? The front door!

I ran down the hallway screaming. "Fire! Fire!" I could feel the flames shooting out from behind me!

I screamed even harder "FIRE! FIRE!"

Except my sisters were too busy singing "Higher, Higher."

I screamed "FIRE!"

They sang "HIGHER!"

I screamed "FIRE!"

They sang "HIGHER!"

This was a fucking disaster! We were all gonna die!

I turned the corner and saw the screen door. All I had to do was get past the kitchen, push hard, and I would make it to the front yard where I could throw it on the ground and stomp it out. Was I going to make it? My feet were pounding against the ground harder than ever before. All I had to do was push on the screen door and I would be home free.

Right when I reached for the door, the fire reached my finger-tips. I instantaneously let go and my little body kept running. Before I knew it, I stood in the front yard realizing I had dropped the flaming sheets of paper. They must have hit the ground. And if they hit the ground, they must have already set the house ablaze. I had no doubt that, if I looked back, our home would be filled with smoke and I would hear my sisters screaming from inside.

But the only thing I heard was Stacey laughing from the doorway. "Scottie, why are you running around screaming fire at the same time we are trying to sing 'Higher?' Are you making fun of us?"

Even Sara was laughing in the background. They thought them

singing "higher" while I screamed "fire" was a joke. They thought it was funny. Didn't they understand that we almost died?! How could they have not seen all the flames as I ran by?

Stacey noticed the sheer terror in my face while I was bent over panting in the front yard. She figured out that I may not have been joking around after all.

"Umm, what's going on?" she asked without any laughter.

I ignored her question and ran past her, back into the house, to see everything for my own eyes. *Did our house seriously not catch on fire? How is that possible?* All I saw were a bunch of ashes all over the ground.

"I ALMOST SET THE HOUSE ON FIRE!" I cried out my confession. I grabbed her and hugged her tightly, feeling so thankful that they were safe and that we went to church so that God would like us enough to keep our house from burning down.

"What are you talking about?!"

"I was in Mom and Dad's bedroom, and I was playing with Dad's burny thing, and I set a bunch of papers on fire, and I tried to run them out of the house, but I burned my fingers, and so I dropped them, and I thought they were going to set the house on fire."

"So wait," Stacey tried grasping what I had just said. "While we were singing 'Higher,' you were *actually* running around with fire?"

"Uh-huh," I said sniffling and snotting all over her shirt.

"Oh my god, that's hilarious," she returned to laughing. "Wait until we tell Mom and Dad."

"You *can't* tell Mom and Dad! They'll kill me! Why are you laughing? You and Sara almost died!"

"No we didn't. Stop being so dramatic. It was just some paper."

I couldn't understand why they didn't understand the gravity of the situation.

Stacey made me clean up the ashes and when my parents got home, she told them all about it. After being a little concerned at first, they wound up laughing too. The whole family found it amusing. I wanted to shake them all like babies and scream! What if I killed my sisters? Or worse, what if I killed the cat?

"Well, I am just glad that everyone is safe," mom said.

Who were we? *The Brady Bunch?* Clearly, this was the worst thing I had ever done and my parents weren't belligerently screaming at me. Somehow they didn't believe that I had put my sisters, the house, or the cat in any danger. I knew the truth; I had almost murdered them all.

There's the old adage that says when you play with fire, you're going to get burned. And for the first time, I learned it firsthand. Literally. I had first degree burns on the fingertips of my primary hand. Maybe my parents figured that it was punishment enough when they saw me walking around, shaking from more adrenaline than a young boy should ever have. My dad still got punished. That night, we could hear them yelling with their door shut. After that, he stopped bringing home any medical tools from his work.

This was fine by me. I no longer had any desire to play with them. Except for many years later, in our next house, I would once again make a habit of snooping in their room. Eventually, I accidentally stumbled upon my father's gun. Don't worry though. After almost being burned alive, something as dangerous as a gun didn't seem all that tempting anymore.

THE SCAR OF DAVID

In Colorado, we have this silly social rivalry thing between the natives and the transplants. The natives argue that they are true Coloradans since they have lived here long before we became the first state to legalize marijuana and the massive influx of stoners rolled in.

The transplants argue that they are Coloradans because they take more advantage of all that the state has to offer. In their defense, the transplants do seem to ski more. The natives respond by slapping a bumper sticker on their car identifying themselves.

When comes the other argument of what makes a native a "native." Do you have to have lived here for a decade? Two decades? Do you have to have been born here? It all depends on who you ask and whether they've had their morning coffee.

Technically, I was born in Oklahoma in a town called Enid. But due to my father's love of raising hell in the hospitals where he worked, the family moved around a lot; five times before I even reached age one. My mother hated it. When we landed in Colorado, she threatened him that if we moved one more time, she would leave. He took her threat seriously, and so the suburbs of Denver became our home.

My family originated out of Texas which, in many ways, was the opposite of Colorado. Our cowboys were sooo different from their cowboys. And every summer, we returned to the south for an obligatory visit with my mom's side of the family.

In Texas, the women had big hair, the men had big bellies, and the food was country-fried everything. While drinking and driving isn't legal in the state, it *was* legal to drive with an open container in your car - something my uncle (and his big belly) always took advantage of.

Then, there was the humidity. I didn't understand why Texas felt so damn hot. It was like sitting in a steam room while wearing a sauna suit and reading Sauna Digest (if such a publication existed). We could only find relief in my aunt's kick-ass pool or places with heavy air-conditioning.

My favorite of the air-conditioned safe havens were the craft shows. The men didn't do the craft shows, but I was more than happy to join the ladies. They'd host them in these big warehouses and there'd be all these tables with all sorts of weird things that the Texas women would make, like bird feeders made from license plates, American flags made from scrap wood, and centerpieces made from cowboy boots. I would have to run around and touch all of it with my dirty fingers.

The craft shows in Colorado didn't have nearly as interesting things and, since we didn't have such an urgent need for air-conditioning, I would have preferred to stay home in my robe and watch *The Mickey Mouse Club*. Maybe I would do a little "Mousercise" while I was at it.

But that never worked out. With my dad working a lot and my sisters wanting to satiate their own craft show cravings, I would have to go too. The upside to the Colorado craft shows was that they had amazing breakfast burritos.

Sara and I would beg our mother for money to go buy some. She would only give us enough to share one. Splitting burritos in half was not easy so we always fought over who got the bigger piece. Once we scarfed it down, we'd run back to plead with her to buy us another. She always caved and never did learn that it would have just been easier to let us buy two right off the bat.

The burritos acted as more food bribery for me. This would keep me from stomping around and whining and complaining about having to be there. Once, when a craft show didn't have any breakfast burritos, my mother didn't have the energy for one of my freak-outs. She relied on her next tactic: hush money to go pick out a present for myself.

I wandered off alone to see if I could find any crafty treasures. These places probably didn't have as much potential for stranger danger. If any old lady wanted to kidnap me, the worst she could do would be to take me home and feed me unlimited amounts of caramels.

The search for a present took a lot more effort than it did in Texas. The items didn't feel as outlandish. Mostly I encountered crocheted cozies for tissue boxes and oven mitts with fabric patterns of apples. At this rate, I would never find anything.

I eventually came upon a table that sold those small stained-glass mosaic ornament things. People would hang them in windows via a suction cup and a hook. Whenever the sunlight would shine through that window, they looked extra pretty. I already had a few of them, but still, a boy can never have too many pretty things hanging in his window.

I scanned the table to see if there were any new shapes or colors that called out to me. The flowers were boring. The hummingbird was kind of cool. And then I saw it, the strangest/coolest glass mosaic ornament I had ever seen. It was like a star but different from any other star. It had six points instead of five. I counted them repeatedly. In a way, it appeared to be like two triangles overlapping on top of each other in opposite directions. The more I stared at it, the more it blew my mind. I had to have it.

The old lady vendor informed me that I didn't have enough money. I ran back to my mom in an absolute state of panic. If I didn't get that star soon, someone else totally would.

"Mom, Mom, Mom, Mom," I tugged at her shirt. "Mom, Mom, I found what I want! I need more money!"

"Hold on, honey. I'm looking at something."

She was looking at birdhouses - nicely painted ones made from real wood rather than license plates. Mom always looked at birdhouses and yet she never bought them. According to her, birds were dirty. Years later, she solved this conflict by purchasing the birdhouses and then sealing up the hole so no birds could actually get in there. Those poor birds must have been so confused.

"But Maaaaahm," I whined. "We need to go get it now!" That star was worth more than all the breakfast burritos in the entire world! I kept tugging at her shirt and begging until I could break her birdhouse hypnosis.

"Okay, okay. Here's some more money, but take Stacey with you," she said, handing the extra money to her, not to me.

By now, Stacey had gone off to college and I hated it when she went away every semester. I'd wait all summer like an army wife waiting for her soldier. With her long black hair, I saw Stacey as the most beautiful girl in the world. When I grew up, I wanted to be just like her.

Mom whispered to Stacey, "Make sure he doesn't buy anything stupid."

I grabbed my sister by the hand and we raced back over to the table with the window ornaments. The amazingly neato star was still there.

"That! That's what I want!" I pointed at it.

"Wait!" She asked. "That star?"

I confirmed her unnecessary question while trying to grab the money out of her hand.

She laughed. "You can't have that!"

"What? Why not?" I didn't see this coming. Why could I not have possibly the most amazing thing I had ever seen?

"Because that is the Star of David," she said.

I looked at her blank-eyed, not knowing what in the hell she even said.

"Scottie, that's a Jewish thing."

"What is a Jewish?" I asked, getting impatient.

She laughed again. "People aren't *a* Jewish. They *are* Jewish."

I really didn't need her linguistic lessons at the moment. I just needed that money. I tried prying it out of her hand again.

"Jewish people believe in Judaism," she continued. "It's a different religion. We are Methodists. We don't believe in the same things that they do."

I didn't get it. If these Jewishes made such cool stuff, why wasn't I one of them and why couldn't I have this star? Perhaps Stacey was making this all up because she was jealous of this star. After all, I found it first. Besides, no one ever told me that there were *other* religions out there. Why would I just now be hearing about this? I decided to call her bluff.

"So, then, what *exactly* do these Jewish people believe in?"

Stacey's laughter slowly turned into irritation. "I don't know," she snarled. Her nostrils always flared when she got angry.

"Well, if you *don't* know what Jewish people believe then how do *you* know that I *don't* believe in the same things?"

I thought I was clever as shit. Stacey did not.

"Okay, that's it!" She grabbed me by the hand and pulled me away from the table. "We're going to find Mom!"

"Fine!" I shouted. "Yes! Let's go find Mom! She'll buy me the star!"

Mom had moved on from the birdhouses to the tissue box cozies. The moment I saw her, I ran over so I could talk first.

"Maaaahm, Stacey won't let me have what I want!"

"What?" she asked slightly startled.

"I showed her what I wanted and she won't let me have it."

Before my mom could rescue me, Stacey butted in. "Yeah, but Mom, he wants the Star of David."

"But we aren't Jewish," my mom said.

My jaw dropped. Did I really have to go through all of this again? Apparently, I did.

"Why do I need to be Jewish to have this star?" I asked.

"Sugarfoot, your sister is right. You can't have that."

"But Maaaaahm, I want that star more than anything I have ever wanted in my whole life."

"I know, Sugarfoot. Really though, since we aren't Jewish, you just can't have it. You will understand when you are older."

Even if I did have the tendency to act a tad dramatic, I didn't necessarily throw a lot of tantrums. That said, without having gotten one of those insane breakfast burritos, and now not being able to have the Star of David, I was about to be pushed over the edge.

I grabbed on to the belt loops of her mom jeans and began yanking her. "Please Mommy, I need it!"

The more she tried to shush me, the louder I got.

She snapped. "If you don't stop, we are going to leave!"

She left me no choice but to throw myself on the ground and kick and scream. "WHAT DOES JEWISH MEAN?! WHY AREN'T WE JEWISH?!" I yelled out so that everyone at the craft show could hear.

Mom picked me up off the floor, telling me how terrible I was behaving. She followed through with her threat. We all left the craft show empty-handed. God, my sisters were pissed.

In the days after my tantrum, I had undoubtedly been scarred for life. I would glance over at my window ornaments and all I could see was that missing star. *What if I never see it again?* I got a bit paranoid thinking I might forget what it looked like. I had to figure out how to draw the Star of David so that I could, at the very least, keep the memory alive.

I would simply draw one triangle, flip the paper and draw a second triangle on top of it. Basically, I drew two triangles overlapping on top of each other in opposite directions. You'd think I had a knack for geometry, but no.

The dimensions were a little off, but I made my star. And the more I did it, the better I got at it, which made me excited to do it even more. I started drawing the star on anything and everything I could.

If I drew pictures for my relatives or my parents' friends (or basically any adult on the street), I would be sure to include my special star. It was clearly becoming my signature item. I could only imagine how impressed they all were with it.

They'd be thinking: *What a lovely picture Scottie drew for me. Wait a minute! What's this? Over here? It's a kind of star. Why that's not like any star I have ever seen! Where in the world did he come up with this? It's so unique! Scottie must be a creative super genius. Here, let's give him an Atari game system.*

But it never worked out that way in real life.

At least my teachers at school liked it. They would look at my drawings and gush about how fantastic they were, often calling attention to the extraordinary stars. Although they never offered me an Atari game system. This seemed strange because with all the responsibility teachers had for the children, they obviously would be swimming in pools of cash.

"Are you Jewish too?" another kid asked one day at school. He had seen my drawings.

"No, I am not," I pouted. "My parents won't let me be." It took a moment to sink in, but once it did, I immediately perked up. "Wait. You are Jewish?" I asked him.

He confirmed it, but was getting antsy about recess steadfastly approaching.

"What is it that makes you Jewish?" I asked him.

"What do you mean?"

"Well, what do you believe?"

He shrugged his shoulders. "I dunno. God?"

This instantly gave me hope. "Yeah, I believe in God too!"

"Cool. Wanna go play on the swings?"

I wanted to grill him on more details of what it meant to be a Jew. However, if we didn't go grab the swings ASAP, all of the other kids would nab them up first - especially the girls. They'd get cooties all over them. I had to get my priorities straight. First, swings. Then, Judaism. Having a new Jew friend at school did help a lot. He couldn't quite explain how our religions differed either, but he at least could tell me more of what it was like to be Jewish.

Christmas was called Hanukkah and I *loved* the thought of getting my presents spread out over eight days. I could savor it more that way. Plus, you get to light candles each night (not that I wanted to play with fire again).

I learned about delicious challah bread, the fun of dreidels, and eating kosher. The kid couldn't clarify what kosher meant, though, I liked the idea of having a very special dietary need. I daydreamed of going to restaurants and saying to the waiters, "Oh, I can't eat that. It's not kosher." I said it to my mom, which earned me a threat of going to bed without any dinner at all.

And then there were the yarmulkes - the tiny caps you can wear on your head. It was like a fashion accessory. It would hide my dad's bald spot. Really! Why weren't we Jewish?! It was quite obvious that Jews had to be like *the* luckiest people in the world. Even though I still didn't realize what it all meant, I knew I wanted to convert.

By this point, my teachers had assumed that my family was Jewish, a fun fact that didn't occur to my parents until the next parent-teacher conferences. In that slightly awkward and embarrassing moment of having to correct them, my dad decided the time had come for us to have a talk while tucking me in bed (which he didn't do unless Mom told him to).

"Scottie, this has got to stop," he said. "We are Methodist. Not Jewish. People are getting confused."

"But I *am* Jewish," I protested again. "I want to convert. Then people won't get confused anymore."

"Well, if you want to convert, we won't stop you. But since the rest of us aren't going to convert, you won't get to do some of the same things we do anymore."

He was starting to use those Jedi mind tricks, and it worked. I asked him to tell me more.

"First of all," he said. "You wouldn't be able to go to church with me, your mom and your sisters. Jewish people go to synagogues."

As much as church bored me, I did like going to Sunday school and singing in the choir. But surely synagogues have these things too, right?

"You'd also have to give up Christmas. I mean reeaaally give it up." Dad continued. "You could only have Hanukkah."

"Yeah, but I get more presents that way," I said.

"Not necessarily. While Hanukkah has eight days of presents, you only get one present each day. Santa brings you more than eight presents now. And you couldn't have a Christmas tree or eat candy canes or your mom's cookies, and you couldn't sing Christmas carols."

Who needed Christmas carols when I could easily just sing Hanukkah carols? I already had the dreidel song down pat (I made it out of clay). But no candy canes or cookies? What else is a child supposed to eat during the holidays? Bacon?

"Oh, and you can't eat bacon anymore," he said.

"What? Why?"

"Jewish people don't eat any part of the pig. That's part of eating kosher. You can't have ham or bacon or bbq sandwiches anymore. You couldn't even have BLTs with us."

At this point, my dad started to paint a very bleak, disturbing reality. Family BLTs were the highlight of the summer. Except I despised lettuce and tomatoes, so really, I would have toasted bread with bacon and Miracle Whip all over it. It was amazing. If you took away the bacon, though, what would I have left? A bunch of toast and zippy off-brand mayo? That's no way to live!

Once dad kissed me goodnight, I laid in bed an unsure man. I stared at my nightlight wondering, *maybe Jews didn't have it so easy like I thought.*

The next morning, I decided that I may not take the path of conversion after all. But this didn't necessarily mean I was going to give it all up either. I'd just be an honorary Jew on the down-low. Down-low Jews still get to have Christmas trees and bacon. My parents considered this to be a decent compromise.

Growing up, we fortunately got to have a second summer trip that didn't involve Texas. This trip revolved around going to the convention for my father's profession. It perfectly murdered two birds with one stone. He'd rub shoulders and drink with his cohorts while we explored a different city each year.

The year we went to Washington D.C., my mother decided it would be "fun" for us all to go to the Holocaust Museum. I had never heard of this Holocaust thing. My grade wasn't reading *The Diary of Anne Frank* and *Schindler's List* hadn't come out yet. I had no knowledge of what any of this was about.

Upon getting to the museum, I automatically became disinterested. All the walls had large black and white photos that were all blurry. If they didn't have photos, they had lots of words to read. *I DIDN'T COME TO*

WASHINGTON, D.C. TO READ, I thought. Thus, I let my brain wander off to think about something else - most likely about my love of ketchup.

I got so lost in my own daydreams that I was missing everything in the museum. That is until we entered a strange room where there sat a huge pile of shoes. Everybody kept staring at the shoes and they all seemed extremely sad. This snatched me back into reality.

"I don't get it. What are we looking at?" I asked my sister Stacey.

"Keep your voice down!" She whisper-yelled at me. "These are thousands of shoes from some of the Jewish people who died."

"JEWISH PEOPLE DIED?!" I blurted out.

Now several other people - total strangers - had shushed me.

"Oh my god, Scottie! That's what this whole thing is about. Haven't you been paying attention at all?"

I brought my voice down to Stacey's level. "Like how many Jewish people died? Like ten thousand?"

"Uh, try like six million."

"SIX MILLION JEWISH PEOPLE DIED?!" I lost control of my quiet-voice again. Not only were other museum-goers getting incredibly annoyed, but they were also getting incredibly offended too.

How could this have happened? How could no one have told me about this? During all my childhood Judeo-delusions, no one ever bothered to stop and tell me that six million Jewish people had been killed by the order of a horribly evil dictator!! A life of menorahs and gefilte fish flashed before my eyes. I guess being a Jew is all fun and games until you learn about the world's largest genocide.

When we walked out of the museum, I got sick to my stomach, more so than all those times I ate too much ketchup. The image of it all was just too much to handle. To make matters worse, I realized how entirely ridiculous I had been for my behavior over the last years.

Here I was, pining over a religion and a culture that I truly knew nothing about. I wasn't any kind of down-low or honorary Jew. I was merely a brat who didn't get what he wanted at a craft show. I never took it seriously. I simply found it entertaining. And now I felt terrible about it.

They say imitation is the sincerest form of flattery. But when my imitation was linked to one of the horrifically definitive events of that culture, it became less about flattery and more of a parody. Because of this, the next time I found an interesting new culture, I would be more respectful about it without jumping in head first.

To this day, I remain a bit of a Judeophile. I have a giant tattoo on my arm written in Aramaic Hebrew, and my partner and I have wedding rings with inscriptions of modern Hebrew. It now all comes from a more educated place with a sense of cultural respect. Except for that one time, in my twenties, when I asked a guy to wear nothing but his yarmulke for me. It wasn't as hot as I hoped it would be, but my heart was in the right place.

POTLUCK POISON

Right before entering the first-grade, my family moved to the northern part of the suburbs in a community called "Hunter's Glen." Like most ritzy neighborhood communities, the name hardly meant anything. Dad found a good deal on a large house that Mom had dropped hints about wanting. She ended up weeping at the signing because she didn't think we could afford it.

Our new house sat on a cul-de-sac. I'm sure you haven't heard of those. They're *very* unique. They're like streets with houses that don't go all the way through. If you drove on to the cul-de-sac, you either lived there, were visiting someone, or made a mistake and needed to turn around immediately to leave. It all felt very exclusive.

Hunter's Glen was mostly made up of cul-de-sacs. It had a community pool, tennis courts, and even its own lake. Our house even had a second story! CAN YOU BELIEVE IT?! A WHOLE SECOND STORY!!

Sometime after moving in, I asked my mother, "Are we rich?"

She glared at me suspiciously. "I'd call us 'upper middle class.'"

I didn't know what this meant, but I knew it wasn't as exciting as telling people we were rich. I still accepted this answer though, as it did imply that we had some kind of wealth.

All the boys on our cul-de-sac were about the same age, yet, somehow, I lucked out that none of them were in my same grade. This worked perfectly to my advantage. If I did something stupid at school, it rarely spread beyond the classroom. I could live a double life: School Scott and Cul-de-sac Scott.

Michael, the oldest kid on the block (two years older than me, to be exact), happened to be the coolest kid on the block. He played sports like a champ and girls liked him. When he discovered his dad's collection of lady magazines, he let us all come over to look at them (when he had the house to himself).

We'd sit in a circle, each with an issue in hand, slowly turning the pages with enthusiasm.[4] When we reached the end, we'd pass the magazine to the left. Being boys in grade school, the plethora of naked women really just blew our minds more than anything else. I personally felt more excited about the fact that I was included in this experience.

We all idolized Michael. When he got into building model cars, we got into building model cars. When he stopped playing with Teenage Mutant Ninja Turtles and switched to nothing but basketball, we did that too. Although I suspect that when most of us returned home, we all got in a bit of much needed "turtle power" time before dinner. How could we not? They were heroes in a half shell.

In light of Michael's coolness, I realized how cool I honestly was not, even for Cul-de-sac Scott. My comrades could tell there was something questionable about me. I couldn't play sports and girls didn't like me. My parents luckily helped me step up my game one year when they bought us a gigantic trampoline for Christmas.

Some of the kids would go on to get their own trampolines, none could top our size or my imagination. All the other cul-de-sac kids would come over and jump on the octagon beast with me and my sister, Sara, for hours. This must have been what Kelis really sang about in her 2003 hit

---

4. Or should I call it "enthusigasm." No, wait. Enthusiasm is better.

song "Milkshake."

After a couple of years, Michael announced that he and his family would be moving to Durango, a small touristy town in southern Colorado. I couldn't bear the thought of my best friend moving away (even if I wasn't *his* best friend), especially if this meant the dirty magazines would go with him.

I begged him to leave at least one issue with me, but he turned me down in fear that his dad might notice it missing. This made his departure *that* much more emotionally distressing. I would at least still have my sweet, precious trampoline. Although, when Sara got too old to play with the trampoline, it was only a matter of time before she would ruin that for me too.

"You know those guys just like you for our trampoline," she would say.

I'd screech back at her, "SHUT UP! PEOPLE LIKE ME!"

Despite our love to torture each other, Sara and I were super close. For a brief period, I slept in her room every night. I'd get out my cot (that my parents originally got me for Boy Scouts) and set it up next to her bed so we could have "sleepovers." I loved a good sleepover, and her living across the hall made it all-the-more convenient.

I always considered Sara to be as equally beautiful as Stacey, which sounds somewhat narcissistic, considering she looked like the girl version of me. Despite the fact that she was four years older, strangers often mistook us for twins.

Once Sara entered high school, she ripened into a nasty, vile teenager. Her fifteen going on sixteen was nothing like Liesl's sixteen going on seventeen (again with the Liesl). No nice boys came to innocently sing songs about her lady transitions in the garden. Sara's suitors wore acid wash jeans and smelled of cigarettes. Being the middle child, it should've come as no surprise that she made her way to the rebellious side. This meant I had to lose her, to some degree, as a best friend too.

In my last couple of years in elementary school, the stupid things I'd do just got stupider. Not only would kids in my grade talk about it, but the other grades as well. For instance, when I started having trouble with another kid in class, my mother said I should let him know how I feel.

On the playground, I did what my mother suggested. I told him that I'd been very upset with him. Except I pronounced it "upsest." I'd heard other people pronouncing it like this and I thought it was simply a fancy way of saying it – like the different ways of saying "caramel." Some people say "car-mal." Others say "care-ah-mel." The latter is obviously the fancy version.

I imagined that saying the fancier version of "upset" would have scored me major points on the playground. If there was anything that could impress a potential bully, it was being extra fancy with your words. Although, due to my fancy pronunciation, the word I actually kept saying was "obsessed." Every fucking fifth-grader somehow knew what this word meant except me. Any remainder of my cul-de-sac coolness quickly plummeted with the other boys.

This led me to befriend the smelly kid in our class. He was poor and lived with his alcoholic mother in the various trailer parks of the men she dated. Sleepovers at his house were absolutely no fun. We would have to sleep on the floor. His new, older "step brothers" would often smoke (like Sara and her boyfriends) and play "punch buggy" in spite of the fact that there were no buggies around. I'm genuinely surprised none of them ever tried to molest us. And that's not a joke.

While I was sad that the smelly kid[5] was not wealthy, he and I made a great team. I would defend him when the other kids would make fun of his odor, and he would defend me when they would say I acted like a girl. I eventually worked it out so that all the sleepovers happened at my house. In time, we welcomed in a third lovable loser to our eclectic circle

---

5. I should note that one day I would accidentally run into this old friend as an adult and he smelled perfectly fine, just in case he reads this.

of friendship. The two of them liked my trampoline, and they also liked me just as much when it was taken down for winter.

One day, my parents told me that my aunt's husband would be receiving some kind of an award from his Rotary Club. They thought it would be fun for all of us to take a small road trip for the big event. This did not sound like a good time to me or my sisters.

My sisters used their age as their "get out of jail free card." Mom and dad would have never left a sixteen-year-old Sara home alone in fear that they'd come back to scuff marks on the hardwood floors from a keg, and vomit stains on the Ethan Allen furniture. Since a twenty-four-year-old Stacey didn't want to go either, she could at least stay behind to chaperone the family hellion. My parents deemed me too young to stay behind with them.

Even though Mom knew I didn't want to go, she also knew I would at least enjoy going to the banquet. Given that banquets were fancy, I could totally say things like "I am completely obsessed with caramel." The other banquet goers would delight in my witty nature as they swirled their decanters of brandy (or whatever people drink their brandy from). As an added bonus, I could wear a necktie, even if it was merely a snap-on.

"And I'll contact Michael's parents to see if they would have time for you two boys to get together. Maybe you could have lunch," my mom said.

I sat up like when a ventriloquist shoves his hand inside the puppet. Amidst my banqueting daydreams, I had spaced that my aunt and uncle lived in Durango. I hadn't seen Michael in nearly a year. Since he hadn't kept in contact with any of us, he had no knowledge of my ever-increasing status as a cul-de-sac loser. AND WE COULD HAVE A WEEKEND SLEEPOVER!

"Can I stay with Michael?" I asked my mom.

"What? Like at his house with his family?"

I nodded excitedly.

"No, Sugarfoot. We are only going to be there for two days. You should spend both nights with your father and me. Besides, you need to spend time with your cousins and aunt and uncle. They're your family," she told me.

"Pleeeeaaaase," I begged.

"Oh, alright," she caved early on this one. "I'll see if his family is available the night we get in. But that's it. The next night you have to stay with us after the banquet."

The van felt empty without my sisters along for the six-hour ride to Durango. Since I didn't have them to entertain me, I spent most of the time pressing my parents for the banquet details.

"Will we get to wear name tags?" I asked.

"I don't know," they said.

"Will there be entertainment?"

"I don't know."

"Will there be a cash bar?"

"You can't drink."

"What's a Rotary Club?"

I had heard about many kinds of clubs in my life thus far: the book club, the after-school club, the clean teeth club. I worked particularly hard at getting into that damn clean teeth club. The dentist gave me the badge to prove it. But what in the heck was a Rotary Club and why would I want to join it?

When Dad started to explain it, he came in three seconds too late. I had already started to daydream about a room filled with a bunch of men dialing rotary phones over and over again. My aunt's husband must have dialed the most rotary phones in the least amount of time. I could see why someone would have won an award for this.

I checked back into reality right when my dad finished explaining it all. I missed every single word and got too excited for my next question to ask him to repeat it. As a result, to this day, I still have no idea what a Rotary Club is. But please, don't tell me. At this point, I'd prefer to live in a world where it is literally an old-fashioned phone dialing entourage.

"Will they serve hors d'oeuvres before the main course?" I asked my next question.

"I'm pretty sure it will be a potluck," my mom said.

My heart sank instantly. No banquets that served potluck food were ever fancy. They were the opposite of fancy. There would be no waiters in black vests refilling my water. There wouldn't be a man in a corner wearing a chef's hat, shaving off thin slices of roast beef. Not that I liked roast beef. I just liked watching them shave it. I had packed my clip-on tie for nothing.

I absolutely loathed potluck dinners. While 95% of the dishes had one ingredient in common (I will get to that in a second), the food somehow never fit well together. One casserole would be something south of the border with corn chips whereas another would be some kind of cheesy, pasta thing filled with canned meats.

With potlucks, you had no clue what kind of ingredients were used or what kitchen or person any of it came from. If someone looked grubby and unkempt, how could you trust their kitchen would be clean enough to prepare food? If somebody at the banquet was disheveled and I couldn't figure out which dish was theirs, then all of it - the whole thing - would be tainted!

Even if you *could* figure out who made what, the food would remain tainted because of that one, single god-forsaken ingredient I hinted at before: cream of mushroom soup. It was the quintessential king of casseroles and I believed it to be absolute poison. My reasons for this were threefold.

First, I didn't trust anything made from mushrooms. They're a fungus. They grew in damp spots in our backyard *and* the forest. Adults constantly told us to never touch them, let alone eat them. Sure, these edible ones were deemed safe, but how safe? How did we truly know? Worst of all, they had an icky texture that could only be described as "thick."

Second, I didn't trust anything that kept the shape of the can it came from. This was creepy and I wouldn't have it. I wouldn't have it with my peanut butter. I wouldn't have it with my cranberry sauce. And I especially wouldn't have it with my soup. Soup, of all things, should not remain in the shape of a can.

Third, I didn't trust anything that could sit on a shelf for two years and not kill you. I didn't necessarily understand processed foods at the time (I was practically raised on them), but I did know that foods *should* spoil. Whatever was in the soup that stopped it from spoiling would slowly kill you as well.

So, when it came to potlucks, with all the poisonous cream of mushroom soup casseroles from all of the unknown kitchens, none of it was a risk worth taking. At least the first evening I could eat at Michael's house with his mother's ultra-clean kitchen.

When we got to Michael's house, he and his dad weren't home yet from his basketball game. My parents still dropped me off as they had to get on to my aunt's house. I awkwardly sat there with his mom and little sister, not knowing what to say. Twelve-year-old boys don't really have a knack for small talk.

When Michael finally walked in, he seemed shockingly different than the kid I grew up with. He was no longer a little older than me, but rather *a lot* older. He had gained a few more inches on his height, not to mention lowered a few more octaves in his voice.

A small bit of his dashing blond hair had made its way onto his upper lip. The guy had freakin' hit puberty and now I didn't know how to greet him. *Do we hug? Do we shake hands?*

He mumbled, "Hey."

I said, "Hey," back.

This unfortunately set the tone for our conversations at dinner. Michael summed up his new school and friends in about two minutes or less. I could hardly talk much about my own life. I certainly wasn't going to discuss my recent increase in bullying and newfound poor friends.

Between him hitting puberty and my fall from cul-de-sac coolness, I wound up trying to act extra cool to overcompensate. With Sara's friends impressing each other by talking extra vulgar, I figured I could connect with Michael this way too. This just resulted in him saying things like "Dude, that's not funny. Don't say things like that in front of my sister."

On their way home, Michael's dad picked up a rental movie for us to watch. They must have not consulted with my parents first because they rented *Dead Calm* - a darling film about a married couple stuck out at sea, on a boat, with a murderous lunatic onboard.

The fact that his parents deemed it fine for me to watch this made me feel surprisingly mature. His sister had to go to bed, but I almost wanted her to stay so that I could peg her as the scaredy-cat of the room. Without her, I tried to cover up my fear by cracking more inappropriate jokes. This time it resulted in Michael saying things like, "Dude, that's not funny. Nicole Kidman is afraid for her life."

After the movie, I waited for Michael to suggest that we rummage through his dad's dirty magazines. But he made no such suggestion. He said he was ready to crash. He got on the couch, turned over, and passed out. He didn't even bother turning out the lights. Did this mean I had to turn out the lights?

It appeared as if I had struck out with Michael the entire night - first with dinner, next with the movie, and now with the magazines. He didn't show any sign of liking me at all anymore. What had I done wrong?

I tossed around relentlessly in the non-Teenage Mutant Ninja Turtle sleeping bag his mother gave me, thinking about Nicole Kidman. Sure, her baby died and she had been kidnapped by a mass murderer on a boat while her husband had been left stranded in the ocean. But at least she had friends who liked her. I assumed.

To say I felt disappointed was an understatement. I couldn't pinpoint where it all went wrong. Then, the next morning, it hit me: I had officially become a loser. Michael could tell. Because the harder losers try, the more obvious they look about it. I reeked of desperation and my nerdy, pre-pubescent ways quickly got me canned.

When Mom picked me up, she asked if we had fun. I pretended like the whole sleepover was a ghastly good time. I didn't want her knowing that her efforts to make the sleepover happen had been a total bust. Nor did I want her knowing about her son's official loser status. Regardless, she could tell something was off.

That evening, when I didn't act quite as excited about my tie, Mom suggested I still wear it. With the banquet being held in a church recreation room and not getting to watch anyone slice roast beef, it hardly seemed worth clipping on (sorry, God).

By the time we arrived at the banquet, I was starving. This gave me no choice but to eat some of that potluck poison. As I got in line to serve myself the various dishes, I got nervous. *Should I have a scoop of "Martha's Macaroni Crab Surprise?" Who in the hell is Martha? Does she bathe and does she make sure to use conditioner in her hair?*

I took a chance and ate some anyway. After that first bite, I felt fairly certain the "surprise" was that Martha's dish didn't contain a single ounce of crab. While Martha's main course may not have measured up, some of the other dishes weren't downright terrible, even if they did contain two-year-old fungus soup.

I stuck by Dad's side, hoping he would strike up conversations with any gentlemen who would potentially be swirling their brandy, but no such luck. Come to think of it, they probably didn't have any alcohol there at all. I mean, we were in a church for God's sake!

Dad wanted some second helpings of food. Seeing as how I wasn't experiencing any frightening symptoms, like dry mouth or double vision, I figured I could have a little bit more too. After we got grub, Dad chatted with the president of the Rotary Club in the corner. Rubbing shoulders with presidents at least made things a bit fancier.

When their talk turned to various Rotary-related things, I didn't have much to add to the conversation. My mind wandered off into the distance so that I could continue to feel sorry for myself. I replayed the previous night with Michael in my head over and over again. *Why can't I be more like the other cul-de-sac kids? What can I do differently? Why can't I just be popular?*

A short time later, I glanced up at Dad. Something wasn't right. He appeared pale and his skin was sweaty.

"Dad? Are you okay?" I asked him.

He furrowed his brow and took a gulp of nothing. He blinked his eyes. "Yeah. Yeah, I'm okay." He didn't seem entirely sure of his answer.

I gave him a few seconds to rethink the question. "Are you sure?"

Before he could answer again, his eyes stopped focusing and he began to wobble. Dad fell back against the wall, dropping his plate of the many mismatched casseroles. Martha's surprise spilled everywhere.

"Dad?!" I started to freak out. "What's happening?"

He clutched at his chest. He looked to be in severe pain.

"Scottie," he groaned. "Go get your mother."

Everything inside me went blank. I couldn't move an inch. The potluck food really *had* gotten to him. The sheer terror of whatever was happening far outweighed the terror of Nicole Kidman getting tortured the night before. I couldn't run off to hide behind a blanket or crack jokes to brush it off. This was real life now and I froze up in total fear.

"Somebody dial 911! He's having a heart attack," the president yelled out.

"SCOTT!" I could hear my mother cry out all the way from the other side of the recreation room. She came running, shoving people out of the way to get to him. To this day, I will never understand how she knew it was for him that the president yelled out for the 911 call. At that moment, their love was telepathic.

"DAD!" I began screaming repeatedly. "DAD! DAD! DAD! DAD! DAD!"

"Someone! Get the boy out of here!" Another person yelled.

The commotion unfurled as the room got loud and everybody filled with panic. Two adult arms grabbed me around the shoulders and pulled me back.

"NO!" I screamed, trying to fight it. "STOP!" I grabbed at their hands and kicked my feet.

It was no use. Whoever they were, they were too big for me. It didn't matter how many times or how loud I screamed. I got dragged away. As the frightened crowd of people leaned in to block my view, I could no longer see my mother crouching down over my father's seemingly lifeless body. I was taken to a room where a couple of adults tried to calm me down.

"It's okay, son. Your father is going to be okay."

Except they didn't know that. None of us did. My dad, my hero, my partner in crime, the man who had done everything to protect us, was dying in the next room and there was nothing I could do. How could they take me away? I was going to miss his final moments!

We could hear the sirens of the ambulance as it approached. Once it arrived, my aunt burst through the door, grabbed me, and took me to the car.

"Where's my mom?" I cried.

"She's in the ambulance with your father. We're going to follow them to the hospital."

Next thing I remember, all of us anxiously sat in the waiting room in silence. My mother stared at the floor. My aunt closed her eyes, resting her forehead upon her hand while my uncle stood in the corner. I barely remembered the drive. Everything had become such a blur in those last moments.

When the doctor walked out to give us an update, I felt like I had to vomit.

"Good news," he said.

On that account, I did not have to vomit.

"It wasn't a heart attack."

We simultaneously let out the big breath we had been holding in all that time. Tears were shed, and emotional "thank you" cards were sent to God. I apologized to God for acting so pissed that the banquet had been held in a church rec room and that it wasn't catered by professionals.

"While we know it was a cardiac episode of sorts, at this time, we're not quite sure what exactly," the doctor continued. "We would like to keep him here for another day or two to run some testing." He turned to my mother, "But your husband has declined this option and is requesting to be released."

My father not only lived, but he also went back to being his stubbornly ironic medical-professional self, going against the very same medical advice he'd offer up to a patient of his own. Mom's moment of relief was instantly cut short.

"Wait here," she said to the rest of us as she walked off with the doctor, most likely to try to talk some sense into my father.

"I'll call Stacey and Sara," my aunt said.

"And watch Scottie," Mom called back to her as if our big relief would instantly cause me to forget my woes and run off gallivanting for wheelchairs to play with. In her defense, I did always try to play with wheelchairs.

The doctors mainly wanted to do a heart catheterization - a procedure where they inject dye into the heart's blood vessels (via a tube through your leg) to get a better view of the arteries. Whatever kind of matriarchal level my mother tried to take the discussion to, my father wasn't having it. If he were to have any testing, he wanted it done by his own doctors that he trusted back in Denver.

On our road trips, Dad typically did all the driving. That said, as part of a compromise, he would not be taking the wheel during the drive back home (per the doctor's advice of avoiding any additional stress). This caused Mom her own great deal of stress as she hated driving through the mountains.

As Dad got discharged the next morning, Mom and I laid down the back seat of the van while my aunt gave us blankets and pillows to make it all as luxuriously comfy as her K-Mart brands could offer. Dad crawled in to reluctantly make himself at home. He was still pale and now had tubes running up his nose from an oxygen tank. Seeing him like this made my stomach churn.

Mom white-knuckled it the whole way home. We tried talking about things that wouldn't interest Dad so that he could rest. For the most part, this limited us to lots of discussions about the articles she recently read in her Good Housekeeping magazine. Each time we hit a bump in the road, we paused, reacting as if it could trigger another cardiac episode, or perhaps an actual heart attack.

She had driven so cautiously that it tacked on a couple of hours to the trip, and night had fallen by the time we got home. The moment we walked in the door, Stacey ran up to hug Dad harder than a doctor would have medically advised.

"Where is Sara?" my mom asked, noticing that our homecoming had been one hug too short.

"Oh," Stacey looked down. "She's out with her friends."

"SHE'S NOT HOME??!!!!!" My mother said, with exactly two question marks and five exclamation points. You could easily hear each punctuation mark in her voice.

"I told her she had to be back by 10 p.m. though," Stacey said, somewhat in her own defense.

I was stunned too. How could our sister not be home after our father almost had a heart attack? What was going through her mind while hanging out with friends at a time like this? Then, something occurred to me: from the moment that my father's back hit that wall, I never did think about Michael or my lack of popularity again. I was so upset at myself for putting so much of my energy in the wrong places.

Once Dad went to his own doctors, we would find out that the cardiac episode was due to a partial blockage (about 50%) in the arteries. At the banquet, his heart rate had slowed down and he had some chest pains, and this caused him to faint. Some indigestion could have also helped trigger it. Thus, the potluck wasn't completely off the hook after all. But, without having all that information at the time, our father's life still felt like it was hanging in the balance.

When the 10 p.m. hour rolled around, Sara did not come home. Nor did she come home at 11 p.m. or 12 a.m. My father had already gone to bed, so I decided to do the same. As one could expect, I didn't sleep. I was filled with anger at my sister for ignoring her curfew and with worry that she might be dead in a ditch somewhere. Mom, Stacey, and I now had two lives to worry about.

At 1 a.m., she finally showed up. With her bedroom being next to mine in our nice, two-story, cul-de-sac house, I could hear the muffled sounds of their argument. Nothing was "nice" about it. At this precise moment, my mother and my sister would become enemies for the remainder of her teenage years.

I kept ruminating about how I really *had* lost Sara as a best friend. I didn't fully realize it until this happened. It far outweighed the loss of Michael as a friend. He could go and have his puberty and his dirty magazines. I didn't want it. I just wanted my sister and my mom to stop screaming at each other.

For future reference, Sara would go on to become one incredibly kind woman who we all positively admire and love. She would have two daughters of her own who, at the publication of this book, have yet to rebel against her. But there's still time for that. One's getting a bit sassy. So, we shall see. The idea of this currently makes my mother laugh. The two of them talk on the phone more than anyone else in our family.

As I laid in bed that evening, listening to the two of them try to keep their voices down, my mind kept racing. *If this is what it takes for Sara to be popular, then I don't want to be popular. This isn't who I want to be.*

I have to admit that this would remain true only for so long. Because occasionally, time heals our wounds a little too well. When we forget life's more teachable moments, we go on to repeat that same mistake over again. Eventually, I'd return to getting consumed with things beyond my family.

HELL HATH NO FURY

I once had a super clever idea for a prank. Or, technically, I had a clever idea of creating a prank from a silly accident I saw on the popular TV show *America's Funniest Home Videos*. I decided Sara needed to be the victim of this prank as she was not revolting against my parents on a regular basis.

Ever since we were little, Sara and I loved to play pranks on each other. I'd put a fake spider in her sheets before she turned down her bed. She'd switch out the cassette tapes in my Teddy Ruxpin. I would take her Barbies, rip their heads off, and stack them naked in a pile. She would try to convince me that our parents had secretly adopted me. We had fun.

At this point, Sara's ebb and flow with the family had become fairly dicey. Some days, she acted fine. Other days, she wanted to scratch all of our eyes out. I wouldn't have put it past her either. A few years back, when I was acting like a total brat, I blocked the stairway so she couldn't take her shoes up to her room.

"Scottie! If you don't move, I'm gonna hit you in the head with my shoes!" She threatened me to knock it off.

I called her bluff. She didn't have the guts to do such a thing. Then, out of the corner of my eye, I saw a blur of shoelaces headed straight towards my face. As it turned out, she did have the guts. I immediately (and deservingly) got smacked by her shoes. She immediately (and unnecessarily) felt guilty for it. I milked this guilt for weeks.

Stacey fortunately moved back into our house the year before. Her initial entry into the workforce after college did not go as planned. She couldn't afford to live on her own. Stacey felt awful about it, but the timing couldn't have been more perfect. She became a liaison between Sara and my parents.

Stacey also became my new best friend, replacing the empty seat that Sara had left behind. I needed it now more than ever too. As you could've imagined, the time I spent in middle school did not go well. My poor friends went to a different school while the bullying came along with me to mine.

I'd get nauseous every morning at the thought of going to school and had to take exactly two TUMS beforehand to settle my stomach, which is weird because TUMS is for heartburn, not nausea. Perhaps those chalky fruit flavors somehow soothed my soul. One time, I forgot to take my morning TUMS and, right when I walked into the school, I threw up into a trash can. A girl saw me, screamed, and everyone looked.

When things at the bus stop got really bad, Stacey gave me rides whenever she could. She and her boyfriend (who also lived at home with his parents) let me hang out with them constantly. I mean, who wouldn't love hanging out with an awkward, gangly, effeminate middle-schooler?

Stacey was not the type to play pranks though, most likely because she was a grown woman. This made for another reason that Sara had to be the victim. However, if Sara didn't play along properly, I had no problem with switching gears to make Stacey the target. The prank was *that* good. It had to be done to someone.

On the afternoon of execution, the three of us happened to be in the kitchen at the same time. While Sara waited for her friends to pick her up,

Stacey and I were trying to figure out if it would be a good idea for me to go with them to see the movie *Exit to Eden*.

If you don't remember, *Exit to Eden* was an S&M/sexual fetish comedy where Rosie O'Donnell and Dan Aykroyd played undercover cops. The tagline for the movie was something about them having to "flash more than their badges" to solve the case. Yup, that really happened.

"Hey, want to see a new game I learned about?" I asked.

They feigned enough interest for me to at least start explaining it. Simultaneously, I acted like I was a bit parched and needed a glass of some refreshingly delicious H2O. Out of habit, I accidentally dispensed ice into my glass first. I do not recommend this. If you would like to pull this prank on someone, only use water and no ice.

The game was simple. Take a small funnel and stick it in your pants. Then, tilt your head back, place a quarter on your forehead and balance it so it doesn't fall off. When ready, tilt your head forward to drop the quarter and see if you can get it to successfully land in the funnel.

"Let's see you do it," Sara said after I finished explaining it.

Uh oh. I hadn't anticipated this. I should have practiced it beforehand. But I can hardly practice the piano. Mom is super pissed that she bought the piano now. Wait. Why am I thinking about the piano? Oh yeah! The prank! Will this game even work? Or will it look so impossible that it's not worth a try?

I had to put my money where my mouth was, or at least where my forehead was. I proceeded to stick the funnel down my pants and tilted my head back with the quarter. When I launched my head forward, the quarter landed directly in the funnel.

EUREKA! IT WORKED!

In fact, I was *so* amazed that it worked that I had to do it again. Sure enough, the quarter landed in the funnel a second time. Who knew I had such a knack for dropping things down my pants?! This was awesome! I went for a third time.

"Here, I wanna try it," Sara said, yanking the funnel from my groinage.

I was having so much fun that I had almost forgotten about the prank. Now, she played right into my hands. She stuck the funnel in her pants and leaned her head back with the quarter. I then took my glass of water and pour it down the funnel, soaking the front of her pants. Amazing, right?

"Goddammit, Scottie!" She screamed, knocking the glass of water out of my hands.

If I hadn't put ice in there, she might not have had such a visceral reaction. This is why I do not recommend the ice in your water. If you use warmer water, perhaps the victim won't sense it so quickly and you can soak their crotch a bit more. Furthermore, ice water on the crotch may be a little *too* cruel.

The cup had luckily been made of plastic. This gave me the benefit of not having shattered glass everywhere. I merely had to clean up a few ice cubes with some water.

Stacey laughed. "Where did you come up with that?"

Naturally, I took all the credit.

"You are such an asshole!" Sara said stomping off. "These are my favorite jeans. My friends are picking me up any fucking minute!"

I didn't understand why she was *so* pissed. It wasn't like she could get a weird ice water based yeast infection from it (I think). It wasn't as if I had pulled a "Carrie" on her by pouring pig's blood down her pants. All of her jeans looked alike anyway. She would just change into another pair and it would be exactly the same.

Besides, her friends were total douche nozzles. They didn't deserve her - not in the way that I deserved her. I'll admit that, while I had Stacey now, I was still slightly burned that Sara stopped wanting to hang out with her little brother. But seriously, her friends were dicks.

I longed for the days when Sara would try to prank me back. Her last major attempt came a couple of years prior when she brought home a Ouija board to try and frighten me on a regular basis. She particularly enjoyed preying on the fact that, as a kid, practically anything slightly scary terrified the hell out of me.

For example, when I was six years old, I saw a commercial where a woman's laundry machine ate her. It was the store's cute way of saying the appliance needed to be replaced. But there was nothing cute about it. After witnessing that, I couldn't go near our laundry machine for years (literally years).

By the time I entered middle school... I kind of, sort of, maybe still wondered if monsters lurked around in my closet. Our family cat happened to play a major role in this one. If the old saying about cats holds any truth, that curiosity kills them, Harlow should have not lived to be nineteen years old.

She had this strange obsession with pawing open people's sliding closet doors and hiding inside them. It would even startle my mom when she'd reach in to get our laundry and Harlow would pop out of the hamper. Harlow liked sleeping with me the most, which then meant she especially loved getting into *my* closet.

Thus, at an appropriately monster-fearing age, things especially got creepy when the lights turned off and I'd hear the closet door shaking, sliding its way open. I knew it was Harlow. It had to be. But what if it had been a giant, green ghoul with razor-sharp fingernails and a long tongue that would perfectly taste me before chomping away? I didn't want to take any chances on getting tasted. I had to stack my stuffed animals in front of the closet doors to thwart our cat.

With all that in mind, Sara's plan with the Ouija board seemed brilliant... in theory. Opening the doorway to talk to dead people should certainly scare her little brother. That is unless her little brother had a strong urge to open the doorway to talk to dead celebrities.

I most often asked the board if I could speak with Elvis. He would sometimes show up and tell us how he planned to murder my entire family in the middle of the night. I skipped over that part so that I could ask him if he approved of his daughter dating Michael Jackson. He apparently didn't like it.

This memory resurfaced on the day that Michael Jackson died. I wondered if his bizarre brief marriage with Lisa Marie would make things a bit awkward when he and Elvis accidentally bumped into each other up in heaven. Either way, I was certain that God was, like, the *best* mediator ever.

After lovingly pouring ice water down my sister's pants, Sara didn't make any attempts at retaliation. The Ouija board sat there, all alone, collecting dust. Without the payback, did any of it mean anything? If a tree falls in the forest and no one is around to see it, does it even crush a squirrel? At least the cat still loved to occasionally torture me with the closet door thing.

By this age, I had to figure out different ways of blocking her from the closet doors since I no longer had stuffed animals. I tried using large stacks of back issues of "Highlights For Kids" magazines with a pillow on top. Sometimes, she still managed to somehow paw her way in. This cat could pretty much get to anything.

My parents had bought me a super cool new bunk bed in fifth-grade. Its metal frame was coated in bright red paint and it had a blue futon couch sitting underneath. Like all futons, it unfolded into a double size bed which made it perfect for sleepovers. I could sleep up top while everybody else slept below me - precisely how I liked it.

But Harlow didn't sleep below me. She somehow would get on top to sleep with me. I never could understand how she got up there. It took me a whole ladder to do it. Could cats really jump that high?

The drawback to this awesome bunk bed was that it became more difficult to intervene with Harlow's desire for my closet. I couldn't easily hop up to shoo her away. I'd whisper-scream for her to stop and she'd casually ignore me.

One night, sometime after the funnel-in-the-pants prank, Harlow went at it again. I could hear the closet doors bumping around. I sighed with total irritation. I didn't want to have to get all the way down from the bunk bed to stop her. But if she got inside, I wouldn't be able to sleep until she got out so I could close the closet door.

"Harlow!" I did my whisper-scream. "Stop it! Go away!"

She meowed.

"I'm gonna come down there if you don't stop!"

She meowed again. By this second meow, I noticed they were not coming from the closet doors. The meows came from down by my feet. Harlow was in bed with me. My heart started beating faster. What was going on? Was a sister inside there trying to play a trick on me?

That would have been impossible. I said goodnight to both of them before going into my room. There's no way one could have snuck in there without me seeing or hearing her. And with the light peering through the open crack in my door, I couldn't see anyone else visibly in the room trying to create shenanigans.

The closet doors rattled again. I didn't know what was happening, but I certainly didn't want to stay and find out. I slowly sat up, trying to keep some kind of composure rather than wail my head off. I had to move quietly. I knew it wasn't a monster. They didn't exist. But in the event they did, I didn't want it to hear me moving around. It might get it more excited.

As I got to the edge of the bed, I heard the closet door slide open just a tad. I clenched my eyes and thought, *Oh, God. Why do I have to have a bunk bed?* All of a sudden, the closet door slammed wide open - fast and hard and completely by itself. I jumped up screaming as is if I had seen a clown get murdered by another clown. My feet shuffled so fast that they couldn't find the stupid ladder.

Harlow leapt off the bed and ran away, basically leaving me for dead. Damn that cat! She was supposed to save me like that *Lassie* dog I never watched on TV because it was totally boring.

Monsters were alive and real, and they didn't just creep out of a closet to come lick their prey. They slammed the doors open with psychotic strength and they lunged forth viciously with a rage of hunger to devour their new favorite midnight snack: the supple young faces of preteen boys.

When I located my escape ladder, I climbed down so fast that I almost fell off. I didn't know how quickly this ungodly creature could move. Judging by how fast the closet door slammed open, I estimated that I had one-tenth of a millisecond to get the hell out. I couldn't stop screaming my head off. I raced for the door knowing that if it didn't catch me, it would at least grab hold of my bedtime shirt to drag me back in and eat me alive.

I flung my bedroom door open, running into the hallway and slamming straight into my parents. With all the sudden commotion, they had already jumped out of bed to come save their boy from this horrible monster that they were probably aware of all along (but neglected to tell him about).

"What's going on?!" Mom said as they grabbed me.

I trembled and shouted, trying to pull them away from the bedroom. "Monsters. God. No. Stop. Monsters. Hurry. Get out. Run. Monsters."

Having encountered a real-life monster apparently caused me to have Tourette's Syndrome. They could barely make sense of what I was saying. I wanted so badly to form complete sentences, but I couldn't. The adrenaline would only let me tick out my words.

As my parents calmed me down, we heard a new noise in the background. It wasn't the distant cackling of an evil, ghoulish closet-demon. It was the downplayed giggling of evil, ghoulish sisters. They couldn't contain it any longer as they ruptured into full-on, hysterical laughter.

At first, I assumed they were laughing at their brother wigging out about monsters yet again. This time, though, I had proof! The closet door slammed open by itself! I couldn't have done that. Harlow couldn't have done that. If she could, we needed to most definitely sell her to the circus for one million dollars.

I gradually figured out that they laughed because they were somehow responsible for the closet door opening. It didn't take long before they let out their confession.

"It was us. We did it," Stacey said.

"How?" I asked, still a fair bit disoriented. "Neither of you were in the room."

"I still don't understand what's going on," mom said.

Sara explained it. "We hooked a string to the end of Scottie's closet door when he was in the bathroom getting ready for bed."

"Yeah," Stacey added. "We played with the string lightly so that he would get all weirded out about it. Once he realized it wasn't Harlow, that's when we yanked it open."

"Although I didn't mean to yank it that hard," Sara said. "I figured the door was going to be heavier than that."

My dad laughed too. "That's actually smart."

As everyone stood there, cheerfully reflecting on how this prank went down, I was also filled with a small sense of joy. Sara *did* care enough to prank me back. Stacey *did* join in on the fun by helping her. And monsters, in fact, did not exist.

Then, I was filled with rage. They had gone too far. Water in the pants was one thing. Hell, I would take another slap in the face with a pair of shoes. But screwing with my fear of monsters was where I drew the line. I already felt dumb enough as it was for still believing in this kind of thing. Now their prank caused me to run around screaming, in front of everyone, like I really had encountered a monster.

Dad was right too. It *was* brilliant. They didn't steal the concept off of TV like I did. They came up with a wickedly original creation on their own, which made my funnel-prank entirely second rate. They out-brillianted me and that wasn't fair. I wanted to be the prodigy of pranks when it came to this household.

I demanded that my parents punish them this instant. They did no such thing. They simply laughed at the amazing, dumb trick, and told us all to go to bed. But how could I go back to bed? Kids don't tend to twitch themselves back to sleep. It was like trying to make a Vietnam war veteran go back to bed after hearing a car backfire.

For the next week, I paced around the house obsessively trying to figure out how to get revenge, like a villain in *Scooby-Doo* who wanted to get back at those meddling kids. I couldn't come up with anything. It was as if I had been so enraged by the whole thing that my brain's "clever revenge centers" had been disabled.

I asked my mom for help.

"What if," Mom gave it some thought. "Oh, I know. What if you took all the girls' pillows and put them in the empty freezer in the basement?! You could sneak them back in their room right before bedtime. This way, they would end up with cold pillows!"

Cold pillows? That was her solution? Mom seemed very proud of herself for this scheme, but clearly, pranks weren't her thing. Plus, with the summer heat lasting long into the fall, the girls would have potentially enjoyed going to bed with cold pillows. At most, it would have made their pillows smell like frozen foods. When I turned down Mom's "prank" by calling it "absolutely idiotic," she refused to help me any further.

I had to think of something, something genuinely good. Since they hit me where it hurt, I needed to do the same for them. *Think. Think. Think.* After a while, it came to me. While I had a tendency to fear monsters, they had a tendency to fear being ugly. Like any self-respecting, warm-blooded American woman, my sisters constantly found reasons why they didn't meet the social beauty standard.

These women, who were already very beautiful, would pile on the foundation, the concealer, the face powder, the eyeliner, the eyeshadow, and the mascara. Chances are I left out five other items because I can't remember them all. They'd blow dry their hair, curl their hair, tease their hair, spray their hair. The list would go on and on.

They'd spend hours getting themselves ready, only to leave the bathroom with a sticky film of makeup and hairspray. No doubt they were the reason Mom hired a cleaning lady to come every two weeks. I had to figure out how to tamper with their beauty, or at least their beauty products.

I went into the bathroom scanning for items to mess with. Stacey's bottle of hairspray called out my name. She loved having big hair. Stacey was practically the leader in carrying this trend over from the eighties into the nineties. She'd toss hair back-and-forth as she sprayed the gunk all over it. Then, she would point it at her bangs to make a giant puff at the front of her head.

I grabbed the hairspray and dumped it out. I filled it with water while singing the lyrics to "All That She Wants," by Ace of Base. Sara equally loved hairspray, but I couldn't do the same thing for both of them. Once one of them discovered their flat-haired fate, the other one would wise up.

I couldn't figure out how to tamper with any more makeup without it looking obvious. I went to the medicine closet in search of some kind of inspiration. Inside, I found the bottle of numbing cream that we all used for canker sores. We got them all the time which had, evidently, been passed down from our dad.[6]

Once I saw the bottle of numbing cream, I knew exactly what to do: pour a dab of the stuff on Sara's toothbrush. She wouldn't see it and it would make her mouth entirely numb.

"All that she wants… is another baby. She's gone tomorrow, boy," I sang to myself as I rubbed the cream into her toothbrush with my finger. "All that she wants… is another baby… ah-way-eh."

I left the bathroom feeling like an absolute badass. While these pranks weren't *quite* as clever as their attaching the string to my closet door, it would blow their minds just as much. I couldn't wait to see the results.

That night, Stacey's boyfriend planned to take her out. I can't remember where. It was one of the things they didn't typically invite me to, maybe an orgy, I don't know. He arrived early while Stacey was still getting ready.

She had gotten her hair all fluffed up the way she liked it and reached for the hairspray to freeze it into place. Within three of the twenty-eight squirts she'd normally use, her hair instantly deflated.

"FUCK!" She shrieked at the top of her lungs. "FUCK!" She did it again.

The whole house heard it. It was impossible not to. This time I expected to be the one laughing hysterically. Instead, I took a big gulp from my now sticky throat. I immediately knew that I had made a big, *big* mistake.

I rushed over to the stairs to go urgently help her. But what would I have done? I didn't know anything about being pretty. And nothing would have made me accidentally come out to my family faster than

---

6. Contrary to popular belief, canker sores do not come from the herpes virus. The two are unrelated. Not that there's anything wrong with having herpes. Some of my best friends have herpes. And for all I know, I could be riddled with herpes (even though I have never had a cold sore).

running to the rescue, shouting "I'll fix your hair!"

Before I could take one step up, she was at the top of the stairs getting ready to barrel down on me. Stacey knew exactly what had happened and shit was about to get real. I turned around and ran - not all that unlike Indiana Jones when he ran away from that giant boulder. Except I was being a coward.

I bolted through the hallway, through the kitchen, and into the living room where I accidentally cornered myself. Right as Stacey got close enough to reach my neck to strangle it, my dad grabbed her from behind to hold her back.

Stacey fought against Dad's grip. Her arms flung out trying desperately to scratch me to death. I was now more terrified of her than the closet-monster who tried to do the exact same thing (with similar fingernails) the week before. As the old saying goes: hell hath no fury like a sister scorned.

"Scottie, what did you do?!" My dad demanded an answer.

"HE PUT WATER IN MY HAIRSPRAY!!" Stacey went limp, sobbing into her hands.

Her mascara ran down her face. So, technically, I managed to ruin two things for her with my one prank. How could I have done this to my new best friend? My stomach turned to liquid and sank out of the bottoms of my feet all over the ground. That's not a metaphor for diarrhea, by the way.

"Scottie, go to your room," Dad said.

"I'm sorry!" I pleaded. "I was only getting back at her for the..."

"YOUR FATHER SAID GO!!!" Mom barked out from behind him.

An apology is not much of an apology when you follow it up by trying to defend yourself. I don't know why I even bothered. The guilt flooded my bones as I slowly marched myself up the stairs to go sulk in my room.

My parents convinced Stacey that she could still salvage the evening and to go get ready again. In twenty minutes, she left the house with non-giant hair that made her feel incredibly plain. I just wished she knew how much she didn't need it to be beautiful. No doubt, now they'd be late for the orgy (or whatever).

As I sat on my bunk bed couch, I thought about the phrase "It's all fun and games until someone gets hurt." The adults said this a million times. Yet, it never occurred to me that this applied to emotional hurt as well.

Stacey had been so kind in letting me hang out with her and her boyfriend. She had done all she could to help me with my rough start at middle school. What if I had lost her friendship?

My sweet tooth for revenge now tasted incredibly sour. What was the point of it anyway? The girls, presumably, would have wanted more revenge afterwards. Then I would have wanted revenge again. It would never end. I guess some dude named Gandhi said it best with the phrase, "An eye for an eye will leave the world blind." He must've poured water down his sister's pants at some point too.

Pranking no longer seemed like a good idea either. Nobody likes feeling foolish, even if it is for silly entertainment. Seeing my sister devastated made me realize that there is no such thing as being harmfully harmless or harmlessly harmful (I still can't decide which one makes more sense).

Once Stacey left and the hallway sounded quiet, I snuck my way over to the bathroom and grabbed Sara's toothbrush to wash it off as frantically as I could. The last thing I needed was her to accidentally swallow her tongue and die in the middle of the night. Then I would be in *real* trouble.

PHYSICAL EDUCATION

You'd think I'd have some epic story of humiliation for my years in middle school, like accidentally peeing my pants during my solo for "You're a mean one, Mr. Grinch." But alas, the solo went perfectly, and when I returned to my position in the rafters, the boy next to me simply said, "Nice job, fairy." It might have been the nicest thing anyone had ever said to me at that school.

"Fairy" became my nickname early on after complimenting another boy's shirt. Usually a couple of times each week, he or his cronies would come up and say something like, "Hey fairy, are your teeth so fucked up cuz you suck dick?!" The teachers never did anything to stop it.

In the end, the bullying I endured was fairly basic. I got slammed into lockers, had books shoved out of my hands, and received numerous threats. But I somehow escaped without experiencing any literal sticks or stones, though, their words certainly did hurt me.

Towards the end of middle school, a group of high school teachers came to explain their plans for an experimental "night high school." It would be the first of its kind here in the USA (one school in Canada had already done it). With the average student having their first class at 7 a.m., they wanted to see if students could respond better when they didn't have to get up at such ungodly hours.

I had no desire to attend a school like this. But I took the flyer home and showed it to my family anyway. They had the same baffling response I did. We all agreed that there was no way I could do it.

Yet, we still decided to attend their open house just in case we needed to tell those convincing teachers, to their faces, how I would absolutely not do it. And maybe, we could also hear what they had to say while we were at it.

This alternative school would still be hosted in the main school I was already supposed to attend. *Well, at least it's not any further away.* Classes would go from 2 p.m. to 9 p.m., Monday through Thursday. On Fridays, it would get out at 8 p.m. *Oh, that's not as late as we worried.*

The teachers expected the school to be small, so they could give students more individual attention. *Hmmm, I bet I could focus better in an environment like that.* And with the cafeteria closed during dinner time, students could go off campus to eat. *I COULD GO HOME FOR DINNER!*

Not that Mom had the finest culinary skills ever. Bell peppers stuffed with meatloaf and "spaghetti pie" was about the most exotic she ever got. However, it would be nice to see the family. Missing out on quality time was my biggest concern (which mostly involved watching TV with Stacey).

At that moment, the family left the decision up to me. The time came to weigh the pros and cons.

PRO: This could give me a clean slate with new students.

CON: I would miss my family so much.

PRO: I could get more attention from teachers who genuinely care.

CON: What about the five hours of television I watched with Stacey?!

PRO: I wouldn't have to wake up so early in the morning.

I made my decision. My parents and I walked right up to those convincing teachers to tell them straight to their faces… that I would be joining the program. My fellow students were a mishmash of rejects and runners-up from various schools. And while some of the rejects were still jerks, any bullying promptly got shut down by teachers who actually gave a shit.

Mr. Ashlund, the science teacher/PE teacher, reigned as the faculty hunk. An avid bodybuilder, he drove an old beat up Mustang with vicious teeth he installed on the front. He was all man. The girl students had huge crushes on him and the boy students bro'd out all over him. I was a mixture of both, which made me try to bypass any opportunity for one-on-one contact with him for the first year.

I often did this: avoiding conversations with heterosexual men that I found attractive. I'd get too inside my own head and overthink it. *If they suspect I'm gay and they know they are attractive, are they wondering if I am attracted to them? Does that make them uncomfortable? I promise I am not trying to sex them up! Or what if I appear as though I am not attracted to them? Will they be offended that I don't want to sex them up?* This inner dialogue caused me to malfunction like a poorly made robot and I'd start bleep-blooping all over the place.

One night, towards the end of the first year, Mr. Ashlund broke my record of avoiding one-on-one contact by asking me to stay behind after class. The second he made this request, I dreaded it. I knew that no matter where I tried to focus my own eyes, it would be the wrong place. If I looked straight into his eyes, he might think I was trying to gaze into them? If I looked down at his crotch, he might think I was trying to look down at his crotch. Bleep. Bloop.

When the other kids left, Mr. Ashlund had me take a seat. He said he wanted to talk.

"I wanted you to know that you are not alone," he said like a therapist/buddy/uncle with bulging biceps.

I have no idea what he is talking about.

"And that you are going to be okay."

Uh oh. Stop staring at his biceps.

"Here, I got these for you," Mr. Ashlund handed me some pamphlets. They had titles like "It's Okay to Be Gay," "Honor Your Inner Rainbow," and "Sword Fighting Won't Send You to Hell."[7]

How did he know? I wasn't a particularly flamboyant kid. I didn't talk with a lisp or anything like that. Not that there's anything wrong with having a lisp. [Th]ome of my be[th]t friend[th] talk with a li[th]p[th]. Although, I wasn't all that butch either. I must have had some kind of "tell" that he, and the rest of the entire world, happened to pick up on.

I wasn't quite sure how to respond. It made me feel anxious, and excited, and terrified, and surprised, and happy, and confused. For a while now, I knew I lacked a certain chemistry with girls while I had some nonstandard thoughts about guys. But I dreaded the label "gay." I didn't want it to be true.

Mr. Ashlund made sure to confirm that he, himself, was heterosexual. But if I needed to talk about this stuff, his door would always be open. I didn't understand why *he*, of all the teachers, was the one to talk to me about it. It could have been Mr. Marsh, the grandfather-ish ex-hippie who taught literature. Or it could have been Ms. Thompson, the ever-so-slightly masculine math teacher who may have been gay herself. Lesbians just love math.

Either way, I knew they would be there for me too. And I was grateful. I could be myself. The faculty would make sure it was okay to be gay. The fact that the most handsomely heterosexual teacher had chosen to be the one to talk to me made me feel sure of that.

Perhaps my unique social awkwardness stood out to Mr. Ashlund, more than the other teachers, due to his also teaching PE class. I never did grow into playing any of those sports games. When I tried, I appeared more afraid of them than anything else.

---

7. Okay, I made that last one up.

I'm sure he also noticed that, whenever it came time to change clothes in the locker room, I was nowhere to be found. Out of the blue, I'd show up to PE ready to go. This was because I changed in a bathroom... in a locked stall... at the empty side of the school... as far away as possible from any potentially visible penises.

I didn't even know if I wanted to see the other guys' penises in my school. None of us were especially good looking. More so, I simply had a not-so-simple problem with getting erections a little too easily. It would seriously happen over anything. I'd get an erection if the wind blew. I'd get an erection if I mowed the lawn. I'd get an erection if I smelled a rotisserie chicken. It was a mess.

Contrary to popular belief, not all teenage boys have this problem. Some get aroused like a normal adult. A select few of us have the misfortune of popping wood the moment we drop trou to turn our heads to cough. I certainly didn't need such things happening in front of my peers. Plus, let's face it: I most likely *did* want to see every single one of their penises.

With Mr. Ashlund being a bodybuilder, it was his main activity for the course. Someday, I'd find a love of weightlifting as an adult, but I hated it as a teenager. For those of us who didn't want to pump iron for an hour, he'd let us get our PE credits elsewhere, outside of the school. This was another cool thing about going to this night high school program: the ability to get credits in alternative ways.

For my external PE credits, I decided I'd go swimming. When my family moved to the Hunter's Glen neighborhood that had its own pool, I took to swimming like a one-armed monkey took to swinging from trees. I managed to do it, and I truly loved it. I was just slower and more gimpy at it than others.

So, for two days a week, I would drive my sixteen-year-old self to the local rec center for an hour before school to swim laps. All the rec center staff had to do was stamp the paperwork Mr. Ashlund gave me. I didn't even have to stay the whole time. But since I loved it - even for a gimpy fish - I often did.

Doing this also meant I could successfully change in a locker room and simultaneously sneak peeks at the various wieners within viewing range. Since the other locker room goers didn't know me (and minded their own business), none of them suspected a thing. I didn't have to concern myself so much with getting caught. I merely had to keep myself properly covered while changing to conceal my own physiological response.

When another guy from school began coming for some pre-class swims as well, I thought my locker room peek advantages had come to an end. A stoner/skater type, he had a lanky, lean body with long hippie hair. He always treated me kindly. Whenever we ran into each other, I stopped behaving like a peeping-tom so that I could attempt masculine pleasantries with him instead.

Then one day, a bizarre thing happened. As he changed a few lockers down, he stripped out of his wet swimsuit and out came a full-on erection. My desire to stealthily get a peek instantly turned into blatantly staring. Once I locked eyes with it, I couldn't stop. He totally noticed, but he wouldn't turn away. Come to think of it, he made no attempts to hide it from anyone in the locker room.

Contrary to what it sounds like, his unabashed raging salmon didn't seem to say much of anything sexual to me. It casually said something more like "It's okay, bro. It happens to all of us."[8] Sooner or later, I'd loosen my own towel in an effort to not try so hard to hide my boner. When he saw, he gave me a sly smile with an approving head nod. "Right on, bro."

If our erections could give each other a high-five, they would have. In the school hallways, he'd always give me that same smile-nod. It was if we

---

8. That's how stoner boners talk.

were secret boner buddies (or "Broners" if you will). I didn't know what it all meant, but I knew that, without a doubt, going to an alternative high school delivered exactly what I needed.

Mr. Ashlund eventually told me that I had to do some physical activity, other than swimming, to continue earning the outside credit. What else could I do? I needed a sport where I wouldn't get hurt, that was super fun, and would involve me getting to go into a locker room.

Stacey suggested that we go skiing. This made sense seeing as how we skied growing up, but it had been a few years since the family went. I was also freaked out after the last time when I accidentally found myself on a double black diamond slope because its chair lifts looked "neat." Getting down that sucker was like a vegan trying to take a stroll through a slaughterhouse.

Doing this for PE credit also didn't involve a locker room. It was just as well though. Nobody wants to be pitching any tents on the slopes, especially with their sister around. Besides, skiing was like riding a bicycle; you don't ever entirely forget how to do it. And, if anything, I could stay on the bunny slope all day to remain nice and safe.

Mr. Ashlund approved of this idea, saying that I would have to do two full days of skiing for it to count towards credit. Both being avid skiers, Stacey and her boyfriend, Glen, had no problem taking me up with them.

The three of us planned to go up early on a Saturday and come back Sunday evening. This way, if I didn't take to it like before, I could at least get it over with all at once. I liked this as it meant we could go lodging. The thing that spoke to me most about skiing was the drinking of hot cocoa and the sitting in hot tubs.

On the first day, I spent my entire time on the bunny slope as planned, trying to get reacquainted with the extremely weird sensation that is skiing. If you aren't used to it, it feels incredibly unnatural and complicated. Stacey and Glen went off to the bigger slopes while I stayed behind to practice my "french fries and pie."

If you have not gone skiing before, let me explain this to you. "French fries" is when you have your skis parallel to each other. This will result in you going incredibly fast. "Pie" (or "pizza") is when you point the front of your skis inward with the backs spreading outward, basically creating a V-shape. This will result in you going incredibly slow. There. Now you know how to ski.

That night, as we sipped away at our hot cocoa, Glen offered up some big-brotherly advice to convince me that I could handle more than the bunny slope. He explained that if you ever end up in a position where your french fries got out of control, you shouldn't automatically try to switch it into pie. One of your legs could slip out of control, which would lead to a disastrous fall.

According to him, the better option was to wait for the appropriate moment to do a controlled fall on purpose. In a controlled fall, you could still bump yourself somewhat hard, but it would result in a far less severe accident than if you were to keep gaining momentum and crashed into a tree. This made total sense.

By the fifth run on the bunny slope the next morning, the ease of it all had gotten incredibly blasé. I had already mastered those food-related positions the day before, and I happened to be tired of skiing alongside small children.

"C'mon," Stacey said during lunchtime at the lodge. "Join us on the blue diamond slope."

"Yeah," Glen added on. "Remember, if things get out of control, find that right moment for a controlled fall to stop it."

"You were always such a good skier. Don't let that last time make you think you're not. Not a lot of us do the double black diamonds."

By the way they were talking to me, I felt like a stupid, whiny baby.

I knew I was capable of a more intermediate slope. "Alright," I said, slamming down my empty cup of hot cocoa as if it had been a shot of bourbon. "I'll do the blue diamond with you guys. But first, let me do one last run on the bunny slope."

"Okay, we will join you on the bunny slope," Stacey said. "Then we can all go over to the blue diamond slope together."

What I neglected to tell Stacey and Glen was that I had concocted up a secret plan. I needed to test out Glen's suggestion of doing a controlled fall. If I literally got in a position where I needed to use this tool, I had to know what it was like first. What better place to do this than on the safe, gentle bunny slope?

Once I stepped off the chairlift, I immediately jetted off, leaving the two of them behind in a trail of my bunny dust. I wanted to surprise them and surpass their expectations. I wanted them to know I was not, for the most part, a stupid, whiny baby.

About a third of the way down, I found myself at a properly stable french fry speed. The time had come to try my experiment. I leaned my body to the left. Nothing happened. I leaned a little more. Still, nothing. Trying to make yourself fall is harder than it sounds. I leaned some more... and then a tad more... and then finally... gravity took over and yanked me the rest of the way down.

As one might expect, my body hit the ground hard. As one might not expect, my body didn't stay on the ground and come to a grinding halt. Rather, it started to bounce back up as if I had done this fall on our trampoline. It's best to imagine it all in slow motion.

As my body bounced upward, it started to do some kind of glorious rotation - not all that unlike a figure skater leaping into the air to spin in those pretty sequenced circles. But figure skaters are high up in the air and wearing skates. I was wearing skis which remained low to the ground. While my body turned, the skis hit the ground at an angle that prevented them from turning with me.

This caused me to go from doing a turning motion into doing a twisting motion. If you can't tell the difference between the two, think about it for a sec. It wasn't good. I sensed a snap inside me. Or maybe it was more like a yank. Either way, it hurt. I pummeled back to the ground and skidded to that grinding halt I originally wanted.

Glen and Stacey had been far enough behind to come to a perfectly demonstrated stop twenty feet ahead of me.

"OH MY GOD! ARE YOU OKAY?!" Stacey yelled back.

"YEAH!" I lied in that knee-jerk-reaction kind of way that we all do when people ask us if we are okay. I was sore, but was too disoriented to tell the degree to which I was.

They cautiously side-stepped their way back up to me. "What happened?"

"I dunno," I lied again. "Maybe my leg hit some black ice or something." I'm not sure if I knew what black ice was or if it existed on the bunny slope. I just didn't want to admit that I had done the whole thing on purpose.

"Do you think can make it down the rest of the way?" Stacey asked.

"Yeah, I should be fine. I just need to dust myself off."

Glen reached out his hands. "Here let me help you up."

As I stood on my feet, a searing pain shot up my leg and into my lower back.

"OH MY GOD! NO! I CAN'T!" I cried out.

"Okay, okay," he said. "Let's get you back on the ground."

As Glen put me back, they quizzed me on what hurt. Was it a bone? Was it a muscle? Oddly, I had no clue. It felt like everything at once and yet nothing in particular.

Stacey asked if I was certain that I couldn't get back down, even if they supported me while we took it slow. Trying not to be overly dramatic, I assured her that this was not an option. Glen decided to go get ski patrol so that Stacey could wait behind with me.

Patrol must have already seen it. A moment after Glen swish-swooshed off for help, a uniformed man skied over to us with his walkie-talkie. He asked me all the same questions. Could I make it down the rest of the way? Could I stand? Where did it hurt?

After giving him my answers, he called over his walkie-talkie for some backup. A few other patrol people showed up carrying a rescue sled. It's freakishly bright orange color happened to draw more people's attention to the idiot who injured himself on the bunny slope.

They removed my skis, transferred me into the sled, and tied me down as if I were a mental patient who wanted to eat their faces. As they slowly sledded me down the rest of the slope, tiny apple-cheeked children whizzed by, staring at me.

The ski resorts medical center presented more like a tiny hospital than a clinic. The patrol transferred me from the rescue sled to a medical bed and wheeled me away from my family into a stall in a small emergency room-like area. Five or six staff members buzzed all around me - removing my gear, filling out paperwork, and hooking up machines. These people definitely had job security.

As they began to remove my long underwear, it occurred to me that I was not wearing any regular underwear underneath. Was I supposed to? I didn't know how this stuff worked. Before I could say anything, they had already managed to strip me completely naked. Then it instantly happened: I straight-up got an erection.

The staff was moving so quickly that none of them seemed to notice. Good! I didn't want them to notice! Except without them noticing, they somehow did not appear to have any urgency in covering me up.

Why are they not getting me a robe? I thought. My boner couldn't just lackadaisically ask them for help like my skater friend's boner would. To a greater extent, it tried screaming at the top of its little erected lungs, "PUT ME AWAY!!!! PUT ME AWAY!!!!"

A woman suddenly popped up out of nowhere. "What is your social security number?" she asked. Actually, "asked" is putting it lightly. It was more like she demanded it.

Was this normal? Do ski resort emergency rooms urgently strip you naked and ask you a bunch of questions while you (every bit of you) hangs out like that?

"Oh… um… I… uh… I… don't know." I couldn't answer.

"You *don't* know your own social security number?!"

I'm not sure if most people know this, but it is incredibly hard to remember nine digits when you are naked and have an erection in front of a half dozen people. I am sure there is some scientific study or pie chart that proves this somewhere. And having a rude woman snap at me for it did not bode well for my dick either.

"Can I get a robe?" I mustered up the courage to ask.

The paperwork woman sighed, practically rolling her eyes. "CAN SOMEONE GET THIS KID A GOWN?!" She shouted behind herself.

Jesus. I couldn't even get a robe. I had to have a "gown." And *now* a few of those medical professionals turned, looked and noticed my boner. *Thanks, lady! As if getting injured on a bunny slope wasn't enough, you just called attention to a teenage boy's most awkward nightmare.*

They threw a hospital gown on me, then jammed an IV in my wrist to pump me full of drugs. If there was ever any chance of remembering my social security number, it was now long gone. Between the drugs and a weird sensation of feeling exposed, my erection refused to resolve itself.

When they let Stacey and Glen back to visit me, I kept my knees bent to create shelter so neither of them would see it. The staff finally offered me some heavy blankets and I gladly accepted knowing that these would do all the hiding for me.

The paperwork woman popped up again. "Do *you* know his social security number?" she interrogated my sister.

"Oh, no, I don't," Stacey said. Why would she know that?

She gave my sister the same glare she gave me. What was up with this woman? "We *need* his insurance information!"

Stacey never tolerated rude people. "You don't need to act like a bitch! Alright?! I will go call our mother to find out!"

They performed an x-ray and some kind of scan, CAT or PET or otherwise, and the results yielded nothing. From what they could tell, no bones had broken and no muscles had torn or sprained. Perhaps it was some kind of minor tissue tear. But that was all the information (or lack of information) the clinic needed to hand me a pair of crutches and kick me the hell out of there. They didn't have time for this. The other injured skiers had begun to pile up.

Stacey and Glen packed up the car in time to get home before the sun went down. I only needed the crutches for one more day as the pain started to subside by then. Though, I made sure to definitely use them in front of Mr. Ashlund.

When telling him, or anyone else for that matter, about the fall or the clinic, I omitted the finer details of it all. And, even though I failed to complete the second full day of skiing, Mr. Ashlund still counted it towards my PE credits. To a large degree, I deserved this. Because between the injury and the erection, physical education hadn't ever felt quite so… physical.

THANK YOU, INTERNET

Here's the thing about coming out of the closet: it's not necessarily a gay thing. It can be for anyone who has kept tough information secret that they now want to share with a loved one. It can be your vegan soulmate who wants to admit she accidentally ate some Cheese Wiz and now delights in putting it on everything. It could be your spouse who saves money by buying things, using them once, and returning them after. It can be your meathead workout partner who loves to crossdress and wants to talk about how it was extremely hard on him when he went to prison (this is a true story that I'll have to write about in another book).

That being said, my coming out of the closet was about the gay thing (and maybe later I'd be the spouse who returns things). My parents had no clue and, as a teenager, I had no intention of telling them. I figured I could save that for my early twenties.

I chose Stacey as the first person to come out to, and it did not go well. It was my fault, really. Historically speaking, she had been the most politically conservative one in our family. Stacey was a product of her environment. Her high school sweetheart was literally the son of a preacher man who most likely didn't boast nice rhetoric about the gays.

Then she got swept up with the "greed is good" Republican mentality of the late eighties. It was the gateway drug for young urban professionals that gradually led Stacey to her bizarre, Kool-Aid-drinking behaviors, like reading Rush Limbaugh books and wearing skirt-suits. Whenever the subject came up, she'd say things like "God made James and Eve, not Adam and Steve."

Not long after Mr. Ashlund gave me those gay pamphlets, when my first year of high school ended, Stacey had a sudden change of tune. She'd talk about how fun it would be to have a gay best friend. I WAS ALREADY HER BEST FRIEND!!! She was clearly trying to tell me something. Stacey was ready to hear it and I was ready to tell her.

Being the kind, loving, incredible, wonderful brother I was, I didn't want to come out of left field with this. I wanted her to have some form of a "heads-up" that it was coming. For this reason, early in the week, I told her I had a surprise for her on Friday.

This method of coming out also held me accountable to actually going through with it. It made it more difficult for me to chicken out. She was anticipating something, now I had to deliver. What I didn't take into account was that when you tell someone you have a surprise for them, they expect a *fun* surprise, not a bombshell.

"What's the surprise?" Stacey asked me all week long. "Just tell me."

"I can't tell you or else it wouldn't be a surprise." *Duh.*

"Is it a pair of diamond earrings?" She'd joke.

When Friday arrived, she got home from work and demanded that we get to this. I kept figuring out ways to stall. For instance, I needed to do my ab workout first. I had become obsessed with wanting to have a six-pack. If I learned anything from pop culture, it was that people liked you if you had a six-pack.

When I finished my workout, I tried stalling again by getting a glass of water. I mean, I had just broken a sweat after all. I was super parched and needed to take five minutes or ten minutes or three hours to *really* quench that thirst.

Stacey wouldn't let me take three hours to drink my glass of water. We sat down on the couch together.

"So, what's my surprise?" She had such an eager grin on her face.

I took a deep breath. "I'm gay." I couldn't wait for the glitter to explode from her head as she discovered that her new gay best friend had been right under her nose the whole time.

But Stacey's grin faded into a grimace. She went wide-eyed like a deer about to be hit by a car. "What?"

Uh, oh. She didn't already know. "Umm, I'm gay. That's the surprise."

"What? Scottie, no. No. No! You are *not* gay!" She appeared to be having a panic attack. Stacey fluttered about in her seat as if she needed to find something to hold on to. "How could you call this a surprise?!"

"I'm sorry. Lately, you've been talking about wanting a gay best friend. I thought you were trying to tell me that you already knew."

"How could I possibly know? Scottie, you're barely sixteen years old. You *cannot* know whether this is the right choice for you."

I found this offensive. "It's not a choice. This is who I am. I've known it for a long time."

"No," she shut this down as if it were up for debate. "This is just because of your new friends that you've been hanging out with."

She was referring to a friend I made that first year of high school. He was obese, so he didn't have abs. But he did have an older sister who was a lesbian, and she had a girlfriend. My social life outside of our house pretty much ended with them.

Stacey couldn't help but cry. "Scottie, I'm telling you… you're too young. Please, don't make this decision yet. Trust me. You're not ready yet."

When she asked me if I had done anything, like sexually, I lied. I decided it wasn't worth it to win this argument by telling her that I had already been there and done that the previous summer. It especially wouldn't help if I told her that it was pretty magnificent. She and I kept going 'round in circles until we had to agree to disagree.

I regretted all of it - not just coming out to her, but by also making it a "surprise." Things had become so horribly awkward. So, if I can offer up any advice, do not preface coming out by calling it a "surprise." What a mind-fuck that must have been for her.

"Don't tell Mom and Dad about this, okay?" she said. "They can't handle it right now, not with all that has happened with Sara."

Earlier in the year, Sara had dropped out of college to go live with her boyfriend. My parents were devastated. They had done everything they could to provide us with a great upbringing. Sara now hardly had anything to do with us. Even Stacey couldn't reach her anymore.

"I don't have any plans to tell them," I said, slightly irritated as if she had equated me being gay with Sara's exit from the family.

In the months that followed, we acted like none of it ever happened. I began spending less time with Stacey and her boyfriend, Glen. They didn't need me hanging around so much anyway. Plus, I had gained a couple more friends at school.

What I didn't know, at the time, was that Stacey had contacted PFLAG (Parents and Friends of Lesbians and Gays) to ask them for resources. She bought books to learn that these homosexuals put their pants on one leg at a time like everyone else. To her surprise, they didn't simply dance their way into their pants via Madonna remixes.

Later that year, Stacey got that skirt-suit dream job and moved out of the house into her own apartment. This newfound distance gave her the freedom to pursue a new dating life after she and Glen broke up. This also gave me space to not rely on her so much and go make those friends I mentioned earlier.

Having friends while going to school at night presented a new challenge. During the semesters, we couldn't quite hang out during the week. Our curfews came an hour after getting out of class. Fortunately for us, the internet had begun taking off around this time.

That's right, young people! I was in high school when the internet became more than just sexy binary code! This meant my friends and I could hang out in the virtual world, talking for hours in chat rooms. Chat rooms were, without a doubt, the safest place for teenagers.

I relished living in the digital world. Not only did it give you the opportunity to change the venue where you hung out with the mere click of eight buttons, but it gave you the opportunity to change your identity as well. I could go into chat rooms and pretend to be somebody else - anybody else. *Thank you, internet.*

My favorite was a photographer named Jack. He strictly worked in freelance, often doing shoots for National Geographic. I'd snag wildlife photos from other sites and post them in the room as if they were my own. Jack was far more interesting than the boy behind the curtain - a greaseball teen who always had food stuck in his braces.

It wouldn't take a super genius to quickly discover the gay chat rooms. Since I was about one-eighth of a semi-okay-genius, it took me a bit longer than it should have. I eventually typed "gay.com" into my web browser to see what would happen, and voila, I had access to a whole world of guys like me.

Most of the guys in these chat rooms were older than me. I didn't care. I just needed to socialize with people who knew what it was like to be in my shoes. I could be myself here. Here, I wouldn't have to change my identity.

Knowing my age, none of these older men tried to hit on me. They were very respectful and some were even super protective of me. The most popular rooms were topic based, which made it tough to meet anyone local. This was a good thing. Teens don't need GPS tools to tell who's around the corner waiting to give them a blow job. Too much access can be a bad thing.

Not long into my Junior year, I started chatting with Roger. He was a fifty-some-odd-year-old Asian man who had lived most of his life in Hawaii. Roger recently relocated to Salt Lake City for work or family or something. He didn't have many friends. Like me, he took to the chatrooms in hopes to find some human connection.

I didn't have much of an interest in getting to know Roger. Being seventeen, he and I had about as much in common as a flamingo and a toothbrush. But I felt bad for the guy. He was noticeably lonely. I knew all about that. I decided to befriend him as a charity case. Doing so made me feel smugly superior.

Talking with Roger also made me feel exceedingly mature for my age. In reality, he just validated everything I had to say. If a fifty-year-old Asian man could justify my behavior, then surely I was doing something right.

We'd stay up chatting late into the night. At some point, he asked if we could talk on the phone. This seemed harmless enough, as long as I could be the one to call him. I had to be stealthy about this. Cell phones weren't all that common and the last thing I needed was for my parents to wake up to middle-aged men calling the house.

Roger sounded strangely soft-spoken over the phone. Considering that we mostly talked about me, I didn't think much of it. I could vent to him about the difficult life of a white, upper-middle-class, suburban teenager. When I griped about not being able to afford an orange pair of boxers I wanted (don't ask), Roger had an idea that surprised me.

"I could buy them for you," he suggested.

"What? No. I couldn't accept that." I said half sincerely. In reality, I absolutely definitely most totally wanted to accept that.

He let out a soft laugh. "You're a good kid. It would be my pleasure to send you the money for it."

"How would that even work?" I asked.

"I could wire you the money," he said.

I didn't have any experience with wiring money. I imagined it was like sending cash over a fax machine. If it meant getting what I wanted, I could certainly figure it out. But my gut was hesitant. *Can I do this? Can I let some old weirdo buy me something that I really, really want?*

Before we went any further, I had to make sure this situation was safe. "You wouldn't expect anything back in return for this, right?" I said.

"What do you mean?" He asked. I'm sure he had some notion.

"I mean that… if I let you buy this for me, you know that it can't *be* for anything. Like I can't owe you anything. Like we can't sleep together." I had to make myself clear on this, which I was apparently struggling to do.

Roger acted shocked. "Of course not. I would never expect anything like that from you. It just makes me happy to see a nice young man like you be happy."

I accepted his offer. He transferred the money and I figured out how to go pick it up. I bolted off to the store to go pick up my boxers. By the time I got there, someone else already bought them. Bright orange underwear was evidently a hot commodity at the time.

I told Roger that I would give him his money back. He said not to bother and to spend it on something else. My list of "wants" certainly had no shortage of items. I patted myself on the back for befriending this guy.

Roger coincidentally had a business trip the following week in Denver. This should have come off as strange given that he said he was a chef. *Do chefs typically travel for business? And do their trips get scheduled a week out?* Regardless, I figured after he bought me a gift, I should have the decency to meet up. One dinner couldn't hurt and he would obviously pay for it. I could never say "no" to free food (still can't).

We met up at the restaurant in the hotel where he stayed. Roger was everything you might have imagined by now: small, quiet, and wrinkly - *way* wrinklier than I expected. He had possibly lied about his age. But I wanted to give him the benefit of the doubt. When dinner wrapped up, he asked if I'd like to come up to his hotel room - that he had another gift for me.

"Um, sure!" I said. "I don't have much time though. I have to head out soon. My parents are expecting me home." This wasn't true. I had plans to meet up with friends. I merely wanted a convincing reason to cut our time short if he got creepy up there.

We sat on the bed as he handed me a plastic grocery bag with an item inside it. I pulled out a package of underwear, one of which was bright orange. They were tiny briefs instead of boxers, though, I wouldn't be nit-picky about it. It was a nice gesture.

"It was sad that you couldn't find the underwear you wanted," he said. "When I saw these, I knew I had to get them for you."

"Oh, wow! Thank you! These are great!" I said.

Then he made a request. "I was wondering if you might want to try them on for me."

"What? Oh, Roger. I'm sorry. You know that's not what this is about," I told him.

"Oh, I know. I didn't mean it to sound like that. It's only because I have never seen underwear like these. I was curious about what they looked like on."

Underwear like these? They were just orange undies. I mean, yes, I was the one who whined about wanting them, but it wasn't as if NASA constructed them from leftover pieces of failed space missions.

"I'm sorry, Roger. I'm not all that comfortable with that. You can have them back if you'd like."

"Oh, no. They are yours to keep. I'm sorry if I made you

uncomfortable."

I didn't want him to feel bad, especially after giving me *another* gift. "You're fine. Thank you for understanding. And thank you for the underwear. I truly do love them."

I gave Roger a hug and said I needed to go. When I left the room, something occurred to me. I drew the line in the sand... with Roger... in person, and he accepted it. I got gifts without having to put out and nobody's feelings got hurt. Roger understood the status quo. He was okay with it. I had legitimately scored a win-win situation. A boy could get used to this.

And get used to it, I did. Roger began wiring money on a regular basis - no more than once a week (because, ya know, that would be weird). Whoever said money can't buy happiness was a dirty liar because this felt divine. I don't even use words like "divine." That's how incredible this was.

When he came back to town a second time, he suggested that I pick him up so we could go on a shopping spree. I had never been on a shopping spree before. I saw them a couple of times on TV. But unlike the television ones, I wouldn't have to rush around and quickly grab random items to beat the clock. I didn't have to beat a single thing - not even a strange man's advances.

"Oh, I like that thing," I'd point out to some unnecessary item.

"You should get it!" Roger would say.

"No. You've already done so much for me."

He'd laugh. "Grab it. You're only young once."

When we drove back to the hotel, he suggested I park to come up as he had another gift for me. This man just spent hundreds of dollars on me, which may not seem like much of a shopping spree, but to a seventeen-year-old in the nineties, it was epic. I couldn't think of anything else I wanted. What on earth could he have for me?

When we got to his room, he explained it. "Doing this wire transfer thing for the money isn't very convenient for either of us," he said. Roger grabbed his wallet and pulled out a credit card. "On that account, this is for you."

My eyes went wide. A bit of drool oozed out of my mouth as I stared at it. This was not just desire drool. It was also dumbfounded drool. Roger had given me his credit card and all I could do was stand there salivating. I did the gracious protest game like I always did and, like he always did, he insisted that I have it.

"Although it's not for running around to buy whatever you want whenever you want," he said.

Oh, now come the rules, I thought.

"It's to help get the money to you faster. I'll give you the pin number, and whenever I let you know, you can go get money from the ATM."

Actually, I am pretty okay with these rules.

"Wow, I don't know what to say," I told him. "No one has ever done anything like this for me before."

"Say you'll take it and have the high school experience I didn't get to."

To my surprise, Roger didn't try to make any sexual advances this time. It was as if he really for reals wanted to see me be happy. I truly hit the jackpot here. *Thank you, Internet.*

Per his permission, I took out money from the ATM two or three times a week. Sixty dollars here. Forty dollars there. Sometimes eighty or a hundred. I got a huge dopamine rush each time I did it. I told all of my friends at school about this new set up. They were all ridiculously jealous and still a tad suspicious.

"Are you *sure* he doesn't expect sex from you?" They'd say.

"Yeah, I drew that boundary and he hasn't tried anything since."

In all icky honesty, I didn't just love this situation for the money. It felt powerful. I could get this man to spend large sums of money on me without having to do a thing. I was the person in control. For someone who grew up as an outcast, I never knew what it was like to have control. I had never dined out on power before. It tasted like a flourless chocolate cake served on a golden plate brought to me by a chimpanzee wearing a tuxedo.

No wonder 90% of billionaires act like total selfish assholes. They get to have tuxedo chimp cake every single day. It's better than heroin. Of course they'd screw over the lower and middle classes in order to keep it.

On Roger's third visit, we went on another shopping spree - buying more CDs, outfits, and underwear. He made his usual invite up to his hotel room afterward and I made my usual attempt to cut it short. I never wanted to spend more time with him than I had to.

"Scott, I am giving you all this money," he said after I told him I needed to leave. "The least you can do is spend some time with me in my room."

I couldn't argue that.

"Here. Lay down with me," he said.

I didn't feel I couldn't argue that either. He *had* spent all this money on me. Now I did have somewhat of an obligation to offer something in return. I wouldn't offer sex. But anything else that gave him a sense of platonic companionship sounded like a valid request. If this meant lying next to each other on a bed, then so be it. This was a small price to pay for a big allowance.

We laid down on our backs, side-by-side, until he rolled over and wrapped his arm around me.

"Doesn't that feel nice," he said.

I tensed up. "Yeah," I lied. It all felt weird, like being cuddled by a giant prune. And, like a giant prune, it made my insides slosh all around in my belly. I clenched my eyes, trying to breathe through it while thinking about how I lied to him all the time.

"I know what I want to get you for your graduation present," he said. I had an inkling that I didn't want to hear this. "What?" I asked.

"I'm gonna get you that new Volkswagen Beetle."

Oh, fuck. I forgot I'd been droning on about that stupid half circle of a car. I didn't mean for him to think I wanted him to buy it for me.

"Roger, you can't buy me a car!"

"Why not?"

"Because my parents will wonder where it came from."

"Oh, well by then your parents will have met me," he said.

"What?! No. My parents can never meet you. They wouldn't understand this. They wouldn't be okay with you being so much older than me. They don't even know I'm gay."

"Oh, no. They will be fine with it," he said. "When they see how good I have taken care of you, they'll love me."

My mind went blank. What could I say to that? His boney fingers slowly made their way along my body, on the outside of my clothes.

"You know," he whispered into my ear while unbuttoning my jeans. "You're going to have to show me what you look like in that underwear." Then he unzipped my jeans.

I immediately jumped up from the bed. "Roger, you know that's not our agreement!"

"Scott, that wasn't our agreement before. Things are different now," he said.

"I'm sorry, Roger. I… I can't. I'm sorry. I have to go." I ran out of the room zipping up my pants as fast as I could. What in the hell just happened?

The next time Roger and I talked on the phone, he apologized for making me uncomfortable again. I told him it was fine. It wasn't. With the talk of getting me cars and seeing me in underwear, this had taken too bizarre of a twist. I knew that my time with Roger (and his money) had to come to an end before anything got out of hand.

In the back of my head, I made the decision to slowly (*very* slowly) distance myself from this man. I couldn't have him going off to kill himself over me. I held back on calling him as much as I did before. This only resulted in him paging me on my beeper more and more.

What's a beeper, you ask? If you were born in the year 2000 or beyond, you may not remember these little devices. Before the fine-tuning of cellphones, people had beepers: a tiny plastic box that hooked to our belt loops. People would dial in the page, and it would magically beep or vibrate, displaying their phone number. If you were out of the house, you were then burdened with the task of finding a pay phone to call them back.

This primitive technology was originally intended for doctors or other important on-call professions. But like smartphones, teenagers hijacked the concept for the ever-so-important task of staying in touch with their friends at all times.

One Saturday night, when I went to the movies with a couple of friends, my beeper vibrated in my pocket. I didn't want to walk out during the film, so I decided I would check the number and call back afterwards. Twenty minutes later, it went off again. Ten minutes later, it happened a third time. Five minutes after that, it wouldn't stop. It kept going off and my gut knew what was happening. My heart knew it too.

I didn't have any money for a pay phone and couldn't call Roger back until I got home. But first I had to check in with my parents for curfew.

"Scottie, a strange man called a couple of times tonight while you were out," my mom said when I woke her up to tell her I had gotten home.

"Really?"

"He called several times after we went to bed," my dad added, not sounding happy about it.

Mom continued. "He said his name was Roger and that it was an emergency. He needed you to call him back as soon as possible."

I ransacked my mental warehouse for a quick fib. "Oh, he's a friend from that coffee shop we sometimes go to. I'm sure it's just dumb teenage drama. I'm sorry. I'll tell him not to call so late."

I ran downstairs, shut myself in the office, and called Roger.

"Where have you been?!" He snapped after picking up on the first ring.

I snapped back. "What are you doing calling my house? You woke up my parents. You know I'm not out to them!"

"You weren't calling me back!"

"I was in a movie with my friends and I didn't have a quarter to use the payphone!"

"I'm giving you all this money and you didn't have a quarter?! You shouldn't have a problem finding a quarter. And if you can't, you *need* to figure out some other way to call me back."

I told him that he was insane and needed help. This is, without a doubt, what you don't want to say to people who are acting insane and need help. It made him more belligerent. I tried switching gears, hoping he'd take pity on me.

"Please, Roger! Why are you doing this?" I pleaded with him. "We aren't together."

"WE ARE TOGETHER!!!!" He screamed. His voice turned into a creepy quiver. "God meant for you and me to meet in that chat room. It was *his* will for us to be together and we *will* be together! Do you understand me?!"

He had never spoken of God before. My mind went blank again. All my words got stuck in my throat. I couldn't say anything.

"DO YOU UNDERSTAND ME?!"

"YES!" I blurted out. "I understand you!" I was so frustrated and scared that I couldn't say anything else.

"Good. Now listen to me you spoiled brat!" How was this the soft-spoken man I originally met? "You have taken thousands of dollars from me and you need to start behaving. I don't care if you are in a movie. I don't even care if you're at a funeral. If I page you, you will call me back within five minutes. If you don't, I will call your parents and tell them everything. Do I make myself clear?!"

"Yes," I whimpered, shaking with actual fear.

When we hung up the phone, I broke down. All this time, I assumed I was the one in control. I assumed I was the one who was manipulating Roger by telling him all those nice things. But he was the one in control the whole time. He had manipulated me.

Remember those closet monsters I mentioned back in Chapter Five? They do exist. But they don't try and drag you into the closet to devour you like I envisioned. They exist in the closet with you, destroying you by shoving you out of it. Roger had been my new closet monster all along. I didn't know what to do. I couldn't ask my parents for help. I couldn't come out to them like this.

As luck would have it, my parents would be going out of town the following weekend. They trusted to leave me alone, as long as Stacey would come by to check in on me here and there. I figured I'd have enough privacy to somehow end this before Mom and Dad got back Monday evening.

Until then, I played along with Roger for the rest of the week. When he ordered me to go get some money out of the ATM, I told him I didn't need it - that I still had some from the previous transaction. This enraged him and he made the same threats: if I didn't go get more money, he'd tell my parents everything. It was like some type of bizarro-world blackmail.

My parents left on Friday so, that night, when I got home from school, I called Roger and told him it was all over. Without delay, he screamed and threatened me like before.

"I'm sorry, Roger," I kept my voice calm. "It's clear that we aren't on the same page about this anymore. I *am* grateful for everything you did for me. But I am not going to be with you. That was our deal. So, I am saying this is officially over. You can't change my mind or threaten me anymore. I'm sorry. We are officially done. Please take care of yourself. Goodbye."

I hung up before he could say anything back. As I predicted, the phone rang off the hook (such a weird phrase). My beeper went off relentlessly. I refused to cave in and answer it, not even to tell him to stop. I escaped it all by going out with friends. I couldn't confide in them about it though. I'd spent so much time bragging about this. I didn't want anyone knowing that my dream scenario had turned into a real-life nightmare.

By Saturday afternoon, the phone calls and the pages slowed down. I thanked God that Roger didn't resort to leaving any voicemails. Another historical fact: voicemails, at this time in history, were left on other devices called answering machines. The messages were recorded on a small cassette tape and, in order to listen to them, you had to play the messages out loud in front of everyone.[9]

That evening, the frantic calling came to an end. *Did this mean I won?* I wondered. *Did Roger tucker himself out and give up?* But on Sunday, someone did leave a message on our answering machine. It was a woman's voice.

"Um, this is Leslie," she said. Her "um" introduction was not passive. It was very, very aggressive.

"I am Roger's cousin and he has informed me that you have been acting very unkind to him and that you've been very irresponsible with his money. He informed me that he lent you his credit card to help you out and now you've been taking money out of the ATM against his wishes. I thought you should know that I am also Roger's lawyer. We have

---

9. Wow! You're learning so much in this chapter, young people. You're welcome.

BREAKING GLASS BALLOONS

records of all the ATM transactions. If you do not contact Roger soon, we'll be handing over these records to the police and reporting this card as stolen. I hope you learn how to treat people better and suggest that you call Roger post-haste or else we will be pressing charges."

Fuck! I was screwed! I was all tapped out of ideas. If I had any chance of putting this fire out, I'd have to ask an adult for help. Therefore, when Stacey and the new boyfriend came over later that afternoon, I had to come out to her a second time.

Two years had passed since I came out to her the first time. She went from not believing in Adam and Steve to being my biggest advocate. She was proud to have a gay brother and it meant the world to me. But, as I explained the situation about Roger from start to finish, she was not proud of what I had done.

"Oh, Jesus," she sighed. "First of all, you are an idiot! How could you do something so stupid?" Stacey had a real knack for not softening her opinions. She didn't run over to hug her brother while shaking her fist at God for bestowing this horrible event upon him. Today, I thank her for this.

"I've been wondering where you've been getting all this stuff," her new boyfriend said. He had been around long enough to notice it.

"How could you think this would be okay?" Stacey said.

"I dunno. I distinctly drew a line in the sand. I made the boundaries and he agreed to it. I thought it would be fine."

"Didn't anyone ever tell you there's no such thing as a free lunch?!"

I had genuinely never heard this saying before. It instantaneously blew my mind. I thumbed through my brain's catalog of free lunch scenarios and couldn't think of a single instance where there wouldn't be a catch attached.

I snapped out of it and continued to launch my worry onto Stacey. "Now they're threatening to press charges. What are we going to do?"

"Don't stress out about that part," Stacey said. "I think they're bluffing. I bet he fed his cousin some bullshit version of the story. You've been doing this long enough that it's impossible to make it look like he wasn't giving you consent. Aside from that, it sounds like she doesn't know you're underage. What kind of lawyer would threaten a minor?!"

She made a good point.

"This guy is smart too," she added. "No wonder he didn't leave any voicemails himself. That way there wouldn't be any evidence against him harassing you."

"Seriously, what do we do? I don't want Mom and Dad to find out I'm gay this way."

"You need to come out to them already, Scottie. I'm fairly sure they've figured it out."

"You think? Whatever. Either way, not like this. They *can't* know about this."

She thought to herself for a second. "Okay, first things first. Do you still have his credit card?"

I nodded and handed it over.

"Okay, let's cut this up and I'll hold on to it. I have to think about what to do next. In the meantime, come sleep at the apartment with me. I don't want you alone in this house tonight."

Stacey and I stayed up late watching music videos on MTV. We didn't say a word to each other, but I could sense her staring at me - her eyes telling me how much she loved me and how disappointed she was in what I did. Her aspirations for money paled in comparison to what I had done. Apparently, green thirst wasn't just a Republican thing after all.

When she went to bed, she gave me a super tight hug, telling me how some terrible people exist out there and not to be so trusting. I didn't have the heart to remind her that I had been a terrible person too.

Around 3 a.m., a loud banging slammed against her front door.

It startled us all awake. Before we could collect ourselves, the bangs happened again.

"OPEN UP!! IT'S THE POLICE!!" A man yelled from the other side.

Stacey dashed across the living room, throwing her robe on. "Oh, God. What now?" She opened the door.

"Is Scott McGlothlen here?" One of the two officers asked straight off the bat.

"Yeah, he's my little brother. What's happening?"

The two officers shoved past her without answering. They looked directly at me. "Are you Scott?"

"Yes. What's going on?"

"We got a call this evening that you committed suicide," he said while the other officer called back on his radio to report that they had found me alive.

My knights in shining armor had come to save the day. "Oh, thank God you are here. You've got to help me," I unloaded on them. "The guy who called you that said I committed suicide… he's a stalker of mine. He won't leave me alone and…"

"WE AREN'T HERE FOR THAT!" The officer snapped. He proceeded to interrogate me on whether or not I had any plans or means to harm myself. Any moment I tried to ask for help, he refused to discuss it further. Their armor didn't shine so much anymore.

Dammit. Why won't he help me? I am so freaking scared.

The officers explained that they had received an anonymous call that I had killed myself. They went to our house and, when no one answered, they broke in to search for my body. They also went to neighbors houses to see if they knew anything regarding my whereabouts. Now the whole cul-de-sac knew some major shit was going down at the McGlothlen house.

After the officers left, Stacey and I went back to the house. The alarm had been set off and all the closet doors were opened. Our cat, Harlow, sat huddled in a corner, terrified from the loud sirens and the large men trotting around. Between seeing her fear and imagining people searching for my body, I felt nauseous.

"Well, the good news is that I think you can stop worrying?" Stacey said.

"Why do you say that?"

"I think this was his final move. This was his last resort to do the most damage he probably could."

"You really believe that?" I wasn't so sure.

"He called the police and told them you were dead. What else can he do?"

She made another good point.

"Let's go back to the apartment to get some sleep," Stacey said. "There's nothing we can do at this point. I have to get up for work in a couple of hours anyway."

"Do you think we're going to have to tell Mom and Dad?" I asked.

"I dunno. I will see if I can reach out to the neighbors to try to answer any of their questions. You go to school like normal. I'll figure out some way to handle Mom and Dad when they get home this afternoon."

I went off to school that afternoon, but hardly any of it felt like normal. Roger weighed too heavily on my mind. Right when I was about to go into Mr. Marsh's photography class, the school counselor came up to me.

"Scott, can I see you in my office for a bit? You can leave your things here."

Even though I hadn't directly met with him before, I liked the school counselor. He was compassionate. Later, I found out he was gay himself.

"I've asked you to come meet with me because, this morning, the school got a phone call that you had committed suicide last night."

"Oh my god. He did it *again*?" Much like this chapter, it felt like this would never end.

The counselor leaned in. "Who did what? Can you tell me what's going on?"

I gave him a general rundown of the whole thing. Each time I had to explain this, it was like chiseling away at a pit of mud with an ice pick. The more I did it, the more tiring it got. And yet I wasn't getting anywhere.

The counselor apologized that I had such a bad experience with the police that morning as if he was responsible for the force. He suggested to not give up on them and still reach out for help. Roger's actions were undoubtedly a form of harassment, and taking his money certainly didn't entitle him to do this.

Once I clarified that I had no intention of harming myself, we wrapped up our meeting so I could go back to class. When he opened the door to set me free, I was startled to see my mother standing there.

"Sugarfoot," she said. "What is going on?"

To this day, I have no clue how she knew something had happened.

The counselor stepped up before I could answer. "Here. You guys can use this room to have some privacy. If you need anything, I'll be next door." He made sure to grab a box of tissues and leave it with us before shutting the door behind him.

Mom asked another time what was happening. Without having a clue as to what she did or didn't know, I would have to tell her everything (as vaguely as possible). I went at the mud pit with the ice pick again and I knew that, somewhere in there, I would have to come out of the closet.

Once I finished the Roger story, Mom sighed. "Okay, you're done with school for this evening. We need to go home to talk to your father and contact the police I suppose."

When she got up, I stopped her.

"Wait, Mom," I said. "Before we go, there's one more thing I have to tell you." It was either now or never.

"Okay," she sat back down. "I'm ready."

I took a deep breath. "The chat room where I met this guy... you know what kind of chat room it was, don't you?"

She lowered her head as tears rolled down her cheeks. "Yes, we know. We aren't stupid."

"Mom, I'm gay," I started to cry as well.

She grabbed for the tissue box and wiped away at her wet face. "I know. I've known for a long time." I guess my parents had suspected it after all.

"If you've known, why didn't tell me?"

"It wasn't my position to tell you," she said. "You needed to tell us whenever *you* were ready."

"I'm sorry, Mom," I hated apologizing for it. No one should have to apologize for this. However, I dreaded that it hurt her.

"Don't be sorry. I admit I don't necessarily understand it and it's not what I want for you, but I still love you the same."

We hugged. We cried. And as we walked out of the room, she added one more thing. "I'm not going to tell your father for you. You have to do that yourself."

We went home, where Stacey and my dad waited for us, so I could relay the whole vague version of the story to him. I capped it off by coming out in the exact same way that I did with my mom, asking if he knew the kind of chatroom I had been in.

"I already know you're gay, Scottie. I blame myself for it too. Maybe if I had been around more when you were a kid, this wouldn't have happened."

"What? Dad? No. You were an amazing father who happened to work hard for your family. Being gay doesn't even work like that. It would have happened regardless. Also, nobody should be taking blame for it.

I'm happy about this."

Stacey chimed in. "And I've known for like two years now. So, if you guys need any books on it, I've got them!" Her tone was lighthearted, almost joyous.

Together, as a family, we called the non-emergency police line. A male and a female officer came out to the house so that I could explain the whole thing one final time. This time, they acted kinder about it, more empathetic than the officers that came to Stacey's apartment.

The male officer dialed up Roger who, to my surprise, answered the phone. When Officer Empathy told him that he was to no longer have any contact with me or my family, I could tell Roger was trying to flip the situation around on me. I wanted to reach into that phone to punch his stupid eyes out.

Officer Empathy thankfully stuck to his guns - not buying any of his story. He reiterated that this whole thing was to officially end. He warned Roger that if he attempted anything else, the police would begin an official investigation.

It all played out so dramatically, like some terrible Lifetime Television movie with a ridiculous name like "Trapped by Temptation: A Mother's Worst Nightmare," or "Secrets of A Teenage Cyber Son: A Mother's Worst Nightmare." All those movies seem like they are about a mother's worst nightmare.

Roger said he would leave us alone. He almost told the truth. A week later, an anonymous letter came to the house disclosing all the various personal things that I had told him. Some of it was true and some of it wasn't. At any rate, with all my secrets and lies, Mom wouldn't know what to believe, including the part about my first sexual experience.

After Mom read that letter, I wondered how much this "free lunch" had cost me. *My dignity. My privacy. My faith and trust in other people. My ability to come out to my parents on my own terms.*

She decided not to notify the police about the letter. We would hold onto it in case Roger attempted something else. Only then would we start that investigation. That ended up being Roger's final stab and it was a good one at that. To some degree, he won. I couldn't stab back, and now my mom knew all the things a teenage son would never want their mother to know. *Thank you, Internet.*

SOMETHING WORSE THAN ADD

Like a majority of the American population, taking tests has never been a strong point for me. It mostly came down to my ADD, which caused me to not read so good (and then say things like "not read so good"). Whenever the class would read aloud together in grade school, my head would slowly drift up towards the ceiling. I'd spend my time wondering if the fluorescent lighting made my eyes sparkle.

When one of the kids near me started reading their part, it would yank me back down to the classroom and I'd panic, knowing that my turn was approaching. I didn't have a fear of reading aloud in front of the entire of the class (kind of). What I *did* fear was having to admit I hadn't been paying attention in front of the entire class. I'd race through the book to figure out which page or paragraph we were on, but rarely found it in time. The kids would laugh. The teacher would sigh. I would want to crawl under my desk.

My fantastic ability to not look at words made me an incredibly bad reader. By third grade, they put in "remedial classes" which always sounded like a fancy term for "almost special ed." Along with a few other students, I had to leave our classroom to go into a tiny, dark room where we would read slightly easier books in order to catch up (which now sounds absurd).

My mother's parenting style was a bit like Carol Brady. This is probably an outdated reference by now, but I can't think of any better example of a mother so deeply committed to their kid's well-being other than *The Brady Bunch*. She would sit with me, literally for hours, while I did my homework, making sure that each time I floated upward (which happened approximately 27 times an hour), she could pull me back to the pages.

For someone who could not read so good (dammit, I wrote that again!), I oddly managed to do one hell of a job with writing stories. No one quite understood this, but they certainly didn't discourage it. While getting praised for my writing was great, it never helped me when it came to standardized testing. They didn't ask you to write stories for these kinds of tests. Instead, you had to read paragraphs, which, as we already established, I was not good at.

These paragraphs took forever to read, and then I had to fill in some sort of bubble with my Number Two pencil to answer questions about what I read. The word problems on the math portion especially messed me up. Reading *and* math combined into one? It would have been more productive to just dig my own grave.

As you can imagine, when it came to taking the SATs in high school, I was completely screwed. I had the same Attention Deficit Dis-struggle as before, and my mother never put me on drugs. Now, I thank her for this. I've read that taking such drugs at a young age can affect the brain later in adulthood. My brain certainly didn't need any more affecting than it already had.

Since standardized testing didn't typically have a written portion, I couldn't ever increase my scores by writing a witty, self-deprecating, short story. This especially applied to the SATs. I think. I can't remember. THAT'S HOW BAD I WAS AT TAKING THE SATs!!!!

Hold on a second. Let's take a break so I can go look up whether or not the SATs had a written portion in which I wouldn't have failed. Feel free to put this book down and go make yourself some tea. Tea is delicious.

*****

Okay, I'm back. How is your tea? That's awesome! Anyhow, I looked it up and I was correct. The SATs did *not* have an essay portion when I took them around 1997/1998. This didn't get added until 2005. Even then, you had to read a passage, analyze how the author "builds their argument," and write an explanation of your analysis. Being that I could hardly read or analyze, this wouldn't have worked well for me either.

Also, with you taking so long to get your tea, I decided to dig up my old SAT scores so I could reveal what they actually were. I have no clue why I still have them (note to self: throw them away). It doesn't matter anyway, because I can't understand what the scores mean. There are dashes and numbers and it reads like some kind of computer code. If I can't read my scores now, what chance did I have at doing a halfway decent job on the test back then?

Even though I cannot figure out how to translate my scores for you here, I can tell you that I did bad enough that my mother decided I should take the test a second time. In all fairness, I didn't do a stellar job at preparing for it the first time around. Studying for the SATs was a bit like trying to juggle knives while riding on a unicycle. I already had so much homework. Now I had to glue my brain onto that thick-ass book too?

I much preferred gluing my brain to the TV with all the amazing primetime television shows I'd record on our VCR during the school night. Each time I would sit down to crack open the SAT study guide, I could hear the television calling to me.

Scooooott. Come watch us, Scott. You know you want to. It's okay, Scott.

You can study later, Scott. Your mother won't beat you. She's too much like Carol Brady, Scott. When TVs talk to you, they're usually creepy about it.

My attempts to overcome the TV's siren call were futile. I'd study a little and then reward myself with a half hour show. Before I knew it, it was 4 a.m. and I had to start getting ready for bed. By this point in my life, I typically slept from 5 a.m. to 1 p.m.

I genuinely did want to do at least somewhat of a decent job on the SATs. It meant a lot to me, and my parents, that I get a higher education. Stacey had graduated from college and she *eventually* got a cool job where she made good money. When Sara dropped out of college to move in with her boyfriend, she did not get such jobs.

If I wanted to get the good jobs like Stacey, I would have to get a good education. If I were to have any chance of getting a good education, I would have to do better at taking the SATs. We signed up for round two, and I successfully fought the urge to watch the television.

The SATs always happened on a Saturday, which seemed like an unnecessary and diabolical plan to abuse teenagers. Why couldn't they have let you out of school during a weekday to take it? That would have been a much better compromise. Instead, I would be getting up at 7 a.m., which did not jive for a kid who went to bed at 5 a.m. This only boggled my ability to focus more, but there wasn't much I could do about it except try to study harder.

Two weeks before this second SAT test, a strange thing started to happen. I began to feel an itch. I felt it in a very specific spot - a very unfortunate spot. This strange itch developed precisely in my crotch. It wasn't horrible. But it was enough for me to take notice and I began to scratch a little more frequently down there.

Since it was mild, I figured it most likely had to do with dry skin. Living in Denver meant living in a dry climate, and dry climates bring on the dry skin. It seemed logical that we could get dry skin in our crotches too. A couple of dozen scratches and some moisturizing soap would most likely fix this itch.

Well, the soap did not help clear this up. It clogged my pores and made me break out all over my chest. Now that itched too. By the week of the SATs, the crotch itch was starting to get worse. Like any sane person, my worry ventured over to the worst-case scenario: crabs!

I ran to the bathroom, dropped my pants, and cranked my head down to do the closest inspection I possibly could. I had never seen crabs before, nor talked to anyone who claimed to have had them. I didn't know exactly what to keep an eye out for. In any case, I didn't see anything.

I needed to get a closer look just to be sure. You can never be "too sure" when it comes to crabs. I ran back to my room, grabbed my desk lamp, and shined it deep into my goods while shifting through each hair, one at a time, as carefully as I could. Still, no sight of anything.

Ruling out crabs was a total relief. It didn't make sense anyway. I wasn't having sex with anyone. But next came that other terrifying thought: if it wasn't crabs, what else could it be? Why was my crotch itching like this?

By Tuesday, the itch became so unbearable, I could hardly study. I had done such a good job at avoiding the TV and now I struggled immensely to focus on any of the words in the study guide. It was driving me so crazy. And, as it didn't show any signs of easing up, I worried that it had to be some kind of medical problem. If I had any hope of getting it fixed, I'd have to see a doctor. This meant having to tell my mother about the mystery itch in my groin.

As much as I want to praise my parents for my upbringing, I have to say that they fell short when it came to talking about the birds and the bees. Luckily, in fourth-grade, my elementary school dedicated one whole afternoon for a sex education class. This was the school's first attempt at doing it with such a young grade, so they didn't do such a stellar job. They divided out the girls so that us boys could stay with the male teacher as he explained how our bodies would soon be changing.

All he said was that we would be getting hair in new places and we might start to smell in new ways. With these changes, we would have to start acting more mature in front of the girls - that we could no longer fart in front of them. HE REALLY SAID THAT!

For the remainder of this first sex education class, we could anonymously write down questions and put them in a jar, and he would dig them out to answer them. We mostly asked questions about AIDS. It was the early nineties so AIDS still weighed heavily on everyone's minds.

I wrote down the question: "If one person has AIDS and they have sex with another person who has AIDS, does the AIDS get stronger?" I'm not sure why I asked this. I think I was envious of all the other boys asking good anonymous questions about AIDS that I wanted to ask one too.

When the teacher read my question aloud, he said loudly, with almost strange certainty, "NO, THE AIDS WON'T GET STRONGER!"

How does he know the AIDS won't get stronger? I thought.

My father never sat me down for any kind of father-son-talk. I'm guessing that, by the time he realized his son was going to be a homo, he gave up on the idea. He wouldn't know what to say. It'd be useless to talk about girls. And Dad certainly didn't know how to talk to me about the boys, so he stayed away from it.

My mom, on the other hand, did make an attempt at a father-son-talk. While the two of us were in the car one day, she decided that she needed to talk to me about wet dreams. The car ride took the most awkward of turns.

Mom explained it so cautiously that it made it all the more confusing right off the bat. I pictured some very weird, dramatic scenes, like waking up in the middle of the night in pools of strange fluids after flooding the bed with all of it.

I freaked out. "What am I supposed to do if this happens?"
She tried using her sweetest tone to keep me calm. "All you have to do is get up and put your sheets in the laundry machine and run it."

I was now especially horrified. *I will have to do my own laundry... in the middle of the night? What am I? Some kind of animal? I have ever done laundry before. What else would I even sleep on? Other sheets? Where do I get those? And how do I put them on a bed?*

I panicked. "If this happens, can't I come wake you up so you can do it for me?!"

"NO, NO! Do *not* come wake me up!" She panicked herself. The thought of her son waking her up in the middle of the night to tell her he had a wet dream was way too much to handle. She clearly regretted bringing it up. "You are old enough to at least change your sheets. Just put the old sheets in the hamper, get new sheets out of the hall closet, and put them on your bed. That is all you have to do."

This was the *one* thing she decided to talk to me about and, ironically, I never once went on to have a wet dream. For months after that, I'd go to bed terrified that I'd wake up sopping wet from top to bottom. She never talked to me about any such thing again and it would be at least another year before I would learn how to do my own laundry.

When I told her about my itchy crotch, mom jumped to the same terrible conclusion I had too. *Crabs!* I assured her that I had checked myself over thoroughly and didn't see anything like that. She called the doctor to get me in as soon as possible. He unfortunately didn't have any openings until the following Tuesday.

I couldn't sit idly by to wait for the doctor. I became obsessed with figuring it out. I sat in different light sources to meticulously inspect myself two or three times a day, still not finding anything.

By Wednesday, the itching had spread along my inner thighs. As I stripped down and gave them a comprehensive look, I noticed little brown dots occasionally stuck to some hair follicles. They reminded me of the brown dots that show up on your arm hair when someone gives you an Indian Burn. Had I somehow managed to give myself an Indian Burn in my crotch? Nah, that would be impossible. I think.

I tried pulling the brown dots away, but they stuck on like glue. I ripped out a hair to observe it. It looked like nothing, but had to be something - some sort of clue to solving this mystery. I would have to show my mother. With the dots being on my thighs, I wouldn't have to let my mother see my junk to get her opinion. My family wasn't that open about our bodies. Mom leaned in to observe my thigh hair and was still at a loss.

On Friday, during my 180th groin inspection, I finally did catch something. It was a little white spot that resembled one of those fuzzies of fabric caught in your pubic hair. I presumed it was one of those fuzzies, but decided to pick it out to have a closer look.

Like the brown dots, the white fuzz did not want to come out from the hair so easily. It took five or six tries to get it. Once I got it in my fingertips, I made sure to hold on carefully as to not accidentally blow it away.

As I held it up, I squinted my eyes to give it the most accurate view possible. Suddenly, a tiny leg popped out of it. I gasped. Then another tiny leg popped out. Before I knew it, the white dot had several legs and was moving.

"OH MY GOD!" I screamed out loud to precisely no one. I was home alone. "I DO HAVE CRABS! I DO HAVE CRABS!"

I began running around in circles. When you discover you have crabs, really, what else can you do? I twitched and talked to myself like a crazy person. "I have crabs I have crabs I have crabs I have crabs I have crabs."

I ran to the phone to call Mom's emergency cell phone number.

She strictly used it for work and as a crisis hotline for the family. This classified as a "level five crisis."

"I *do* have crabs," I told her hysterically.

"Are you sure?" she said.

"Yes, I am sure. It had legs and moved around on my fingertip. It kind of looked like a crab too."

This sounds strange, but it was true. It had the same shape as those awful things that live in the ocean. I hated crabs. I even hated crab cakes. These creatures were creepy and they didn't have *that* much flavor. Now, I had their miniature counterparts crawling around the sides of my genitals.

"Hold on," my mother said. "I will be right there." She dropped everything at the store and came home.

When she got home, Mom asked me to go over exactly what I saw. I explained it as best as I could. Lord knows I didn't want to show her. She didn't necessarily want to see either.

"Have you been sexually active?" she asked me point blank. This was not the conversation I wanted to be having the night before my big test.

"No, I haven't been," I told her. "I swear."

I assumed she meant at this particular time. Per that assumption, I was being absolutely honest about it.

"How could this have happened?" she asked.

I pondered on it. "It must have been on that toilet seat!"

The CDC, at some point, declared that crabs from a toilet seat would be incredibly rare. They can't live long without body heat and they can't walk on smooth surfaces. But this was the only plausible explanation. I could have gone into that bathroom stall without knowing that some gentlemen left behind a crustacean friend or two.

"What should I do now?"

"I don't know," she said.

"You're a nurse! How could you not know?"

"I'm a recovery nurse! We don't help patients who are recovering from crabs! We are just going to have to wait to see the doctor on Tuesday."

"So I am going to have to take the SATs tomorrow while I have crabs?!"

"I am afraid so," she said.

It was the cold hard truth. These vermin had set up shop all over my man parts and they had no plans of leaving. There was nothing we could do. We didn't have the likes of Google yet to search-engine our way to an answer.

That night, I couldn't get any sleep. Scratching myself didn't feel like an option anymore. I worried I'd get one these little creatures on my finger and spread it around. The last thing I needed was accidentally getting a crab in my eye before the big test.

As the testing kicked off, my concentration plummeted to a new low. Not only feeling stupidly exhausted, but the itching itself had evolved into a new unbearable sensation: bugs crawling all over me. The ability to read each question was now rivaled with my continuously squirming in the seat.

I longed for the days when I *just* had ADD. This was way worse. When the test ended, I knew that the outcome would not be good. All I wanted was a normal life via a decent SAT score. Now, because of these things, my future was destroyed.

Tuesday could not come fast enough. When my mother said the time had to come to head to the doctor, I was like one of those puppies who runs and jumps in the car to wait for the owner to hurry their ass up. I wondered what the treatment would be like. Would he prescribe me some kind of highly toxic bodily pesticide? Would he have to do some kind of laser therapy on me?

In his office, the doctor asked what had brought us in to see him.

"I have crabs," I told him.

"Alright. Let's go ahead and see what we got here," he said as if he didn't believe my expert opinion.

The doctor asked my mom to leave the room, which she was more than happy to do. He asked me about my sexual history and I found this interesting. If I could get this from a toilet seat (in theory), should this really be considered an STI? It wasn't actually an "infection." When it comes to crabs, the acronym should stand for "sexually transmitted infestation."

I pulled down my shorts and laid back on the table as he snapped on some rubber gloves. He shined a bright light on to my midsection, leaned in for a close look (too close), and, one second later, he abruptly jumped backwards, nearly all the way across the room.

"Whoa! Yes! You *definitely* have crabs!" He seemed almost frightened.

Perhaps this was not the most professional response. Apparently, the infestation had gotten extremely bad. They had become big and strong with all the blood they had siphoned off me. I had no idea since I hadn't looked back down there after their initial discovery.

Feeling grosser now, I pulled up my pants while the doctor invited my mother back in. He informed her of the situation more calmly rather than leaping around the room in terror like he did with me. She thankfully didn't have to know that, due to waiting so long, the crabs found their new home quite accommodating and set up their own little tent city.

But what about the brown dots I had been seeing? Those were the eggs that the crabs had been laying in my hair this whole time. *They laid eggs on me? They hatched eggs on me? Little crab babies grew up to be big strong crab adults?* This information made me want to barf.

"Fortunately, crabs are very easy to treat," he explained. "All you need to do is apply some head lice shampoo to the area for the allotted time in the directions."

WHAT?! THAT'S IT?! THAT'S THE SOLUTION?! You mean to tell me I could have gone and taken the SATs totally crab free if we had simply used some head lice shampoo?! Couldn't you have told us this information over the phone? Are you sure we don't need lasers?!

After the doctor, we stopped by the store to pick up the lice killing shampoo. When we got home, I urgently ran upstairs, into the bathroom, and stripped down to begin the process. The directions said to rub on the shampoo, then leave it on for ten minutes, but no longer than this. When that part was done, I would have to take a tiny comb and brush it through the hairs to remove the eggs.

Directions like this drive me insane. What if it takes me one minute to fully cover the area with the shampoo? Should I still leave it on for ten minutes? Or does that mean I should leave it on for nine minutes? If it goes to eleven minutes, will it harm me?

Even as a kid, I had fairly hairy legs. When I hit puberty, this caused me to have a hairy butt as well. I knew they had to be hiding back there too, so I coated my rear in addition to my groin and legs, opting to wait the full ten minutes after this. When the timer dinged, I stepped into the shower to wash it all off. I could literally see the crabs falling from my body. They had gotten *that* big. No wonder the doctor jumped.

I tried using the comb to remove the eggs after drying off. The comb was, in fact, pretty useless. The eggs were not coming out. And to make matters worse, I could see a couple of crabs still moving about on my thighs. It appeared as though the shampoo didn't fully work either.

I freaked out and covered myself up to go tell my mom the terrible news.

"The shampoo isn't working!" I shouted as I ran into her room.

"Are you sure?"

"Yeah, a bunch of them washed away. But when I went to go brush away the eggs, I saw more of them crawling around! And the dumb comb doesn't work. The eggs won't come out. I need to shave it all off!"

"You want to shave it all off?"

"Yes, I have to - everything - all of it!"

I had never "shaved" anything before. When my facial hair started coming in, my dad bought me an electric razor since that's what he used. That wouldn't suffice this time. I needed the hairs essentially gone - right down to the very skin. If my sisters could shave their legs every day, how hard could it be?

My mother handed me some shaving cream along with one of their lady razors so I could start this whole process. Being that my upper body didn't have much hair, I didn't worry so much about that. I only needed to focus on everything from the waist down.

I got the hang of shaving my legs surprisingly quick (or maybe it was no surprise at all). The tricky parts, like behind the knee, were tough. I went over those carefully to avoid any cuts. When I was close to finishing, a new terrifying thought hit me: how on earth am I going to shave my own butt?!

This had to be done and it was the one spot I couldn't see. Even if I did it carefully, I felt like I still had a high risk of cutting myself, especially in the more tender areas. *What if I hit a vein or an artery? Do we have arteries in our butts? I don't want to cut myself and accidentally bleed to death out of my ass.*

I knew what I had to do. Not a single part of me wanted to admit it, but I had no other choice. I would have to ask my poor mother to shave my rear for me. I went back out and admitted my defeat.

"Mom, I need your help."

"What's wrong now? Is the shaving not working?"

"No, I think the shaving is working. It's just that... well... I can't see where I am shaving when it comes to my butt so I'm scared I will cut myself. I need help."

"Are you saying you need me to help you shave your butt?"

I nodded. I imagine she didn't know I had enough hair back there to warrant this.

She sighed. "Okay. C'mon. Let's get this over with."

My mother joined me in the bathroom as I bent over the tub and rubbed the shaving cream all over my backside. I let her take the liberty of guiding the razor along those tricky curves and crevices so that this could be done safely.

I don't think that Carol Brady would have ever done this for Greg. If she did, it was probably because she did a hit of acid. I think. I've never done acid so I don't know what it does. But if Carol Brady was dropping acid and shaving her stepson's tush, Alice, the maid, should've seriously called child services.[10]

My mother did it without acid, or any drugs for that matter. She didn't even have a glass of chardonnay first. For that, she deserved an award instead of a call into child services. She saved her son from the brink of insanity. If I hadn't gotten this help, I would have, without a doubt, lost my mind. Man, I better have gotten her one incredible Mother's Day card after this.

I couldn't tell which made me more self-conscious: having crabs while taking the SATs or having my mother shave my butt. If nothing else, I am proud to say that, in this story, I didn't get an erection at any time during any of it. In case you weren't sure, both crabs and your own mother are major boner-killers.

As Mom got up to leave the room, she asked that we never speak of this again. I had no problem agreeing with that. Assuming that none of the other guys in my high school had to have their mothers shave their asses, I didn't want them finding out about mine. I never did tell anyone... until now... in this book.[11]

As of the publication of this book, I had gotten crabs two more times

---

10. As the story goes, the actress and actor who played these characters had a slightly controversial off off-screen romance. So, who knows? She could have been shaving his ass behind the scenes all along.

11. Oops!

and did figure out a more solid way to get rid of them. The secret is to leave the shampoo on for twenty minutes rather than ten (although I'm sure a doctor would advise against this). A trim job certainly does help to work in that shampoo more thoroughly, but shaving your whole body isn't necessary.

When I got my second round of SAT scores back, some areas had improved and others had suffered. The overall score was about the same. This made me wonder if having crabs isn't all that different from having ADD. My thoughts constantly distracted me by crawling around my brain, much in the same way these parasites distracted me by crawling around my crotch.

In the end, these SAT scores were good enough to get me into a halfway decent college. Like the ADD, the crabs didn't stop me from getting a degree so that I could have a professional job I hated like everybody else. But, like most rational human beings, I'd take the constant ADD over the occasional crabs any day.

Now if you'll excuse me, I need to go take a shower.

THIEF OF HEARTS

I ended up graduating high school a year early. Now, before you jump to any conclusions thinking I'm some sort of mega-genius, let me assure you that a "Doogie Howser" I was not. I was just as dumb and distracted as the next guy. Also, if you don't know who Doogie Howser is, then excuse me while I bend over to pick up my cane off the floor.

This happened by way of our night high school running on an experimental trimester system along with some extra credits I earned for volunteering at a hospital. Due to me being a somewhat young, Mom deemed it a good idea that I go to community college for a year first before moving on to a four-year school (which would actually take me five years to complete).

My parents proceeded to get my three graduation presents. First, I got a new computer. All college students needed computers to access the many learning opportunities (and not pornography).

Second, they made me get a job. I tried working at Walmart first. But between the disgruntled employees, the even more disgruntled customers, and the increasingly-disgruntled-me, I lasted a meager three days. I'd rather have accidentally vomited on someone's attractive baby than go back there.

I made my way over to Target. They didn't pay as well as Walmart, however the management didn't suck. When I took a liking to being a cashier, they let me be a cashier. They worked with my school schedule. They put bags of popcorn in the breakroom that I could shovel into my mouth. And, to be perfectly honest, I kind of *liked* wearing the red and khaki combo.

Third, my parents abandoned me. Dad had whistle-blown his way through all the hospitals in Denver. He couldn't find any more work in Colorado. No one would hire him. They all feared that he'd rat them out for corrupt practices. In order for Dad to find a job, the folks had to move six hours away into the panhandle of Oklahoma - the state that looks like it's giving New Mexico a prostate exam.

Stacey had bought her first house and I went to live with her. Mom and Dad paid rent to her on my behalf, which may have been cheaper than paying for student housing. Either way, I had my own bedroom and bathroom upstairs and my own living room in the basement. This gave me a lot of privacy for all that studying I had to do (and not pornography).

When the time came for me to move on to the four-year college, I chose to attend a state college located in downtown Denver. It was also a commuter campus, which made it all the more appealing. I didn't want to have to deal with getting assigned a dorm-mate only to have him get all weirded out with me being gay. And this way, I could keep living with Stacey.

In the middle of the summer, before my first semester there, my friend Rey (a fellow gay kid in high school) got hired at The Gap. He called me up and said I should apply along with him. They were opening a new store so they needed a fresh bunch of employees.

This made absolutely no sense for me. I didn't have a knack for fashion. Remember what I wrote five paragraphs ago? I said that I liked wearing the red and khaki combo at Target. I clearly knew nothing. I told

Rey I would remain at Target where I belonged.

One of our favorite summer activities was to go to the "sixteen and up night" at the local gay club. They drew big X's on our hands so they didn't accidentally serve us alcohol. There, I learned I had a love of dancing and a fear of flirting. I pretty much maxed out at two seconds of eye contact.

On one particular evening, as my dancing feet turned me around in circles (I may not have been a very good dancer), I saw a group of very attractive guys looking over at me and talking. I turned away quickly. *Are they making fun of me?* I wondered.

When I turned back, one of them was walking in my direction. I scanned the room to find the exits in case he said horrible things to me and I had to get out of there fast.

"Hi," he said.

"Hello," I responded.

"How are you?" He had a very thick Latino accent.

"Uh, I'm good."

"My cousin… he think you are hot."

This was not what I expected him to say (not the broken English, but the compliment). He pointed over to the group and there he stood - one incredibly handsome Mexican man. He looked like Mario Lopez's less attractive brother. That doesn't sound like much of a compliment, but an unattractive Mario Lopez is still moderately freakin' attractive.[12]

"Oh, well tell him 'thank you,'" I said.

"Do you want meet him?" his cousin asked.

"Um, okay. Yeah. I want to."

"Ok. He do not speak much English. I will translate."

HE DOESN'T SPEAK ENGLISH?! I already struggled to talk to cute guys. What in the hell would I say to someone who doesn't speak English?

We walked back over to his group and he introduced us. "This is Roberto."

---

12. Just to clarify, Mario Lopez no longer appeals to me. I wish him all the best.

"HI! I'M SCOTT!" I said both slowly and loudly at his face. I didn't know how to properly talk to people who didn't speak English.

The two of them spoke in Spanish.

"Roberto say he think you are hot." That had technically already been established, but I didn't mind hearing it again.

"Tell him 'thank you.' I think he is hot too."

Our awkward banter went on like this for half an hour. I had no idea where this could go. After a while, the cousin said, "Roberto want to go home with you. Where you live?"

I told him the area in which I lived, and it just so happened that they lived on the same side of town. Could this get any better? Except, wait... I had never brought a guy home to Stacey's house. That could be super weird.

But how often does something like this happen in a lifetime? Three times max! Besides, Stacey had to work in the morning, so she'd be asleep. If we were quiet, I could pull this off. I agreed to take him home.

On the car ride back to my place, I tried making conversation by slowly asking him the simplest things I could.

"How old are you?"

"I am twenty-one."

Oh gosh. He is three years older than me. And he really thinks I'm cute?

"Do you live here or are you just visiting?"

He sat there silent. "I no understand."

I tried to rephrase it. "You... live... here?"

He perked up. "Yes, I live here!"

"What... part... of town... do you... live?"

"I no understand."

As we made our way to my basement living room, I put my finger up to my lips for the universal sign of "shhhh." He seemed to get it. We made out. We took our clothes off. And, while he didn't have any muscles like

Mario Lopez, I still got to semi-live-out my "Saved By The Bell" fantasy. Admit it. If you were coming of age in the early nineties, you surely had a "Saved By The Bell" fantasy.

When things finished, I picked up his pants off the floor to politely hand them over. I noticed the label. It was from The Gap.

Roberto noticed me looking at it. "I *love* The Gap." Evidently, he could say that. "I love fashion."

"Oh, yeah. Me too!" I lied.

As we got ready to leave, he stopped and noticed one of my CDs lying on the floor. He picked it up. "I love it!"

"Oh my god. Me too. That's one of my favorite artists."

I'm fairly sure he didn't comprehend any of that. It didn't matter. He started going through all my CDs, showing them to me. "I love it. I love it. I love it."

He and I had the same taste in music. This was incredible. We genuinely did have something in common. I so wished he could speak English. I wanted to talk more in-depth about these musicians we both loved. And I sort of didn't want him to merely be a hookup. I wanted to get to know this guy.

Taking him home proved to be a bit of a challenge. He couldn't give directions so much as he could just point out which streets to go down. We got lost approximately three times.

When we pulled up to the apartment building, he gave me a hug. "Goodbye," he said.

Roberto opened the car door and got out, glancing back at me one more time. By the look in his eyes, he was interested in getting to know me too. I wanted to give him my number. Before I could figure out how to say this, he closed the door and walked off.

The next morning, I immediately called Rey to ask him for the phone number to apply at The Gap. For the interview, I tried wearing an outfit that could potentially be seen as fashionable. It might have involved a vest. Let's not worry about the details. All I can say is that, somehow, I got the job.

I didn't technically quit my job at Target. They treated me so nicely there that I didn't want to risk losing a good thing. I told them I had to take a leave-of-absence as I would be taking some intensive pre-courses before starting at the new school. I'd also need time off through the first semester after that. Somehow they believed it and said I could have my job back when I returned.

My initial start with The Gap did not go over great. All the other employees looked so trendy with their form-fitting outfits and nice haircuts. They knew that, because they got this job, they were hot shit. I didn't know how to think of myself as hot shit. I only ever saw myself as cold shit. But, not long after the store opened, I found my niche.

For a month, I went back to the nightclub hoping I'd run into Roberto. But he was nowhere to be found. I didn't see his friends either. When I asked Roberto if he lived here, maybe he thought I meant something else. It became clear that I possibly wouldn't see him again. This was for the best. I needed to focus on my school work instead of boys.

While going to school, I had a typical college student diet. Heating up frozen foods was about the limit of my ability to cook, and fast-food became a main source of nutrition. I ran around filling my mouth-hole with low-grade cheeseburgers and burritos. How I didn't have a heart attack by the time I got my degree remains a total mystery.

When I had the shifts at Target, I would sit in the backroom, swallowing down fistfuls of that free popcorn from, what I can assure you, was a trash bag. To this day, the mere smell of popcorn makes me want to go pour sanitizer all over my mouth.

One night, I didn't have anything to microwave, so I decided to be extravagant and treat myself to some Taco Bell. I made my order at the speaker and paid my money at the first window. As I pulled up to the second window to get my bag of greasy beef(ish) filled tortillas, there he was: the guy I spent a whole night whispering sweet-hardly-anythings to.

"Is you!" Roberto was shocked.

"Oh my god! Roberto. Yes. How are you?"

"I am good. I am working here. I am learning English," he said, like a Latino robot.

"That's great!"

We were both so completely stunned. Roberto wasn't sure if he should be embarrassed about working there and I wasn't sure if I should be embarrassed about ordering their most disgusting item. But we continued to lean out of our respective windows anyway, grinning like fools and figuring out how to talk to one another. The car behind me honked, startling us back into reality. I had to move on. But I wasn't done swooning yet.

"I will see you again?" I asked.

"Okay. Yes. Good."

I drove out and pulled into a parking spot so that I could have a moment to take it all in. *Should I go back through the drive-thru so I could see him again?* I thought. *No. I would look like a stalker. Play it cool, Scott. Now you know where to find him.* Okay, that last part still kind of made me sound like a stalker.

This situation seemed like it came straight out of romantic comedy. We had an awkwardly wonderful time together only to lose each other, ONLY THEN TO FIND EACH OTHER THROUGH A DRIVE-THRU WINDOW!!! If the wisdom of Meg Ryan and Sandra Bullock taught me anything while growing up, it's that you know you've found true love when you meet again in the most coincidental and comical of ways.

In the coming weeks, I would make many, *many* trips to Taco Bell in hopes of seeing Roberto on one of his shifts. Sometimes I would pile friends in the car so we could all go look at him. I wanted them to see how beautiful he was. I eventually handed him my number through the window and he gladly took it. A few days after that, I'd receive a voicemail full of adorably fragmented sentences.

"Hi. This Roberto. You not in your home. I call you tomorrow. Okay?"

I was devastated to miss his phone call. He didn't leave his number, so I couldn't call back. Then I became even *more* devastated when I realized I had a shift at The GAP the next day. If I went into work, I could miss out on the potentially most amazing man I had ever met.

The next morning, I woke up early enough to give my manager a call long before the store opened. "I'm so sorry," I groaned into the phone. "I got some food poisoning last night. I don't think I am going to make it in today." I rarely ever faked sick, but clearly, true love was at stake here. Though it's surprising that I had to fake it with all the burritos I had eaten.

"Oh, Scott!" She screamed. "You sound horrible. You need to get to the hospital now!"

Shit. She wasn't supposed to take it that seriously. I continued to gag, groan and make big gulpy, swallowy sounds. "My dad is a doctor. He told me I just needed to rest and drink lots of fluids and that I should be back to normal in a day or two."

A couple of hours later, Roberto called and asked if we could spend the day together. Just like that, we had our first date filled with tons of almost-conversations. He explained (as best he could) that he had come to the United States on a student visa and he stayed in the country after it expired. We both knew this meant he was here illegally, but neither of us dared to say it. This somehow made him hotter to me.

The following months felt magical. Roberto and I managed to make each other laugh hysterically regardless of our language barrier. As it turned out, we really did have a lot in common. And he happened to be majorly impressed that I worked at The Gap.

He continued to learn his English at a rapid speed while I slowly picked up Spanish here and there. His cousin liked me and I found a new social circle, even if I couldn't hold a conversation with 90% of them.

The one thing I struggled to understand was how Roberto and his cousin could afford clothes from the likes of The Gap, on taco wages, when I could hardly afford them with my store discount. Once I earned the official title of "boyfriend," they let me in on their own secret discount of the five-finger kind.

I might have done a lot of stupid things in my life so far, but shoplifting hadn't been one of them. I was *way* too scared. I would totally screw it up. If I tried sneaking an item out the door, there'd undoubtedly be one of those exploding blue ink packs hidden inside. Next thing you know, I'd be getting arrested while looking like a smurf.

I told Roberto and his friends that what they were doing was dangerous and wrong... in my head, that is. I wouldn't dare say any of it out loud because if I did, ya know, they may not like me and stuff. So, like anyone in love, I criticized my new beau in silence.

Upon letting me in on their secret, they made it *very* clear that I worked at one of their favorite retailers. They knew I could help them steal from my store so they'd have less of a chance of getting caught. I knew all the security measures. I knew that we didn't have any alarms or exploding blue ink packs. It made for the perfect set up. I couldn't argue it.

Without further ado, they piled into my car so that I could drive us there. Did I mention that none of these guys drove? I had to drive us everywhere all the time. Nobody ever gave me money for gas either. I didn't care though. I just felt happy to belong to this group of beautiful Mexican men.

As we walked into the store, my co-workers were surprised to see me coming in on my day off. I told them we happened to be at the mall and that my friends wanted to check out the store. I proceeded to show the guys all the sweet spots without cameras.

We split up and I moseyed over to my favorite section: the clearance section. Rummaging through the items, I picked up a belt to check out the tag. It was 70% off! I could afford it. *But what if I stole it? I wouldn't have to pay for any of it*, I thought. On the one hand, I didn't really want to do this. On the other, guys like me didn't get guys like Roberto. I wanted to keep impressing them. I wanted to keep fitting in.

I made sure no one could see me and slipped off the tag. I typically didn't wear belts (which made this all the more odd to steal), so I had the space to slip it on. I lifted up my shirt and slid it through my loops. If someone came around the corner, I could act like I was casually trying it on. But nobody did. I put my shirt back down and walked around normally, trying my best not to accidentally faint on the table of new cashmere sweaters.

Roberto and his cousin grabbed me when they were ready to go. As we made our way out of the store, my heart wanted to pound its way out of my chest. I could sense someone coming up from behind to detain us and then, suddenly… nothing. Not a single thing happened. We walked out the door and got away scot-free.

The moment we got to the car, they pulled out all the items they snuck into their bags from a previous store, gushing over their free finds. I wanted to join in the fun too.

"Look, guys! I got a belt!" I said, sliding it off to show them.

They appeared moderately impressed.

"It was on sale too, like 70% off." I was very proud

"You stole the belt that was on the sale?!" Roberto acted shocked.

"Yeah."

"That is so stupid! Why you steal things on the sale?! We can afford that!"

His cousin began laughing, which took my pride and stomped it into the dirt. After disappointing Roberto, I knew I had to do better. If I was going to make this relationship work, I needed to get some street cred by stealing things at full price. I still couldn't bring myself to steal as often as they did. But when I did, I made sure it counted.

When working at The Gap started to turn south, I did what any rational person would do: I began robbing them blind. I'd wear a slightly baggier shirt so that I could slip on one of the store's shirts underneath. Or I'd intentionally not wear socks so that I could start my work day by putting on a pair or two of theirs. I was like Robin Hood - stealing from the rich to... well, keep it all for Roberto and myself.

Stealing from an employer you hate is absolutely, positively delicious. But in the end, you won't ever *really* feel vindicated by doing it *(Yes you will! Don't listen to him!)*. It just offers a temporary relief and, before you know it, you want to steal again *(Which gives you more relief!)*. Therefore, if you're ever tempted to take that notepad or that stapler from the office, I wouldn't recommend it *(Take it! I'll keep an eye out while you stuff it down your pants!)*.

Once The Gap reduced my shifts, I quit and returned to Target. The red bullseye welcomed me back with open arms and I decided that I would not steal from them. It was only fair seeing as how I lied to them so that they would hold the job for me.

Then the day came when we got caught shoplifting. We were at Hobby Lobby trying to steal some special markers so that we could design our own t-shirts. The nice lady-employee asked if she could help us find anything. We said no and, when she left the aisle, broke the package open to start sliding them out.

All of a sudden, the lady-employee came back and saw us. "I know what you're up to!" She yelled. "I'm calling security!"

We dropped the markers and bolted for the front door. All the other patrons stopped dead in their tracks as we zipped by. We somehow made it without any security guard tackling us. Roberto and I jumped in my car and got the hell out of there.

"That's it! I am *done* stealing!" I told Roberto when we got back to my house.

"Stop worry," he said. "We are fine."

"YOU DON'T KNOW THAT!" I was a complete wreck. "What if they had security cameras in the parking lot?! They could've gotten my license plate number and figured out where I live. The cops could be showing up here any minute! I can't put Stacey through that!"

The cops never did come to our door, but I still meant every word. The image of getting arrested right in front of my sister scared me straight. After that close call, I never did steal again.[13]

After a year of being together, Roberto and I thought we reached the point where we should move in together. Mom was not crazy about this plan. She struggled with the notion of her son living with his boyfriend. But Roberto and I had been together for over a year by now.

We were obviously committed. Plus, Stacey now had her next boyfriend living at the house - a British man that she'd one day marry. They could've used the space to themselves. Mom reluctantly agreed so long as they didn't have to pay any more than what they paid for me to live with Stacey.

We found an apartment in the same building where his cousin and their friends lived. Roberto got a new job at a different Taco Bell and would have to pay, at most, a couple of hundred dollars a month to cover the rest of the rent. Like any exciting new venture with someone you love, it was all rainbows and Leprechauns.

Shortly after, I learned that living with someone is very different than dating someone. The first sign of trouble came when Roberto asked me

---

13. Okay, so maybe I went through a small phase where I'd take a bottle of Tabasco from Chipotle in my to-go bag. But they gave that stuff away for free, so it doesn't count. Right?!

to decorate our apartment while he went to work. I spent all afternoon hanging up framed posters of our favorite bands. When I picked him up and brought him home, he was pissed, saying that our place looked like a dorm room.

Roberto hated work and would often throw tantrums until his manager would let him leave early. I'd have to drop everything in the middle of studying to go pick him up. The minute we walked in the door, he'd throw his clothes all over the floor and sit at the computer in his underwear, scouring eBay for good deals on Prada or Dolce & Gabbana.

One good thing was that Roberto loved to cook. He made corn tortillas from scratch and the best chile rellenos I've ever had, even to this day. Except, when he did cook, he made an insane mess in the kitchen. The sink would overflow with dishes from just one meal. The walls would be greasy from all of the relleno oil splattering everywhere. It would take me double the time to clean it all up than it did for him to prepare the damn thing.

Still, I adored this man. His broken English made for him saying the most adorable things. We loved watching the same shows and movies. We made each other laugh hysterically. We listened to the same music and could talk for hours about our favorite artists.

Roberto taught me how to use chapstick. Before him, I thought our lips were *meant* to feel like sandpaper. He showed me how to dress better by wearing t-shirts that actually fit me and taught me not to be so self-conscious about my thin, bony body. Having him as my boyfriend made me 10% more confident about myself.

Sure, he wasn't generous or kind. But we were two birds of a feather and we flocked together. The time had simply come for me to learn how to tolerate the other bird's less desirable habits. This man genuinely made me happy in spite of it all. I chose him for better or worse.

Then, one day, an unexpected thing happened. I got out of class early (which was rare). Roberto was supposed to be at work and all I could think was how nice it'd be to have the place to myself. I barely ever got any alone time. When I walked in the door, I saw him sitting there on the floor, pulling CDs out from my CD rack (his CDs sat on a different rack).

"Um, what are you doing?" I asked.

"Nothing," he said in a way that already assumed guilt.

"Why are you taking my CDs out?"

You could see him trying to come up with a legit reason. "I'm just going through them."

"Roberto, *why* are you going through them?!"

"Okay, fine! I was going to take them to the used CD store. On eBay is a shirt of Dolce & Gabbana and I almost going to win it. I need a few dollars more."

"Wait! You were going to sell my CDs?! Roberto, you're stealing from me!!!"

He scoffed. "Oh, God! Stop being so dramatic! You don't even listen to these anymore!"

"That doesn't matter. They're still mine." I walked over and shoved my way in, trying to put back the music I had collected over the years. "If you want to sell CDs for a shirt, then sell your own!"

"Whatever," he said, getting up and headed towards the door. "My music is better than yours anyway!"

He left, and there I sat on the floor, trying not to bawl while figuring out how to put each CD back in its place. Had he done this before? I scanned my collection to see if anything else was missing. I couldn't tell. That's what I got for having over six hundred CDs.

Come to think of it, I couldn't figure out how Roberto could afford any of these high fashion items, even off eBay, with as little hours as he worked. Taco Bell couldn't pay *that* well and, if they did, I would happily wrap a hundred burritos every single day. *Could he be sneaking money out of my wallet?* I would unfortunately never know.

At this point, Roberto and I had been together for nearly two years. I had proclaimed to everyone how much I was in love with him and that I wanted to spend my life with him. Now, I wasn't entirely sure if I knew the man. I thought about all the other ways he could have lied to me and wondered what people would say if they found out about this.

When he didn't come back to the apartment that evening, I had gotten the alone time I wanted so badly. However, the longer it took for him to return, the more my alone time turned into loneliness. And the lonelier I got, the more I started to think about the various ways I had deceived him.

Working at The Gap would have never interested me. I purely did it to impress him. I lied about liking fashion, I even lied about liking some of the same musicians as him. If I hadn't heard of them, I'd go catch up on their music behind his back to act like I'd known it all along.

I had been a wolf in cheap clothing, running around with deceptions like these hidden underneath my shirt so that I could get this man to love me. I didn't want to lose that. Roberto may have gotten caught trying to steal from me, but he had no clue that I was his thief as well. I had stolen his heart and now I was nothing without him.

Upon his late-night return, I apologized to him instead of the other way around. I did this partly because he was hurt that I accused him of stealing. Even though it was true, the accusation offended him. I also did this due to the fact that I didn't want him figuring out what I had been taking from him all this time.

I imagined this whole relationship would've been like those romantic comedies. We found each other in a drive-thru window and, therefore, were meant to live happily ever after. That's what those movies taught me. I guess we never really know what happens to Meg Ryan or Sandra Bullock after those credits roll and real life begins.

On a grander scale of things, this wouldn't even come close to the worst that could happen in a relationship. But when it comes to romance, boats of all sizes will still make those ocean waters ripple. Because, as 97.4% of you know, there is nothing else out there that can make us feel more foolish than falling in love.

BUSINESS ABROAD

One night, around 3 a.m., a strange sound startled me awake. Roberto must not have heard it as he continued to lay there, still passed out. I got up to go look out the window. Our eighth-floor apartment overlooked the alleyway and I wanted to make sure nothing awful had happened.

We didn't live in a bad part of town. But still, it was the city. Batshit craziness can go down in an alleyway, especially when it's next to a bar. This usually made our alley fill up with drunk people laughing too loud or fighting too loud or making out too loud. To get them to shut up, Roberto and I would throw eggs at them which, more often than not, became our own form of entertainment.

On this particular night, though, I didn't see anything in the alley - not even a group of feral cats trying to shoot up some heroin. I decided to let it go and get back to bed. As I crawled in, I didn't lay down right away. I sat there, staring at Roberto while he was still fast asleep.

Lightly running my fingers along his cheek, it still surprised me how someone could have such beautiful dimples even when he wasn't smiling. I took my pillow and clutched it around my chest as if I were hugging the angel who had brought us together. How could I love one man so much?

Then I took my pillow... and slammed it against Roberto's face! His body jolted awake as the pressure abruptly hit him. He could hardly breathe. His hands began thrashing around, trying to get me to stop. It was no use. I just held the pillow down on him tighter until his body gradually went limp.

Roberto was dead - like extensively dead - like the kind of dead where his eyes stayed open. It was super creepy, so I took my two fingers to gently close them. I didn't know what to do next. *Should I call 911? Should I call my family? Should I call a psychic hotline?* It all seemed so overwhelming.

Before calling anyone, I needed a snack. I was completely famished. Suffocating someone really takes it out of you. I checked out the fridge to see what we had: frozen pizza or frozen corn dogs. What goes best with murdering your boyfriend whom you dearly love? Definitely frozen pizza.

Suddenly, it was my body that jolted awake. It had all been a dream - a wonderful, *wonderful* dream. This was essentially what our relationship had transformed into. Deep, profound love followed by a deep, profound desire to kill one another. Our line between love and hate had become so paper-thin that a butterfly could bust through it.

I had somehow become so tired of this man. He constantly made fun of me for whatever reason he could find. He would spend money we didn't have on useless fashion. And then there was his stupid large penis. I know big penises sound fun at first, but when it's attached to the insufferable person you've chosen to be with, all of those extra inches are just more of them to hate.

We would get into major arguments two or three times a week and break up once or twice a month. I'd walk down the alleyway to our friend's apartment, blubbering and proclaiming that it was over. We'd then turn around to "try to give it one more shot." My counts could be off, but I think we gave it approximately 138 "shots" throughout the course of our relationship.

This had become *so* toxic. Something *had* to change. We couldn't think of anything else other than taking time apart. But how? We lived together and were still flat broke (despite the fact that my parents still helped me pay for things). We couldn't afford separate places.

A solution soon found us. Because I was the kind of person who threw his identity out the window for his boyfriend, I had declared Spanish as my minor in college. The school's Spanish department happened to have several study abroad programs.

My attempts at becoming bilingual had floundered. It felt super awkward to try to talk with Roberto or his friends in Spanish considering that we had always done it the other way around. I was a Gringo trying to become an honorary Mexican and I couldn't get the hang of it. Total submersion could do wonders for me.

I chose a program in Guadalajara and would be gone for the summer. The students and I met with the professors to learn about our experience abroad. The adventure would kick off with a four-night stay in Mexico City (a place where people get murdered more often than in New York, but not as frequently as in Atlanta) followed by a few days touring the Mexican countryside before starting school.

Before going, they prepared us for the Mexican way of life. The people in Mexico apparently had no sense of time. If someone suggested meeting up somewhere at a specific time, it was literally that: a suggestion. They could really show up whenever - no more than an hour or two later - because, you know, anything more than that would be rude.

The plumbing also sucked in most places, so people didn't flush toilet paper after wiping their butts. They had little trash cans next to the toilet where they threw away their wipes instead. Our professors told us we had to do the same.

Then came the age-old advice of not drinking the water. It had numerous bacteria that could cause stomach infection - aka "traveler's diarrhea" - aka "Montezuma's Revenge." We were to bring *lots* of tummy medicine just in case.

But enough about diarrhea. Let's move on to sex.[14] Before I left, Roberto and I made an agreement. We could sleep with two - and only two - other people while I was away. Technically speaking, this was not an entirely new concept for us.

On a couple of occasions, we both struggled to keep our wieners properly locked up. This made us feel lousy about ourselves, as if we were failures at being decent human beings. That was until we slowly discovered that hardly anybody else in relationships was keeping their wieners locked up either.

So, we decided to experiment by allowing each other some sexual grace every now and then. You might think that doing this was a shockingly bad idea for a couple with such chaos and you would be 1,000% correct. Knowing what I know now, I do not recommend this if the relationship is on the rocks. Non-monogamy is best experimented with when the relationship rests in a state of bliss.

But it somehow felt right at the time and, to our surprise, it was the one thing that went well in our relationship. It was one of the few things I didn't regret about my time with Roberto: learning to "do sex" with other people. Okay, now that I say that out loud, I see how terrible that sounds.

The day I had to leave, we cried wondering what we had done. How could we think that spending the whole summer apart would help fix everything? Roberto refused to come to the airport when Stacey arrived early that morning to take me, partly because he wanted to go back to bed.

When I met up with the other students to check in for our flights, a bunch of their boyfriends or girlfriends had come to say goodbye. I

---

14. Slick transition, eh?

watched them in envy as they all cried up until the last possible moment of being together. Well, the girls cried. The boys? Not so much.

Guadalajara turned out to be perfect for me. I FREAKIN' LOVED IT! Nobody had told me that it sometimes got referred to as the "The San Francisco of Mexico." It was a major metropolitan city with a high gay population (even if a large portion of them were in the closet). There were thirty bars I could go to and I still wouldn't be able to visit them all before the end of the summer.

On top of that, my blue eyes and practically translucent skin made *me* the foxy foreigner. Everywhere I went, people looked at me the way I once looked at Roberto. Thus, I was going to need *way* more than two hall passes to sleep around.

The next time Roberto and I talked on the phone, we both eagerly gave one another unlimited passes to said halls. I should've been suspicious as to why he wanted this too. But who cared? I was too busy feeling kind of sexy.

I talked openly with some of my fellow students about how Roberto and I did this. They, by all means, thought we were out of our minds. But here's the interesting thing: by the end of that summer, every single one of them, who had boyfriends or girlfriends back home, cheated on their loved ones in some form or another. Even the Mormon girl (who was engaged) gave a guy a hand-job in a nightclub.

Anyway, my being the oddity of the bunch gave me the opportunity to break away from our group co-dependence. While they hung out with each other, I went out on my own to meet strangers. If someone found a McDonald's, they'd flock there without hesitation. Me? I'd let strangers take me through markets to get the most incredible barbacoa tacos that I have ever tasted.

These strangers quickly became friends and they didn't speak a lick of English. So, I could only lick them back in Spanish. Before I knew it, my bilingual abilities skyrocketed. I was finally becoming an honorary Mexican.

When I originally outlined this book, I hadn't intended on writing anything about my time studying abroad. I had so many little stories that couldn't fit in one chapter, yet none of them had enough significance to make their *own* chapter. Nor did any of them play out as exceptionally embarrassing.

Don't get me wrong. I made an idiot of myself in Spanish just as much as I did in English. Once, when I joined some of these new friends out at one of our favorite nightclubs, one acquaintance leaned in to ask me the strangest thing.

"¿Te gusta el cambio?"

El Cambio means "change" in English. And, like the English term, this includes the definition of getting money back after you've paid for something.

That question didn't make any sense. I must have misunderstood him. "¿Que?" I asked him to repeat it.

He said the exact same thing, "¿Te gusta el cambio?"

Why is this guy asking me if I liked change? Who cares what I think about change? Did he want to know if I had any preferences on the peso vs the dollar? Or was this some weird-ass way of asking if I collected coins?

I had to clarify. "¿El cambio?" I asked, taking my index finger and tapping it in the palm of my other hand (as if this was some universal sign of when someone gives you money).

The guy looked at me as if I were the one who was completely insane. "!El cambio!" He took *his* index finger and swirled it around the air above his head. He was definitely the crazy one.

I gave up and offered him a half-assed answer of "Sure, I like change." I mean, in the end, who doesn't like change? I mean it's kind of annoying to have to lug coins around it your pocket. But still, it's money.

Twenty minutes later, it hit me. This nightclub had been closed for two weeks to revamp the place and "change" some things. The acquaintance was being nice, trying to make conversation by asking what I thought of the "changes" they had made.

All of my embarrassing moments functioned like this: my trademark microbursts of idiocy - nothing worthy of major storytelling (though I think I just told that story). It didn't seem reasonable to write a whole chapter containing a ton of tiny stories on how my brain still managed to short-circuit on itself in a different language. That is until I remembered this one notable story: the time I took a side trip to Puerto Vallarta.

This story came to mind during a recent coffee date with a friend. He talked about his trip to Puerto Vallarta and I told him about how I had quite the unfortunate adventure there during my studies abroad.

"How far away was Puerto Vallarta from Guadalajara?" He asked.

"It was about a five-hour bus ride," I told him.

"Ah, so Guadalajara is towards the west side of Mexico?"

I shrugged. "I dunno."

This baffled him. "Uh, you don't know where Guadalajara is?"

"Nope. If you brought up a blank map of Mexico, I would have no idea where to point for Guadalajara."

"But you just said you lived there for a whole summer! How do you not know where Guadalajara is?!"

I shrugged my shoulders again. "I dunno. I studied Spanish, not geography."

See? MICROBURST!

Our school was strictly for students studying abroad. The building was small but beautiful. Covered in tile, it opened up to the outside air with gorgeous plants surrounding every corner. Each day felt like going to class in some exotic location. The teachers were kind and the school director, a semi-closeted gay man, took me under his wing. He taught me how to find things like bathhouses and hot dogs wrapped in bacon and jammed with cheese.

For some extra money, the school offered side excursions for the students, one of which went to Puerto Vallarta. Those who came back from the first weekend of this excursion raved about it. The school would luckily be doing a second one in a few weeks.

I had always heard people talk of Puerto Vallarta. It sounded like the perfect, touristy, tropical getaway. I could spend the days kicking back on the beach and hit the bars at night - a perfect blend of relaxation and partying. When a few of my fellow Denver students said they were going, I decided that this would be the one excursion I would splurge on (and by "I," I mean my parents).

I got even more excited when I found out that Dean was also on board. Upon meeting this fellow American student, I didn't have the slightest clue that he might remotely be gay. He had a big, beefy build with a shaved head and a full beard - the kind of guy that you could look at and somehow know that he sported the most glorious manly chest hair under his shirt.

Dean was a real man's man, basically the complete opposite of Roberto. This made me crush on him more, which helped me realize that perhaps Mario Lopez could not have been my type after all. Being under the impression that he was straight, I avoided him at all costs.

Then the day came when one of our teachers decided to do some strange exercise. She matched up students at random, asked us to think of an animal that fits our partner and explain why. I got matched up with Dean and had to figure out flattering-animal-compliments without coming off like some queer who worshiped the ground he walked on. The only thing that came to mind was a bear, because of him having the total bear body type.

As my turn approached, I tried desperately to think of nice qualities of bears that have nothing to do with hot burly man bodies. I stumbled through my words as I described Dean. (Imagine this in Spanish), "Dean is like... a bear. He is... ummm... like big and powerful... majestic... and um, very protective of the ones he loves." MICROBURST!

Afterwards, Dean approached me and thanked me for all the kind words. We went to lunch at an Americanized restaurant where he ate appetizers and confided in me about a guy at our school that he liked - a cheerleader who was fit with perfectly tanned skin - basically the complete opposite of me. I was crushed that my crush was crushing on someone else.

He became my only American gay friend that summer, so it worked out perfectly that he had chosen to come on the same Puerto Vallarta trip. This meant I could have a partner in crime for the bars, and maybe he'd get drunk enough to be willing to take his clothes off with me.

The trip to Puerto Vallarta went south before we even got there. As the bus approached our destination, people talked about how the political election would be on that following Monday. Mexicans evidently take their elections *very* seriously. Starting at midnight on Friday, all the bars would close down for the entire weekend. WE HAD CHOSEN TO GO TO PUERTO VALLARTA WHEN ALL THE BARS WOULD BE CLOSED! Strike one. This sucked. Sure, I would get to still lay out on the beach, but what fun, interesting shenanigans could come of that?

Dean didn't stay in the same hotel as me. I shared a room with some Denver girls I made friends with during the first part of our trip in Mexico City. He and I agreed to meet at a certain hour to walk our way to a bar that he knew of. Although we wouldn't get much time before it shut down, it would be something. We arrived at 11 p.m. with about one hour to make the most of our trip.

By virtue of our white exoticness, we did strike up a conversation with a group of incredibly gorgeous men - the kind with square-jaws and rock-hard stomachs. I never got to associate with guys like this back in the United States.

This group absolutely loved Dean, but who didn't? Even if you weren't into bears, you were still into Dean. Seriously, if I could remember Dean's actual name, I would still try to track him down to this day.

A few of them also chatted with me, including Gustavo, who was one of the muscle-iest of the bunch. They literally bulged. And each time I struggled with my Spanish, he kindly switched over to English.

Dean leaned in and said, "One of these guys is the owner of the bar. Since they are about to close, he's inviting us back to his place where they're gonna keep the party going. Wanna go?"

"Hell yes!" I replied.

We super-intelligently hopped into the cars of men we hardly knew. I sat next to Gustavo and he put his hand on my leg, giving me an honest smile. Something about him appeared genuinely sweet, as if he had a soft heart underneath those hard muscles.

We drove up the side of the mountain to an incredible house, a mansion by Mexico standards, where more guys greeted us on the back patio and around the pool. The owner of the bar clearly did well for himself.

Right off the bat, I did what any insecuierdo (my term for an insecure weirdo) would do: I made a beeline to the vodka. Alcohol had become my dear friend in Mexico. It loosened me up which legitimately helped me speak Spanish more fluently. It gave me the confidence to make-out with guys in bars and scream "NO SOY TURISTA" ("I'm not a tourist!") at taxi drivers who tried to rip off the gringo as he stumbled his way home.

A little alcohol went a long way for me. Now, at this wealthy house with all these beautiful people, I bypassed the "little" and went for "a lot." Within the hour, I got majorly blitzed. The room was spinning. I was slurring. Anytime someone tried to speak Spanish with me, I'd stare them straight in the face... and immediately go cross-eyed.

I wobbled my way into the living room and laid back on the couch to pass out like any respectable drunk person should. Minutes later, two guys sat down on each side of me. One began kissing my neck while the other unzipped my pants.

Like any respectable drunk person, I responded by kissing and unzipping their pants back. Or at least I tried unzipping their pants. In reality, I probably bounced my fingertips all over their crotches. I could hardly open my eyes to see what they looked like. But their faces felt attractive. I'm sure a blind person would agree with me.

"Vamonos al otra cuarto," one of them said, suggesting we go to another room.

We stood up and they both quickly grabbed on to me as to make sure I didn't smash onto the floor. We made our way into the laundry room. One guy pulled down my pants and went in for a blowski as I leaned back against the dryer. The other kissed me and I became lucid enough to know that this was incredibly hot.

Then, all of a sudden, they were gone. I was standing there all alone, in the laundry room, with my pants around my ankles and a soppy knob. However much time had passed between sleeping on the couch and this moment must have gotten me 10% more sober because I finally blinked my eyes open and got the room to stop spinning. When I pulled up my pants, I noticed my wallet was gone.

I got robbed while getting a blowjob! Strike two.

Typically, I keep my wallet in my front pocket to avoid getting pickpocketed.[15] But this one time, I had slid it in the back pocket in an attempt to look normal in front of all these attractive people. I at least still had my ID in my front pocket. I had shoved it in there after showing it to the doorman at the bar. But everything else was gone, including most of

---

15. I also do this to avoid sciatica. Sure, it looks nerdy but it's worth avoiding a lifetime of back pain.

the cash I had brought for the weekend.

I stumbled out to the back patio where Dean, Gustavo, and the bar-owner sat at a table. I plopped down in a chair, declaring, "Someone stole my wallet."

"Oh no! That's terrible," Gustavo said. "Are you sure it was stolen? You think you could have lost it somewhere?"

"No, it's stolen," I said, slurring. "I was in the laundry room and then with these two guys and [HICCUP] and with then one of them was giving me a blowjob and then alls-a-sudden they were gone and then when [HICCUP] I pulled my pants up my wallet was gone."

Dean tried to console me in his very masculine way. "Damn. That sucks, buddy. I'm sorry."

Next, the bar-owner chimed in. "I am *so* sorry this happened to you in my home. Do you know who did this?"

I lifted my head up to see if anyone looked familiar. No one did.

"Here. Let me make it up to you," he added.

Oh, thank God! He is going to give me some money!

"Let me give you some cocaine?"

Okay, nevermind.

"No, I don't want any cocaine!" I told him.

Some people reading this may be like "Whaaaa?! You didn't take the cocaine?!" Here's the thing: at this point in my life, I hadn't experimented with any kind of drugs. None of my friends ever mentioned the word "cocaine," much less suggested we do it. The bar-owner's offer sounded so random to me. It could only be akin to him offering me a black-market baby to make up for my loss.

I'm surprised I didn't cry. But I whined a lot. "What am I going to dooooo? How am I going to get hooooome?"

Gustavo stood up and came over. "Here. I am going to take care of you tonight. Come with me. I make sure you are safe."

The next morning, I woke up next to Gustavo in his bed. He laid there in his underwear while I still remained in all of my clothes. I took this as a sign that he kept his promise. He gave me a safe place to sleep and didn't try to steal anything while performing sexual acts on me. Gustavo had been my knight in shining Mexican armor.

After admiring his chivalry, I moved on to admiring his body. I couldn't believe I woke up next to someone like this. His biceps were like bowling balls. His pecs were like bowling balls. His shoulders were like tiny bowling balls. This whole man was like one giant bowling alley with a six pack (almost an eight pack).

Gustavo woke up to me staring at him, which he graciously didn't get creeped out by. He asked how I felt. I told him I was a little hungover and feeling dumb, but that I would be fine. He leaned in for a kiss. I accepted it even though I hadn't brushed my teeth in twenty-four hours.

Gustavo mentioned that everybody had planned to take a boat out to a private island and he asked if I wanted to join them. A private island? This could definitely turn this weekend trip around.

"But I don't have my swimsuit," I told him.

"You don't need your swimsuit. It's clothing optional," he said, as if I could totally do that.

"I can't go naked in front of other people!"

He laughed. "Why not?"

"I dunno. It's weird."

"You look good," he told me. "But okay, okay. If you are not comfortable, I take you back to your hotel so we can get your things."

We got to the hotel with enough time for me to brush my teeth, take a shower, and basically shed off the grimy swamp monster I had turned into the night before. I made sure to grab my bottle of SPF one billion. If being pale made me attractive in this country, I sure as hell wasn't gonna lose that.

Gustavo suggested that I could bring my toiletries with me in case I wanted to "sleep" at his place again. I liked this idea *a lot*. It meant many more hours of unlimited access to his six-to-eight abs.

When we got to the boat, I nearly jumped as I saw Dean had also joined this outing. I didn't know where he had spent his night or who he had been with, but it didn't matter. It was one thing to jump in a car with a bunch of strangers. It was quite another to do it on a boat. As much as I trusted Gustavo, I needed a trusted friend on board too.

The island was less an island and more of a giant rock with a large platform in the middle that kind of made a beach. It at least had sand on it. Any time someone wanted to go in the water, they'd take their swimsuit off. Why even bother wearing one?

The group talked about it being the bar-owner's birthday and discussed their plans for the evening.

"What would you like for your birthday," his boyfriend (who was American) asked.

"I would like some special cake," he said.

I found this to be one of the weirdest things I had ever heard. *Of course he wants special cake,* I thought. *It's a cake for his birthday. That's what makes it special! Duh!*

"Aren't all birthday cakes special?" I said, thinking it was witty.

The few guys that heard me gave an odd look. It took me a moment to realize that the bar-owner had actually said "special K," and he wasn't talking about the cereal. He meant ketamine, the delightful horse tranquilizer turned street drug. MICROBURST!

Dean stood up, slipped off his swimsuit, and headed for the waters. I figured I should get in a good swim too. This way, I could doggie paddle in circles around Dean to get a better view of him naked. In the water, he asked why I still wore my swimsuit. I told him the truth: that I was allergic to casual nudity.

When he got out, I decided to stay put so it wasn't too obvious that I followed him in there. As I bobbed up and down alone, I thought, *why not take off my swimsuit? Everybody else is doing it. It will be normal.*

But the water was kind of cold and my penis was extremely unhappy with me. And I'd be damned if I got out of the water with an angry penis. It wouldn't make any difference. I could never, ever, most definitely, unquestionably, absolutely, positively, no ifs, ands, or buts, without a doubt ever take off my clothes in front of people anyway. This whole "naked thing" just wasn't for me. No way. No how. No thank you.

Gustavo and I didn't join the crew for the bar-owner's birthday, which was fine by me. Having never done drugs before, I didn't want to start with "K," no matter how special it was. We had a quiet dinner followed by going directly back to his place and directly back into his bed.

He didn't have the nicest apartment. For window shades, Gustavo had used cut up sheets. They did the trick to prevent any neighbors from seeing all the stuff we did in the dark hours, but when the morning came, they failed to stop the light from coming in. Being used to it, Gustavo stayed fast asleep. I, on the other hand, woke up promptly.

As I came into consciousness, something seemed off. The light hadn't been the only thing that woke me up. When I moved, I noticed that my butt felt a smidge wet. My eyes shot wide open as I simultaneously gasped. I knew exactly what happened. Montezuma's Revenge had gotten to me. I shit the bed. I SHIT THE BED IN FRONT OF THE FIRST GUY I HAD SEX WITH WHO HAD MUSCLES!!!! Strike three, Puerto Vallarta. Strike three.

It wasn't a ton, but it was enough. What was I going to do? How was I going to hide this? I counted my blessings that I hadn't been a naked guy. I had worn boxers to bed which caught the brunt of the backdoor debris. While Gustavo laid there naked, I laid there soiled.

I got up very carefully, hoping that none of it got on the bed. No such luck. A little bit of it did. I didn't know what the proper order was of cleaning up after you shit the bed. Do you start with yourself before tending to the sheets? Or the other way around? I decided to clean myself first and held my boxers very tight as I scampered across Gustavo's apartment. The last thing I needed was to be Hansel-And-Gretel-ing it from the bed to the bathroom.

I took off my boxers to get what I could in the toilet. The rest I'd have to wash off in the sink. *Please, don't let Gustavo wake up and catch me washing shitty boxers in his sink!* But then I didn't know what to do with my sopping, wet underwear.

Using the shower to wash myself didn't seem like a good option. If I turned it on, the sound could wake Gustavo. The good news was that he had a roll of paper towels in the bathroom. The bad news was that, with all of the bad Mexican plumbing, I couldn't simply flush these paper towels down the toilet.

Like the wet underwear, I'd have to stuff them in my backpack... next to my toiletries. Later, I could dunk my entire backpack in bleach. After that, I would set it on fire. And then after that, I would take the ashes and flush them down the toilet. *Take that, Mexico! I flushed a whole backpack down your toilet!* Granted, I would be too lazy to do such a thing.

Once I got myself cleaned, I took some wet paper towels over to the bed to clean the small spot, praying that it would come out. No such luck again. It left a small stain - about the size of a nickel - big enough that Gustavo would eventually see it.

"Fucking Puerto Vallarta!" I whispered to myself as I scrubbed it. "When will this godforsaken trip ever end?!"

With it being election weekend, I thought about how this country needed to make a new law where all citizens are required to have brown sheets (or any other dark color). That way we Americans can clean up with dignity when we do our business in their beds while abroad. Because really, that's what escapes our butts in the middle of the night: our dignity.

Alas, Gustavo's sheets were some light stripy thing. Once I got out as much as I could, I slid back into bed and waited for him to wake up. When he did, he tried kissing me to initiate a round of morning sex. I normally hated morning sex (I still do), but I would have actually gone for this just to hit the bowling alley one last time.

I had to push Gustavo away instead, telling him I didn't feel good. Although I didn't give details, it was that rare instance I told the truth in order to get out of a sticky situation (oh, Jesus, it was so sticky). This also gave me an excuse to not see him for the rest of the day. When he would later discover the small stain, it would be understandable as to what happened.

That night, I slept at the hotel so that I could shit the bed in the same room with my girlfriends, who neither had muscles nor the potential for sex with me. I should have stayed there the whole trip. Naturally, my bowels decided to remain perfectly intact.

I have never returned to Puerto Vallarta to this day. A part of me remains convinced that this tourist destination had a vendetta against me. It makes me sad whenever my friends tell me how much fun they have during their vacations there. Maybe one day I will give it a second chance and try my best not to shit all over the entire city while I am there.

When the summer semester ended, I couldn't get back to Denver fast enough. Roberto and I literally ran to embrace each other at the airport. He brought me a flower, which he had never done before. We hugged so hard that we squeezed water out of each other's eyeballs. Taking this time apart had been exactly what we needed. We decided to go back to full monogamy so that we could focus solely on the two of us - focus on getting back to what made us great.

A month later, Roberto and I officially broke up – for real this time. We had become so lost in thinking how our relationship was meant to be, that we never stopped to think, in all the blatant ways, how *not* meant to be it actually was. Without question, taking this time apart had been exactly what we needed.

We would go on to make the next major mistake of trying to "remain friends" after breaking up. Once we started dating new people, new jealousies were more than happy to rear their ugly heads. I would never have to see his large penis ever again though. And I guess I made it through without murdering him, so that's good too.

That summer in Mexico taught me a lot of wonderful things. It taught me that tequila tastes *ah-mazing* with grapefruit flavored soda.[16] It taught me that taking advice from total strangers will land you in some incredible places. And it taught me that blowjobs are fantastic until someone robs you.

That summer, Mexico also taught me a lot of terrible things. It taught me that you shouldn't get wasted on tequila and grapefruit soda the night before you go on a tequila factory tour. It taught me that taking drinks from total strangers can land you in some scary places. And it taught me that, no matter how hard you try to avoid it, if you stay in Mexico long enough, Montezuma's Revenge *will* find you.

16. By this time in the story, I refuse to use the brand name "Squirt."

A PINK FEATHERED FELLOW

Back when I switched from the community college to the state college downtown, things didn't start off so solid. Between math class and astronomy class (to which I kept accidentally calling "astrology class"), my grades took a dive. But I struggled mostly with ethics class.

Contrary to how this sounds, it was not due to me being an unethical person. I just couldn't quite understand what an "ethics class" meant. None of it ever made sense to me. I partly blame the teacher for this. He was about as interesting as the chalk he wrote with. Although I think he used a dry-erase board. Still, if he had written with chalk, it would've been him.

It wouldn't be until the end of the semester that I'd realize this class was about the philosophical approach to decision making along with the difference between right and wrong. That certainly sounds super interesting to me now. But, at the time, it bored me out of my mind.

I went to class early one day hoping that, if I had some extra minutes to read ahead, I might be able to figure out what this mind-numbing man was talking about. A few other students had done the same. I took a random seat and cracked the book open. Before I could read the first word, somebody tapped on my shoulder.

I turned around to see one of the most beautiful girls I had ever met. I am not even pandering to her. She was positively gorgeous with short blonde hair and light makeup that accented her lovely face (instead of making her look like a sexy clown like some of the ladies on campus).

"I *love* your shirt," she said.

This was not a compliment I received often, and it made less sense coming from someone like her. She looked like she stepped right out of a fashion catalog. I looked like I stepped out of a homeless shelter. What could I possibly be wearing that she would like?

I glanced down to see it: Garbage. Not literally though. It was the name of my favorite band and I had worn their shirts all the time.

"*You* like Garbage?!" I asked.

"Oh my god, yeah. They're like my favorite band!"

"Really? MINE TOO!!"

She reached out her hand with a bushy-eyed disposition that I had not been accustomed to. "Hi! I'm Sinead!"

"Like O'Connor?" I asked a question that she had unfortunately heard all too often. She graciously let it slide so that we could talk some Garbage. I was grateful for this, because finding someone who loved Garbage as much as I did was like finding an African polar bear.

Ever since I was a kid, my musical tastes had floated in and out of obscurity. I was about five years old when Gloria Estefan warned everyone that the rhythm would get us all. This was a terrifying message for a child. *What if the rhythm does get me? Will I be okay? Will the rhythm try to hurt me? Why doesn't the rhythm just leave us all alone?* But Gloria had it right. The rhythm ended up getting me. And it got me to the tune of weird nineties dance music.

In sixth-grade, I saw an episode of *Beavis and Butthead* that featured a music video by the campy Euro-Pop group called Army of Lovers. The men looked like hairy women and the women looked like wealthy hookers. They sang all choir-like about crucifixion amongst a backdrop of 122 irresistible beats per minute. The next day, I went to school and asked the other boys if they had seen that very same brilliance. This did not help my popularity.

As I slid into my teen years, my interest in dance music got more mainstream. I ran around buying CD singles for the remixes of LeAnn Rimes' "How Do I Live?" and Whitney Houston's "It's Not Right But It's Okay." Ya know, the hyper-masculine stuff.

It wasn't until I was with one of my friends at the park that I heard Garbage. Their second album, Version 2.0, had just come out, and he couldn't get enough of it. The moment I heard it, I pretty much hated it. The guitars slammed too hard. The drumming slammed too hard. And the lead singer's vocals slammed too hard, and with a lot of anger. There was a lot of slamming, not enough disco balls and fog machines.

The day ultimately came when I got one of their songs stuck in my head. I couldn't get it out. Next thing I knew, I bought their album, which quickly became the best thing since sliced bread (which was invented in 1928). I played it so much that I physically wore out the CD and had to buy a second one. That's not easy to do. And I perhaps had to buy a third one too.

When I saw Garbage live for the first time, that sealed the deal. The fiery red-headed vocalist captivated me with her commanding stage persona. The music's slamming sound slammed right into my face. She was angry. I was angry. All my years of being bullied came flooding back to me. I needed to let it all out.

I discovered head-banging and slam-dancing (a few notches below moshing). It felt a thousand times more invigorating than normal dancing. That was all I needed. Gloria Estefan's rhythm could go screw itself. I now had rock-n-roll surging through my veins.

Garbage's music was all about being an outsider. The band members saw themselves this way, both in their personal lives and in their music. They combined different genres of various styles to come up with their rock-infused sound.

At the time, bands didn't do this. Genres were segmented. The music industry naturally became suspicious of them, which is how they got their name. Their multi-genre influenced approach and layering of sounds, to most, sounded like a bunch of garbage.

The lead singer, Shirley Manson, represented everything I wanted to be. She was brash, intelligent, bold, sexual, and strong. She spoke her mind and did it with smarts. She'd tease with her skirt and then stick her fist in her mouth to prove she was nobody's plaything. Shirley didn't take shit from anyone. If I had to be an outsider, this was the kind of outsider I wanted to be.

Therefore, meeting Sinead in class confused me. She didn't seem like an outsider. She was *so* beautiful and put together. It reminded me of that classic image of popular girls in high school. But she acted *so* nice - an image that *didn't* fit the popular girls in high school. I naturally felt a tad skeptical about it. How could someone like her have the same favorite band as someone like me?

I learned that Sinead had transferred to our school after completing a year at a traditional campus and hating it. Her dorm-mate would apparently leave half-eaten peanut-butter and jelly sandwiches lying around, or make-out with her boyfriend on the top bunk while Sinead had to listen. Speaking of "ethics," that's completely unethical - only eating half of a peanut butter and jelly sandwich. Furthermore, Sinead missed her boyfriend, so a centralized commuter campus would be a better fit.

Sinead hadn't exactly been an outsider. My sixth sense of superiority had proven correct in that. She did run with the typical popular crowd in high school, doing the typical mean girl things. Then, in her senior year, Sinead's friends switched and started doing the mean girl things to her. Being in the leper's shoes had given her a whole new perspective on things. It made her sick to know she treated people the same way.

Sinead fortunately had a slightly older sister, Deirdre, who had always been an outsider. Deirdre already belonged to the world of dark makeup, moody flannel shirts, and leprosy music. She even kind of looked like Shirley Manson (so, also beautiful).

With her sister's influence, Sinead was already well-versed in alt-rock bands like Smashing Pumpkins, Radiohead, and, of course, Garbage. After going through her terrible high school turn, she took to the angsty lyrics in a more connected way.

Sinead and I... wait... hold on. Can I back up for a second? Sinead's dorm-mate would really only eat half of a peanut butter and jelly sandwich? Seriously?! Who does that?! You either eat a PBJ sandwich or you don't. What a sociopath! Anyway...

Sinead and I formed a study group along with another girl who had jet-black hair and listened to the band Dropkick Murphys. The three of us could not have been more different and yet similar. By the end of that semester, I understood what an ethics class was and pulled my grade up to a C. Over the next couple of semesters, Sinead and I continued to take more classes together like two codependent peas in a higher educational pod.

By the time I met Sinead, my love of the band Garbage had become a borderline obsession. If a tour was going to happen, I knew the dates and when tickets would go on sale. If Garbage was going to play on TV, I knew the date, time and channel. If they were going to be in a magazine, I knew the date it would get released and where to pick it up. Clearly being obsessed meant knowing a lot of dates.

Between collecting all the albums, singles and bootlegs, I had more CDs by Garbage than some people had in their entire music collection. I wore their shirts so much that people called me "Scott the Garbage Guy," and I wholeheartedly loved it. I came to use it as my online moniker which, in hindsight, probably scared some people away.

When the band finished releasing all their singles from the second album, they turned the singles' artwork into symbols. They used these symbols as Easter eggs throughout their other visuals. I proceeded to go get all six symbols tattooed on my lower back. Six months later, I kid you not, the term "tramp stamp" emerged. Coincidence? Well, yes, absolutely. But I didn't regret it one bit.

This obsession has toned down over the years. That being said, while writing this story, I decided to take a break to go count how many Garbage t-shirts that currently sit in my closet. I have twenty-one shirts (college day shirts not included). Like the CDs, I have more Garbage t-shirts than people have in their entire shirt collection.

So, Shirley, if you're reading this and you aren't creeped out, let's do lunch. Have your agent call my agent. That's assuming I have an agent. If I haven't made it as a writer, then chances are I'll be working as a "sandwich artist" somewhere. In this case, you can call my manager at the sandwich shop. His name is Brad and he is the worst.

Sinead didn't get creeped out by my obsession. She loved it. I was like her 24/7 Garbage news source. When I found out Garbage would be joining the other popular nineties pop/rock band, No Doubt, on an upcoming tour, we squealed in ways that dogs could hear. WE COULD FINALLY SEE OUR FAVORITE BAND TOGETHER!

This tour came sometime after Garbage's third album. On this record, they experimented with a pop sound in their alternative weirdo way. A few songs toyed with the idea of gender, and the album's lead single was even called "Androgyny."

For this album, Shirley shaved the sides of her head to go for a more masculine haircut. When she died it blonde, the record label went nuts. Nobody had ever heard of a "fiery blonde head." They immediately demanded that she dye it back to which she immediately refused. What a badass.

With Shirley having all the qualities I wanted to embody, I had no other choice but to go give myself the exact same shaved-head blonde haircut. It made me feel super edgy and rock-n-roll. I stood out from the crowd and didn't care what anyone thought of me. And I couldn't wait to see what everyone thought of me.

The night of the show, we went to the arena early in hopes to get a decent spot. With No Doubt being such chart-toppers at the time, we knew we'd have a big crowd ahead of us. Being such early birds indeed helped us get our worm. Sinead and I wound up standing ten feet away from the stage.

Once Garbage took the stage, we lost our minds. Shirley Manson no longer had that same shaved haircut, but who cared? We screamed. We jumped. We cheered. We danced. No doubt the No Doubt fans who had come early had gotten annoyed with us. This didn't matter either. We were seeing our favorite band live and WE WERE SO CLOSE!!!!

For one of their final songs, Shirley sang "Cherry Lips," a track inspired by a book about a boy who dresses like a girl and becomes a prostitute - clearly a feel-good-song. As dark as that sounds, this song actually has the most upbeat sound of any of their recordings. Shirley dubbed it as an "ode to the transgender spirit." Not a lot of people talked about the transgender community in 2001.

When this song began, our idol busted out a big pink feathered boa. She flung it around her neck and managed to do what I could only describe as "dance-strut" around the stage in the most rock-n-roll way. Whenever she came to our side, Sinead and I jumped higher and sang louder. Our favorite singer wouldn't notice us, but we were already in heaven as it was.

When the song wrapped up, Shirley made her way back to our side of the stage and tapped on the security guard's shoulder. She handed him the boa and spoke into the mic, "Here. Hand this to that sweet boy right there." Shirley pointed directly at me.

SHE HAD NOTICED US! All I could do was stand there, shaking and gasping as if I had won the lottery. Shirley Manson, my hero, had just given me her pink feathered boa. Me! Scott! The kid who always believed he got the short end of the stick. I teared up as this could've been the happiest moment of my life.

After No Doubt took the stage, Sinead and I decided to duck out from our amazing spot to let their fans get closer. It seemed like the nice thing to do since they had put up with us beforehand. We listened to a few songs before curiosity got the best of us. *If we went in search for Garbage's tour bus, could we meet the band? This boa is obviously our ticket to a meet-n-greet.*

We broke away from the concert to roam the halls of the massive venue. Surprisingly we did find the van, but the security guard in front of it refused my pink feathered ticket. He wouldn't even confirm whether the band was in the van or not. It appeared to be a dead end, so we gave up and decided to go back to the show.

As we made our way back through the halls, we came upon a group of girls walking in our direction. One of the girls pointed at us and yelled, "SHE GAVE YOU THE BOA?! THAT'S NOT FAIR! YOU'RE A GUY!"

Before I could think of what to say, Sinead stepped in and yelled back, "IT'S TOTALLY FAIR! HE'S THE BIGGEST GARBAGE FAN EVER!" She was technically correct.

In the weeks that followed, I couldn't shut up about the boa. I went around repeating it like those dolls who, when pulling the cord, can say one of exactly five phrases.

Pulls the cord.

"Hi, I'm Scott and my favorite band is Garbage!"

Pulls the cord.

"Lead singer, Shirley Manson, handed me her pink feathered boa right off the stage!"

Pulls the cord.

"She didn't give it to anyone else. Just me!"

Pulls the cord.

"Would you like to see my pink feathered boa?!"

Pulls the cord.

"Would you like to touch my pink feathered boa?!"

I used exclamation points all of my doll phraseology because those dolls always feel like they shout their joy at you.

My sister, Stacey, found the perfect display case for it. It was a long rectangular wooden frame with glass panels and a wooden base. This way, the boa could sit high up on a shelf in the apartment, for all to see. I think it confused people more than anything else. *Why does this guy have a bunch of pink feathers in a glass case?* But it meant the world to me. It also gave me an excuse to tell the story.

A while after the concert, it came out that Shirley would be doing an upcoming interview in a magazine. This was back when magazines were made from glossy trees rather than backlit screens that screw up our circadian rhythms.

Sinead and I both needed this. It had been approximately sixty-three days, thirteen hours, and twenty-eight minutes since our last Garbage fix. We were slapping our wrists like junkies waiting for our next fix.

The day it came out, I reminded Sinead before I ran to the record store to pick up my copy. When I got home, I didn't flip through it right away. I poured myself a nice glass of cabernet sauvignon first. And by cabernet sauvignon, I mean Welch's grape juice. I couldn't afford wine with all the CDs, posters, t-shirts, and magazines I was buying. Oh, and by Welch's grape juice, I mean the store brand knock-off that had *real* grape flavoring.

Once I swirled my glass and smelled the vanilla, black-pepper tones that didn't exist, I flipped through the magazine. In the first part of the interview, Shirley said something amazing. Next, she said something brilliant. I read further and then she said something incredible. I read even more, and... I stopped. Shirley Manson had talked about the pink feathered boa.

She had been giving one out at every show. But that's not the thing that stopped me. I didn't need to be the only fan who got a boa. Getting to be the one who she handed it to at our show still felt special enough. The thing I didn't expect her to say was that she had been giving them to the most androgynous boy or girl in the audience.

Am I androgynous? I thought. *I mean, sure, I have the same haircut that Shirley had. But she had a boy's haircut so that she could be androgynous. Surely, that must mean I still look like a guy, right? Lots of guys have bleach blond buzz cuts with length on top. Don't they?*

The idea of this made me lose my head. I promptly went over to the kitchen and poured my "wine" down the drain. *Men don't drink wine. What do men drink? Beer? But what would work as a cheap, fake substitute for beer? Sparkling cider? No, that's worse! Men don't drink things that sparkle!*

I know this shouldn't have been upsetting, but my favorite singer had inadvertently called me a nancy-pants. Being an effeminate kid was the basis for all the bullying I endured growing up. I had come to like being an outsider, however, I didn't have a choice in the matter. I at least wanted to be a normal, masculine male outsider. I didn't want to be androgynous.

I looked up at the pink feathered boa sitting in its display case and something occurred to me: Stacey had gotten it at a sports memorabilia store. It was a display case that guys used to show off impressive baseball bats, and I had filled it with pink feathers. My prized possession now mocked me. This wasn't who I wanted to be.

I started to wonder about Sinead. I didn't want her to read this. I didn't want her to know that Shirley Manson dubbed me as "the most androgynous person" at our concert. From grade school to middle school to high school, the same message always got reinforced: people don't befriend boys who act like girls. Sinead wouldn't tolerate her new male friend being femme. Nobody would.

The next day, when I met up with her on campus, the first words out of her mouth were, "Did you go get the magazine?"

"Umm, yeah. Did you?"

"No. I didn't have time, Boo."

Whew. I still had a shot at salvaging this.

"How's the interview?" she asked.

"Oh, you know. It was great, as always."

This should have been the first clue that the interview hadn't settled with me. Normally I would explode with words like "outstanding," "exceptional," or "magnificent." The word "great" was an understatement when it came to my opinions on Garbage.

"Nice," Sinead said. "Maybe I can go pick it up this afternoon after class."

"Oh, no. Don't worry about going to get it. I will borrow it to you," I told her.[17]

"Oh. Sure. Thanks, hon!"

This should have been the second clue. I did not lend out my Garbage magazines in fear that that the lendee wouldn't return them in pristine condition. But I had a plan. I would keep telling her, with my bad grammar, that I would let her borrow it, and then keep forgetting to bring it. Sooner or later, she'd forget about the whole thing (hopefully sooner).

---

17. I know the proper way to phrase this is "I will lend it to you" or "I will let you borrow it." But I had done the study abroad by this time and after learning Spanish, my English got a little jacked up. This was how I talked for many years.

I remained on edge about this diabolical plan for the next few weeks. Sinead would ask about the magazine. I would give her a big old "oops," and promise to bring it next time. Slowly but surely, she stopped asking about Shirley. Then one day, after class, she brought it up again.

"I went and picked up the magazine," she said.

Fuck. She wasn't supposed to do that. "Oh, I was gonna borrow it to you."

"I know. But I figured I should have my own copy anyway."

I shifted uncomfortably in my seat. This was the moment she'd let me know that I was too different to be her friend.

"Well, what did you think?" I braced myself for it.

"It was fabulous. Except for the part where Shirley Manson called you a lady-boy. I'm sorry. Please start sitting at least three desks away from me in class," she did not say. Instead, she said, "It was fabulous. I just love Shirley." And that was it.

As we talked more about the interview, I kept waiting for the bombs to drop, but they didn't. Neither of us mentioned the pink feathered boa and we went on about our day. Sinead continued to treat me like things were totally normal because, to her, things *were* totally normal. This should have made me feel better. It really made me feel worse.

This former mean girl was legitimately a former mean girl. Sinead didn't try to pull my hair, or give me a wedgie, or stab me in the left side of my neck with her ink pen, or whatever mean girls do.

The real embarrassment didn't come from the pink feathered boa. It came from my overreaction to it. In my fear of being different, I had become way too dramatic about the whole thing. It also came from a lack of being good at being different. For a rebellious outsider, I still cared way too much about what others thought of me.

Worst of all, it came from the fact that I had completely underestimated my friend. I should've given Sinead more credit than that. She did defend me against those girls at the concert who didn't think I deserved the boa with my being a guy. In my own fear of being too different, I lost sight of this fact. All the while, that moment she defended me had been the moment our friendship had truly solidified.

Sinead's story of high school redemption had proven unquestionably true. She genuinely became the kind girl who treated people the way she wanted to be treated. It looked so foreign to me that I could hardly recognize it. It made me extra thankful that she tapped on my shoulder that time in ethics class.

I'd eventually learn that I didn't necessarily fall into either category of butch or femme. Like most things in my world, I floated somewhere in between. Shirley Manson most likely gave me the boa because of my over-the-top enthusiasm at the show, and maybe my haircut too.

But if it had been by virtue of being androgynous, it would've been intended as a compliment from someone I admired - not a criticism. Besides, one day I would meet Garbage and Shirley would give me something far better that would last me a lifetime.

In due time, I'd learn that there is nothing wrong with being androgynous. In fact, I admire men who fearlessly embrace their feminine side and I admire women who spend 60% of their time at Home Depot. Gender norms can mess with our minds far too often. I aspire to be like those who have the self-assurance to break from all that.

After graduation, Sinead moved to Philadelphia with her boyfriend when he got a big job promotion. The morning she left, we cried over pancakes. As we stayed in touch - visiting each other often - she became (and still remains) the one person I could honestly call "best friend." And, when the day came that she got married, I got to have the honor of being in their wedding party... standing on her side... along with her awesome sister and the other bridesmaids.

WHEN WORLDS COLLIDE

When a relationship comes to an end, you can essentially do one of two things; A) you can take time for yourself to heal your broken heart, or B) you can immediately jump into another relationship. Can you guess which one is healthier? If you said "A," then you are correct.

Now, can you guess which one I did? If you said "B," you are also correct! Man, you are a good test-taker. Something tells me you'd do great on the SATs even if *you* had to take it while having crabs.

The good news was that, before I jumped into this next relationship, I made a pit stop and got back to the idea of friendships. I moved into a new studio apartment while reuniting with my high school buddy, Rey. Together, we met Eddie - a tall gent who ran around with the rockabilly crowd. Eddie had dark features with a greaser haircut and had lady friends who did themselves up like pin-up girls.

We became like *The Three Musketeers* - that is if *The Three Musketeers* went out boozing it up all the time. Being single and ready to mingle with these guys meant venturing out to the bars and drinking all the alcohols. We somehow dodged more DUIs than I'd like to admit. And I'm pretty sure people love admitting to dodging DUIs.

We embarked on all this partying in the summer before my final year of college. It felt necessary as I thought I missed out on the true college experience by going to a commuter campus. No one ever flipped me upside-down on a keg, stuck a tube in my mouth, and screamed at me to "CHUG CHUG CHUG!"[18]

The three of us went to bars according to their nightly specials. On Thursdays, one joint had fifty cent beer night. On Fridays, another had buy-one-get-one-free night. On Saturdays, the night club offered free well drinks from 9 p.m. to 10 p.m. We took most advantage of this night.

Our favorite landed on Wednesday at a bar called "The Wave." The name really made no sense as the inside had nothing to do with waves - neither tidal, nor brain, nor micro. It was a small dive that had a good dance floor and a kick-ass DJ. Wednesdays were dollar-drink night.

It was on this night that I met Brent. We did the game where we would glance over at each other, and look away. Then, we would smile and look away again, and so on and so on. I eventually walked over to say hello. Or perhaps I swayed my way over and slurred hello. Or, most likely, he walked over to say hello and I slurred back. The next morning, I woke up with his number in my pocket.

I couldn't quite remember what Brent looked like. I had a bad habit of wearing major beer goggles. By my fifth rum and coke, the grim reaper would have been looking kinda sexy. Gotta love a man with a sickle. If I remembered correctly, Brent didn't have a sickle, but he did look like one of those movie vampires. And, for this reason, I was intrigued.

He was so easy to talk to on the phone. We already made each other laugh just by setting up our first date. Brent wanted to set our date for Wednesday night, which meant sacrificing a night of drinking with my friends. *The date better damn well be worth it,* I thought.

When we met up, Brent did indeed match my vampire memories with his jet black hair, pale skin, and piercing blue eyes. He attributed this to the fact that he was half-Irish and half-Mexican. When I informed

---

18. This still sounds fun to me.

people of this interesting fact, they proceeded to label me as being into Hispanic men.

This kind of irked me. I didn't want to be pigeon-holed in my attraction. I mean, every major relationship I had was also with someone older than me (to some degree), but no one labeled me as having a daddy complex. Although, these men did all go by their middle names like my father did. And they all had the same astrological sign as my father. QUICK! LOOK! A BEAR! No? No bear? Okay, fine. Let's continue.

Like a vampire, Brent didn't appear as if he aged. We discovered that we had fourteen years of an age difference between us, which I didn't even see coming. At first, this made me uneasy. But we got along so well. It didn't appear to make much of a difference.

Being a former punk rocker turned physical therapist, Brent really was just a normal guy. He had a nice, normal job, lived in a nice, normal house, had two nice, normal cats, and he had a nice, normal roommate. How he got to all this normalcy, however, was not entirely normal.

Brent had an emotionally abusive father who always targeted him over his younger brother. His relatives on his father's side also treated him horrendously. For example, if he had a sleepover with his cousins, his aunt would make him sleep in the bathtub.

His mother didn't do much in the way of protecting him from his father. At age sixteen, he came out as gay to which his father kicked him out of the house. Brent survived on his own and worked his way up to be that nice, normal adult that I now got to meet.

All of this didn't come right out on our first date. But as we quickly grew close, he let me in on his life just as fast. Hearing all of this made me like him more, knowing that he endured such hardship and survived. It was the complete opposite of my upbringing and, in spite of it all, he still made a success out of himself.

As the two of us grew even closer, he told me about the night his grandmother got drunk and admitted that his father was not actually his biological father. Brent's mother had been pregnant prior to the marriage and asked the man to raise him as if he were his own. This was where Brent got his Hispanic heritage, which answered the question of why he looked slightly different from his younger brother. This was the basis for all the abuse.

Brent still had strong ties to his punk rock roots. When not at work, he wore combat boots, all black, and listened to more aggressive music than I did. This made a supposedly normal guy a lot more interesting. It made him seem rough and rebellious and, well, even more like a vampire. And, like the boy before him, his background rubbed off on me. I found myself getting into classic punk music along with a little heavy metal.

Just because we moved swiftly didn't necessarily mean that things went smoothly. I had remained friends with my ex, Roberto, after our break up, and this bothered Brent immensely. In all fairness, Brent was spot-on. This setup was ridiculously toxic.

In due time, I would purge Roberto from my life. But, for now, I had it in my head that I could have the best of both worlds: a friendship with my ex and a relationship with Brent. We constantly fought about it. Most people would see this as a warning sign to pull up their pants and run. My pants chose to remain down as I stayed on this rollercoaster.

As fall came and I got into my final semester at school, I noticed another thing that troubled me. My friends didn't like Brent. Not only did they not approve of our occasional fighting, but they didn't like the fact that my spending more time with *him* meant less time drinking time with *them.*

On the flip-side, Brent didn't like my friends. It rubbed him the wrong way when I went out with them. He worried that I would crash my car. But more so, he worried they'd try to convince me to date other people or, at the very least, sleep around with other people.

All this relationship rivalry didn't work well for a spaz-master like me. I expected to have a win/win situation (where I was the one who won in both cases). If I was going to have my cake and eat it too (and I really did like eating my metaphorical cake), my two worlds would have to coincide.

There was only one way to solve this: a night of bar hopping for the four of us. Brent could see that drinking with my friends was harmless fun and my friends could see that Brent was a nice guy who would never stop me from going out with them. Then, everyone could just get along.

My suggestion for the bar hopping got met with much resistance. I pleaded with my puppy dog eyes, which, due to all the drinking, looked like that of a bloodhound. And since dog eyes don't necessarily lure in the hearts of the lushes, I had to sweeten up the deal.

I offered to remain sober the entire night and be the designated driver so everyone else could drink as much as they wanted. I'd even buy the first round of drinks for them. Nothing works better on boozers than offering free booze. The three of them agreed to this.

The Friday night that we did this bar hopping adventure commenced just as I had hoped. Before I could fulfill my oath of buying everyone's first drink, Brent stepped in and ordered a round of shots.

I leaned into Eddie, "See?! *This* is the guy I was telling you about."

Again, free alcohol goes a long way. My friends were impressed.

But when the shots arrived, there were four of them. I had evidently been included on the order.

"I told you I wasn't drinking tonight," I said to Brent.

"You can have one," he said. "And we should make a toast anyway."

He made a good point on both accounts. Besides, no night ends badly when starting off with shots. We clinked our tiny glasses together, someone said a very nice thing, and we slurped them down.

At the next bar, I made sure to deliver my promise. While ordering everyone else's drinks, I made the decision to get one more for myself. If all went as planned, this would be a long night. A cocktail here and there would simply give me a slight buzz. I had driven on way more than this many times.

After they each had a few more drinks, Eddie got a phone call to meet up with some other friends at the male strip bar. Everyone agreed to make this our third stop. Now, when I say "male strip bar," I'm not talking about anything fancy. Though the dancers consistently had all of their teeth, this joint was a divey corridor where you didn't really bank on the notion of getting aroused.

My buzz had somewhat worn off by the time we arrived, so I opted for a third drink. The guys were on their fifth or sixth and had no shortage of laughter. Their fun centers were on overdrive and seeing the people I loved enjoying each other, in a seedy bar where mostly naked men left butt prints on a mirrored wall, made my heart feel like Christmas.

When Eddie and Rey whipped out their dollars to tip the dancers, I encouraged Brent to partake in this fun as well. It was the perfect opportunity to show myself as the hip boyfriend who didn't get all jealous about that stuff.

When the dancer I liked came out, the time had come to now put my tip in somebody's hip. I appreciated this guy because he did all of his grinding to rock music rather than twerking to Britney Spears. He was also straight and I was (and still am) a cliché sucker for this.

I went up to the stage. He pulled out the side of his g-string. I slid my dollar in and the dancer gave me a smile while flirtatiously stroking his hand along my jaw. I didn't have a beard yet, so maybe he pretended I was a chick. But, suddenly, Brent came up from behind and slapped the dancer's hand away from my face.

"DON'T YOU FUCKING TOUCH HIM!" Brent screamed. Apparently, *he* was not the hip boyfriend who didn't get all jealous about that stuff.

Being the ultra-classy joint that it was, no bouncer had been available to step in and diffuse the situation. The dancer, genuinely frightened, jumped back and made a beeline for the other side of the stage where his groin would get him more dollars and fewer threats.

"What the hell, Brent?!" I said.

"I don't want other men touching you!" He shouted.

I shouted back, "He was just being nice!"

You could feel my entire night of "everyone getting along" now coming to a grinding halt.

Eddie leaned in. "I think Brent is too drunk. You should take him home."

"But what about you guys? I'm your ride tonight," I said.

"Don't worry about us," he said. "We will find our way home. Do what you need to do."

I felt like if I didn't come back, Brent's outburst would undo all of my hard work. I had to return at least to act like everything was cool. I would tell them that Brent apologized for making a scene and that he wanted us all to have a good night.

I dragged Brent out of the bar as he struggled to make one last charming attempt to threaten the stripper. On the drive home, I wondered how this happened. One minute, he was having a blast. The next minute, he completely lashed out with anger. Perhaps his sexy, vampire heritage made for a less desirable recipe: the drunken Irishman combined with that fiery Latin passion.

We pulled up to the front of the house.

"Okay, I'm gonna drop you off and I will come back later," I said.

He lifted his head. "What? You're not coming in with me?"

"I'll be back," I said. "I'm Eddie and Rey's ride so I need to go take them home. I'll come spend the night with you after that."

Brent didn't like this. "You're just trying to stay out with your friends. That's messed up, Scott. You're supposed to stay with your boyfriend."

"I know. I will stay, but those guys are counting on me. I promise I am coming back."

In truth, Brent had it right. I *did* just want to go end the night with my fun friends rather than stick around with my grumpy boyfriend. I didn't intend on coming back. I was so frustrated by what Brent had done. That stripper, as a matter of fact, seemed like a good guy and gave me the impression that I could have had a shot with him. What if he never took another dollar from me again? How does one forgive that?

Brent started to argue. I tried talking some sense into him. Except reasoning with a drunk person is a bit like attempting to have an extraordinary orgasm with a blow-up doll. You can try and try, but it'll never get the job done and someone is bound to explode. Plus, the mouth is often more horrifying than it is helpful.

I turned off the car as I wouldn't be going anywhere any time soon. By the tenth minute, our argument had become totally circular. The talking had turned into yelling and the yelling had turned into frustration. I pleaded with him to get out of the car.

"YOU WANT ME TO GET OUT OF YOUR CAR?!"

"YES, PLEASE GET OUT OF MY FUCKING CAR!"

"FINE!" Brent opened the door. As he stepped out, he reached over and pulled the keys out of the ignition. Before I could catch him, he ran off to the house.

"GODDAMMIT, Brent!" I shouted.

By the time I stepped out of the car, he already managed to let himself inside, leaving the front door wide open. I now had to find a way to go rationalize with him so that he'd give me my keys back.

As I walked in the dark foyer, I could barely see a thing. Then, without warning, something slammed into the back of my head, knocking me to the ground. I sat up, rubbing my neck and getting my bearings. A dark shadow of a man hovered above me. I realized that, for the first time in my life, I had been punched.

The shadow spoke, "You're such a piece of shit."
Before I could say anything, those combat boots that I thought looked so cool on Brent bashed into my stomach. It knocked the wind out of me, making it impossible to scream out loud. I turned over on to all fours hoping to God I could get my breath back and get out of there.

"Brent, stop!" I said the moment I could speak. "I love you! Stop!"

"You don't love me!" The shadow said. "You don't fucking love anybody but yourself!"

As I began to figure out what was happening, my newly injured gut told me to do something entirely strange. *Do not fight back. If you lay a hand on Brent, our stories will become hearsay. It will be your word against his. If he remains untouched, the story would stay clear: he did this, not you.*

When I got to my feet, his hands grabbed me and shoved me into the dining room chairs. As I lifted myself up, he punched me in the side of my head, knocking me into the wall. The wall fortunately broke my fall and I stumbled my way forward. This momentum helped me make a run for the kitchen.

The moment I turned that corner, I flicked on the kitchen light switch and spun around to see him barreling at me. But the shadow was nowhere to be seen. This brought me a millisecond of relief until it occurred to me that I was a sitting duck. The kitchen had no other exit but from where I came. Everything in my bones knew that he stood there on the other side of that wall, still in the dining room, waiting for me.

I looked over to see their cordless phone. This was crucial as I didn't have a cell phone at the time. Cell phones were on the cusp of becoming the norm and everyone in this story had one except me. I still felt skeptical of this new technology. I saw them as pricy and glitchy and could never truly replace landlines. So, clearly I nailed that one.

Now that I had the cordless phone, I could call for help. I couldn't in there though - not inside the kitchen. If he heard that phone beep on, he'd come charging in to knock it out of my hand and do God-knows-what-else. I'd have to make a run for it to try to get somewhere safe. This meant running back through the dining room where he remained in the dark.

Brent could be standing on either side of the table. If I picked the wrong side to make my escape, I'd run straight into his arms and then game over. But I had to go somewhere. I took a leap of faith and ran out along the outer side of the table. Sure enough, it was the clear side. He lunged forward, and the moment I slipped past him, he tripped over his feet and stumbled.

This bought me an extra couple of seconds as I ran back towards the foyer. I wanted to run out the front door, but it had been shut and most likely locked. We have all seen that in the horror movies a dozen times.

I didn't have enough of a lead to unlock that door, so I hooked left to bolt my way up the staircase. I could feel him trailing behind me. If I so much as tripped, then game over again. Everything was happening so fast and each move counted.

When I reached the top of the staircase, I saw the bathroom and ran in there, slamming the door shut. With the bathroom being so dark, I struggled to get the latch. Brent shoved against the other side, trying to get the door back open.

I dropped the phone and shoved back, throwing us into a game of reverse tug-a-war. I must have wanted it more because I got the door shut - successfully locking it. Flipping on the light switch, I frantically searched for the phone, praying that it didn't break when I dropped it. Thankfully, it sat in the corner, fully intact.

Not having a cellphone gave me at least one advantage. I had everyone's number memorized. My hands trembled so hard as I dialed

Eddie's number, it was a miracle that I hit all the right buttons in all the right order. He answered.

I screamed, "HE'S BEATING ME!"

Eddie laughed. "WHAT?! I CAN'T HEAR YOU!" The loud music and cheering men roared on behind him in the background. "HOLD ON!"

I kept screaming, "HELP ME! HE'S BEATING ME! Brent IS BEATING ME!"

"WAIT! WHAT?!" Eddie caught on. "WHAT'S HAPPENING?!"

The moment Brent recognized that I had the phone, he began pounding his whole body against the door.

"I'M TRAPPED IN THE BATHROOM," I cried. "HE'S TRYING TO BUST DOWN THE DOOR. HE'S GONNA GET IN HERE! HELP ME! HURRY!"

Eddie understood. "HOLD ON! WE WILL BE RIGHT THERE!" He hung up.

I sat against the wall furthest from the door shaking and sobbing. The house was over a hundred years old, which isn't an exaggeration. The door wasn't going to hold. I tried my best to make deals with God.

Dear God, please keep the door from breaking open. I promise I will be a better person (I wouldn't). *I promise I will stop drinking* (I couldn't). *I promise I will go to church* (I'd never). *Please God, just keep me safe until Eddie and Rey get here.*

God knew better though. He/she learned all about my false prayers in the past and thus, he/she said, "No dice."

Within a couple of minutes, my vampire busted through the door. I tried kicking him away, but he managed to grab onto my feet and dragged me into the hallway. He sat on top of me so I couldn't get up and just kept punching me in the face over and over. I threw up my arms trying to block him. It deflected his strikes a few times before he'd knock them out of the way to punch me again.

I kept thinking, *Don't fight back. It's the only way to keep things clear. The second he has a scratch on him, it will become a story of "he said / he said."* It is sad to think this idea had any real merit to it - that one shouldn't fight back to protect their own innocence. As I laid there, taking the many whacks to my face, I thought all hope had been lost.

All of a sudden, new banging noises come flooding into the room. It was the sound of hard shoes - lots of them - slamming their way up the stairs. Flashlights swirled around the dark, unforgiving walls. The weight of Brent's body vanished and, when I stopped clenching, all that remained was a female police officer crouching down to me.

"Are you okay?" she helped me sit up.

My voice quivered so hard I could barely get the words out. "I…. I… dunno. I dunno."

"It's over now," she said. "He's gone."

The lights turned on and there were no more shadows to fear. A medically trained officer came into the hallway to determine if we needed an ambulance or not. As it turns out, when people are that intoxicated, they're too sloppy to hit with such excessive force. It seemed like no urgent care kind of damage had been done.

The two officers escorted me down the staircase and out the door to meet with another officer who needed to hear my version of the story. When I walked out, I saw three police cars with their lights still swirling, along with Eddie, Rey and Brent's roommate all standing there. I'll never forget the look on their faces. It was a strange combination of pity, shock, and disgust.

To this day, I don't know who called the police. They had gotten there too soon for it to have been Eddie and Rey. I suspect it had been Brent's roommate. Maybe he had come home right when the violence had gotten underway. And, instead of getting involved, he made the police call, which was obviously the better choice.

"I'd like to hear your side of what happened tonight," the officer said. He sincerely meant it too. I could hear the empathy in his voice. He was handsome and kind and, best of all, concerned for me.

I saw Brent handcuffed in the back of one of the police cars. Hearing "my side" meant the officer had already talked with him. Who knew what Brent could have said?

I spoke vaguely, "I brought Brent home because he was too drunk and was getting aggressive at the bars. When I tried dropping him off, he took my keys and ran in the house. When I ran in after him, he attacked me."

The officer prodded me for more details. When I finished explaining what happened, it became clear that my plan of "not fighting back" had worked. Considering that Brent didn't have so much as a scratch on him, the officer went with my version of the story.

Many years later, I would take a self-defense class and, without giving any backstory, I asked the sensei whether this was a good move or not. The sensei responded, "It is better to be judged by a jury of your peers than to be carried in a coffin by your friends and family." Touché.

"Is Brent your boyfriend or just your friend?" The officer asked point blank.

I didn't want to answer this. I always suspected that the reason the officers did so poorly during the teen stalker experience was due to their homophobia. If I admitted that Brent was my boyfriend, would this very attractive officer stop being so empathetic?

"What does it matter?" I asked.

It apparently mattered a lot. "Well I will level with you," he said. If he is your friend, then we can let him go if you choose not to press charges. But if he is your boyfriend, we are required to take him to jail tonight and charges will be pressed regardless of what you want."

I didn't know how to respond.

He could see how conflicted I felt. "I will leave it up to you. Is he your boyfriend or is he your friend?"

I looked up and could see him mentally telling me the answer he wanted to hear. *Say it. Say this bastard is your boyfriend so that we can take him to jail.* I turned my head to see everyone else staring at me, telling me the same thing. The officer had given me the chance to determine the outcome. They all now waited for my answer.

I took a big gulp. "He is not my boyfriend. He is just my friend."

Dismay washed over the officer's face. "Are you sure?" He underhandedly pleaded with me to change my mind.

"I am sure," I said.

"And you don't want to press charges?" He asked.

"No."

The officer dropped his head in defeat. Everyone's weird mix of pity, shock, and disgust instantly turned into total and utter disappointment. You, the reader, may also feel a little disappointed in this. But I have to say, while I do not exhibit a lot of rational thinking in this book, this was one of my better moments.

I didn't exactly consider Brent to be the one who attacked me. I mean yes, it was him, physically, but it was not the man I knew and loved. He drank so much that Brent vanished from his own body and an entirely other, far more horrific person took over - that shadow - that vampire - someone to protect him from all the trauma he experienced growing up.

Brent had an incredibly hard life and I happened to be there when all that hardship came bursting out. The last thing I wanted to do was make things even more difficult for him. That didn't seem like the proper solution for this. He'd lose his job. He'd have a permanent record. Brent didn't need punishment. He needed help.

"Do you have somewhere safe to stay tonight?" The officer asked since they couldn't locate my keys.

Eddie stepped in. "You can sleep at my house. We will call your apartment manager in the morning to get you some new keys."

The next morning, I woke up feeling like the Wooly Mammoth had sat on my face the entire night. Eddie's phone rang and it was Brent's roommate letting us know that he found the keys. They somehow ended up in the cat's food dish. Of course. It's always the cat's food dish.

I got up and stood in front of the mirror. The damage could've been worse. A puffy face, a busted lip, and a small bruise around my eye were all that stared back at me. The swelling would go down and I could use makeup to mostly cover the bruise. If anyone were to ask about the lip, I'd just tell them that I had herpes and that they were rude for asking.

I took the remainder of that Saturday to rest and recover. I filled my head with dumb television, my mouth with bad food, and my bathtub with hot water. As I sat there soaking with some sore ribs, I cried... a lot. My worlds hadn't coincided, they had violently collided.

By that afternoon, Brent's roommate reached out to let me know that, even though Brent didn't have much memory of what happened, he was fully aware of everything and he couldn't face me. He left it in my hands on how to start the break-up process. I told the roommate that I wanted to see Brent, asking him if he would meet me in the park in an hour.

I arrived at the park early so I could sit alone on the bench to think about all of the things I wanted to say. The cool weather made for scarce people which gave us the right combo for privacy in a public place.

When Brent walked up, he kept his head so far down that it was shocking that he managed to find the bench. He plopped down next to me. I could feel him tremble - not from the cold but from the pain. Minutes passed before either of us said a thing.

He broke the silence. "I am so sorry, Scott." He could barely get the words out. "There is nothing I can ever do to make up for what I've done to you."

I still couldn't respond.

He continued. "I don't ever expect you to forgive me."

"I don't know what to do," I spoke up. "I am not even sure I understand what happened or what is happening."

"I don't either," he said into his lap.

"I need you to look at my face," I told him. "I need you to see what you did."

I looked up at him as he slowly brought his gaze to mine. His beautiful crystal blue eyes scanned me over, observing my minor but ugly injuries. The tears he had been holding back now shoved their way through. Just as I suspected, this would be punishment enough.

"I don't know if I can live with myself," he wept.

Seeing him like this, I realized that I hadn't been dating a vampire after all. In all actuality, I had been dating Humpty Dumpty. Brent's upbringing sat him all the way up on the highest wall and he had been wobbling on this wall over the entirety of his adult life. The night he beat me was the point in time that he had finally fallen.

"I'm not saying this relationship is over," I continued. "But things have to change in order for me to consider sticking around."

"I can't believe you would consider staying with me. I don't even think I deserve that much," he said.

I laid out my ground rules. "I want you to give up alcohol entirely. I mean it. Not a single drop. We can't ever risk you unleashing that horrible person again."

He nodded his head. "Yes. I will do anything."

"And you have to go to therapy. You have to work through the trauma you experienced from your stepfather during your childhood. I know that is where so much of that drunken rage came from."

"But I don't think I can afford that," he said.

"I can't afford to stay here without it."

He immediately understood and said that he would figure out a way to pay for therapy.

Before all of this happened, I had a nagging suspicion that Brent was not the person I wanted to spend the rest of my life with. I could never quite put my finger on it, but sitting on this bench, seeing Humpty Dumpty so beautifully broken and fragile, I knew that now was not the time to leave.

All the king's horses and all the king's men would not be coming to help him out. And, although it might have been a little narcissistic of me, I felt like I was someone who could put him back together. We had endured that gruesome night together. We might as well find peace with it together. My soul very much needed this. So, at that moment, I decided to stay with Brent.

SCHIZOFRIENDLY

I sat in my office wondering how I had gotten myself into a place like this. It wasn't even "my office." I shared it with two other co-workers. If one of us rolled our chair back, we'd easily bump into each other. Neither of them seemed happy to have me there.

Our computers were about two decades too old. The desks were always mysteriously sticky, and the walls somehow had what looked like coffee stains on them. I was certain this came from the asbestos which always blew directly into my lungs from the air vents.

I wasn't sure if I wanted my phone to ring or not. This was my first career move out of college and I wanted to do a good job. But I had no idea what I was doing. Why did they hire me? I had no experience for a place like this!

The phone would eventually ring, of course, and I would eventually have to answer it. When it did, Reggie's name popped up on the caller ID. This was the man who vowed that he would *never* need my help. He wanted nothing to do with me. Seeing that it was him got me a tad excited. Maybe he wanted me to schedule that dentist appointment for him.

I picked up the phone only to hear a bunch of heavy breathing.

"Hello?" I asked not fully sure it actually was Reggie.

"Scott!" He screamed into my ear. "This is Reggie Elzey, Scott. Scott, you said you'd help me. I'm in trouble, Scott. I need you to help me."

Please, God, let this be some dental emergency. "Calm down, Reggie. Tell me what's wrong."

"It's an emergency, Scott. Them voices - them rich, white, faggot punks - they got to me." He sounded like he was in pain.

"What's happening, Reggie? Are you okay? Tell me what's happening."

He groaned. "I can't... tell you... on... the phone. I need you to come over, Scott. Now, Scott. Please come help me, Scott."

I didn't know what to do. With him living half a mile away, I could possibly go over there and check things out. "Okay, okay. I will be right there."

I hung up the phone, grabbed my keys, and headed to the car. In all the excitement, it didn't occur to me that I had just made the incredibly wise decision to go unescorted to the apartment of a severely mentally disturbed individual who proclaimed to be in danger.

When having to choose my major in college, I wound up entirely confused about what I wanted to do for a living. I truly wanted to be a writer. But that felt artsy and, therefore, not very lucrative or sensible. Marketing sounded like a job where someone could let their creative juices flow. However, my sister Stacey went this route, and her career didn't appear to let any of her juices flow.

As kids, people always ask us that age-old question of what we want to be when we grow up. I always answered the same thing: animal feeder. No more, no less. This must have meant I wanted to work at the zoo as I don't know where else one would get paid to simply feed animals all day.

Push came to shove and I chose to major in sociology, which didn't come across as any more lucrative than wanting to be a writer. When people asked me what a sociologist did, I would say "oh, all kinds of things." Translation? "I have no clue." Honestly though, human interaction fascinated me (and it still does).

Searching for work after graduation translated to throwing resumes at practically every available job I could find online. Sales? Yeah, I could do sales because, in sociology, we know how people work. Office manager? Yeah, I could manage an office because, in sociology, I know how people work. Mechanic? Yeah, I could be a mechanic because, in sociology, I had no clue how cars worked, but I could learn.

After a couple of interviews for sales positions that turned out to be pyramid schemes, I got a call back for a legit job: a case manager at a local non-profit mental health agency called "Open Hearts Community Mental Health." The vague job title made us all feel a little skeptical.

"What does a case manager do exactly?" my mom asked on the phone.

"I dunno. They manage cases," I told her like a lazy teenager. "It's some social work thing."

The job functions said things like "provide comprehensive psychological services," "help clients set and attain goals by evaluating strengths and symptoms," and "ensure clients get access to community resources and services." It all sounded so unclear, but it also sounded important, which I liked.

The notion of working in a psychosocial setting appealed to me even if I didn't know what I'd be doing. My interest in psychology went back to when I was fifteen. The family had taken our usual spring break trip down to visit the relatives in Texas. On this trip, something remarkable happened: a mass suicide in San Diego by a cult known as "Heaven's Gate."

Thirty-eight members and their leader killed themselves in an effort to board a spaceship they believed secretly traveled behind a comet. When they found their bodies, they were all dressed in the exact same black clothing while wearing the exact same brand new, black Nike tennis shoes.

As the media coverage swarmed this event, things got weirder. Investigators found a five-dollar bill and three quarters in each of their pockets. I won't get into the details on how they killed themselves, but prior to their deaths, these folks purchased "alien abduction insurance" in the amount of ten thousand dollars! Every new bizarre detail had me utterly captivated.

My grandparents dug out some old "abnormal psychology" books that my uncle left behind from when he was in college. Even though I never read more than a few pages, I thoroughly enjoyed displaying them on my shelf. And, just like that, I went from wanting a future of feeding animals to wanting to feed the brains of the severely disturbed. Without having gotten a psychology degree, it felt serendipitous that I ended up at a job like this.

When getting the interview, the woman at the mental health center informed me that this would be a group interview. As I pulled up to their building, I saw an overweight gentleman, wearing some tattered sweats, lumbering his way inside. I thought to myself, *if that is my competition, then I am totally getting this job.* I later found out he was a client.

The *actual* four other competitors were far more impressive than sloppy men in sweats. Every single one of them had real-world experience working with disabled or less fortunate populations. They all knew such social-workey terms like "section 8," "food bank," and "human being." The only phrase I knew was "computer."

My forehead got sweaty. I definitely looked like the twenty-something kid who was fresh out of college and desperately grasping at straws for his first job. For the final question, they asked each of us to describe ourselves in three words.

Oh, God! How do I form an entire sentence to describe myself in three words? I got so anxious about trying to form a three-worded sentence that I didn't notice the three contestants before me didn't actually form a sentence. They said things like "Professional, compassionate, and dedicated."

When it got to my turn, I timidly answered, "Generally happy guy." Or perhaps it would have been more like "Generally happy guy?" with a question mark as if I was asking them whether or not this was a sufficient response.

The two lady interviewers glanced at each other, looking confused before glancing back at me. "Um, that must be... nice," one said.

The fifth guy answered like the first three and I instantly knew I had blown the whole thing. A few days later, I got a call for a second interview. I took the time to review some social work/mental health terms and, since this was a dual diagnosis facility, it couldn't hurt to learn a thing or two about some crack, marijuana, and heroin as well. Long story short, I got the job, with a very disappointing $22k/year salary.

My first day of work kicked off with an early morning staff meeting. The mental health office held these several times a week so that the office psychiatrists could get updates about the clients they'd be seeing. When the psychiatrist walked in, the room fell silent as if she had commanded it without a single word. Beautifully brutish, she was almost Amazonian-like with the largest natural shoulders I had ever seen on a woman.

"First line of business," she announced. "I am canceling all of your clients on Wednesday on the grounds that it is the Jewish holiday of [Rushonkandsgokhisgjls] and I will be taking the day off."[19]

She began listing off names as case managers urgently scrambled to tell her their latest updates. "Excuse me!" She interrupted a case manager, slowly twisting her head at me like a Chucky Doll. "Who are you and why exactly are you here?"

"Oh, uh, me?" I stammered. She made me nervous. "I'm the new case

---

19. Technically, I forgot what holiday she mentioned. It was something like that.

manager."

Dr. Amazonianowitz (from henceforth as she shall be known) belted out a condescending laugh. "*The* new case manager?"

I knew what she meant, so I played along as if I was in on the joke. "Oh. I mean I am *a* new case manager. Not *the* new case manager."

She looked me up and down. "Well, welcome," she smirked.

I couldn't tell if I positively loved her or wished she'd fall in a mud pit.

During my first week, they didn't give me my caseload. I did nothing but trainings on the computer instead. I shared that tiny office with two other case managers and tried "shooting the shit" with them on a regular basis.

They never had the time for the small office talk that I always dreamed of. I sat there, bored, staring at the dirty walls with the anti-drug posters. If nothing else, I was able to brush up on what cocaine does to a man's testicles. One of the officemates warned that I wouldn't be so bored for long.

She was correct. The other case managers began purging their unwanted clients onto my caseload and things ramped up quickly. As my schizophrenic and bipolar parade commenced, I got somewhat freaked out. Most of them resembled those folks who stand on street corners with signs asking for money. They smelled just as bad too. Did I mention that, as part of my job duties, I would have to take them places in my own car?!

Some of them wanted nothing to do with me while others wanted everything to do with me. I came face-to-face with the fact that I didn't know how to handle mental illness or how to talk to these clients appropriately. Each new meeting made me incredibly nervous, and I kept defaulting to the way I worked in retail - using a chipper disposition to sell them something they didn't really want.

"The next client I am giving you is sooo great," a case manager named Katie said. She smiled as if she enjoyed licking raw lemons.

I didn't trust her. She always called the clients she gave me "great," and they were the worst ones.

"His name is Reggie Elzey."

"If you like working with him so much, then why put him on my caseload? Why not keep him?"

"As a matter of fact, I *do* like working with Reggie. But I think he *really* liked working with me. You know? A little too much. He is a bit creepy. You will be fine though. Apart from that, he is starting to need more hours than I can give him as an outpatient client. He is a better fit for your team."

The day I met Reggie did not bode well for a first impression. I sat waiting for him in the dirty lounge chair in Katie's office. All the furniture at Open Hearts had obviously been pulled out of the dumpster, even the walls. None of it reflected the beautiful Mary-Poppins-like scene I once imagined when helping the clinically psychotic. Needless to say, getting them to take their spoonful of sugar didn't happen with a nifty song and dance either.

The door flung open. There stood a short, African-American Frankenstein - a man so freaky that he'd surely make the town's children scream in terror. It was like one of those troll doll toys from the nineties made love to Don King (also from the nineties) and had a baby. His body stood limp against crutches under each arm.

"Who the hell are you?" he asked as if he had seen a twenty-three-year-old, pasty white, suburban, boy (which he had).

"Now Reggie, be polite," Katie said from behind. She nudged him further towards the chair across from me. "His name is Scott, and I wanted you to meet him."

As he walked by, he bowed his head and reiterated the need to know who the hell I was. Reggie plopped in the chair, shoving his crutches to the side. He glared at me, sizing me up to see whether I was fit for the kill.

Katie let me know about the crutches ahead of time. Several years ago, the voices inside his head convinced him to walk out into the middle of traffic. He did so, and a car successfully smashed into him. According to Katie, he won a ten-thousand-dollar lawsuit, but couldn't touch the money for ten years.

That didn't make much sense to me. The money didn't seem like a lot when it came to being physically disabled for life, and ten years seemed like a long time to wait to get it. I also kinda felt bad for the person who hit him. It wasn't the driver's fault a schizophrenic man's voices convinced him to walk into traffic on purpose. The driver happened to be in the wrong place at the wrong time.

"Hi, Reggie. Like Katie said, my name is Scott," I acted as friendly as I could so he wouldn't smell the fear on me. Except for excessive friendliness often reeks of fear. "I am going to be your new case manager." I handed him my business card.

"Dammit, woman," he snapped at Katie. "I told you I don't need no damn case manager. I is fine on my own."

"We know you do fine on your own, Reggie," Katie said. "But Scott will be here if you need anything at all. Why don't you tell Scott a bit about yourself?"

The entire room, including the books on her shelf, turned to face me.

"Yeah, Reggie, I would at least like to get to know more about you."

"What do you want to know?" he asked.

"Whatever you want to tell me."

"Okay. I got these problems, ya see?" he said, going straight for what could be the juicy stuff.

"Oh yeah? Like what?" I asked.

"Depends. Lately, it's been them rich, white, faggot punks."

I immediately uncrossed my legs and adjusted my potentially limp wrists.

Katie noticed my discomfort and stepped in to explain. "Those are the voices in his head," she talked about him as if he weren't in the room. "They have different genders, sexual orientations, socioeconomic statuses, you name it."

Reggie got pissed. "I don't need this from you, woman! Them voices is real! They ain't in my head! You always talkin' to me like they's in my head! They's real dammit!" He threw my business card on the floor and got up to leave.

Before he walked out the door, he stopped and looked me square in the nose. "That's right, son. It's them rich, white, faggot, punks and they's always wantin' me to take it up the ass. And I just sit and I yell at 'em, 'I don't wanna take it up my ass. I got a girlfriend!'" Then he walked out the door.

What the hell was Katie thinking? How could she think it would be a good set-up for me, a gay white male who came from an upper-middle-class family and enjoyed listening to punk music, to work with a man who referred to his hallucinations as "rich, white, faggot, punks?" I ran out of her office and up to my supervisor's office on the second floor.

"I'm sure Reggie was only trying to scare you," the supervisor told me. "He has never said anything like that before."

"I'm trying to be open-minded here," I said, frantically. "I don't plan to mix my personal life with my professional life or anything, but, at some point, Reggie is going to notice that I am gay and freak out. He'll try to strangle me with a hammer or something."

I heard Katie laughing at my hammer joke as she stood in the doorway behind me. "I agree. Reggie hasn't ever talked about the voices trying to get him to take it up the…" she paused and said "ass" with a whisper. "He probably wanted to scare you off so I could keep being his case manager. Things like that happen."

"There isn't anyone else who can take him?" I pleaded.

"Everyone else is maxed out on their caseloads," the supervisor said. "Scott, you'll do fine. We all have clients that can sometimes make us uncomfortable. We all just figure out how to work with them and you can too. We believe in you. That's *why* we hired you."

Her comforting words came somewhat close to the Xanax that I was needing. Plus, she reminded me that they had, indeed, taken a chance on me for the job. I couldn't necessarily run around acting all picky about my caseload. Seeing that they did give me my first job out of college, I had to suck it up and, like she said, figure it out.

Each time Reggie came to the office to get his medications, I had the pharmacy call me so I could come try to offer him some assistance. And each time, he threw my business card on the floor. I didn't know what to do. I was required to spend a minimum of four hours a month working with him.

Then came the day when it all changed. The pharmacy called me upon his arrival. I made my way down to the main level to act like I happened to be casually walking by.

"Hey, Reggie, how've you been?" I asked him.

He glanced up at me. "I been fine. You?"

"Good too, thank you." And with that, I ran out of ideas. I tried to ask it again in a different way. "So, has anything been going on lately?"

"No." The conversation came to another halt.

"So, it sounds like you have been doing pretty good."

"Yup."

"And you still do not need my help with anything?"

"Nope."

God, I hated this. "Umm. Okay, then. Bye." I started to walk away feeling completely screwed.

Reggie stopped me.

"Hey now, wait a minute. I is gonna need your help there soon, son. I gots to see me a dentist, ya see? Can you help set me up a dentist and take me there?"

"Sure, Reggie, that is exactly what I am here for!"

I gave him another business card. He didn't throw it on the ground.

Then came that day when he called me screaming for help.

I pulled up to an old, run-down apartment building. He didn't know how to buzz me in from the call box, so he had to come down to get me. I could see Reggie limping down the hall stairs with a cane in one hand. He wore a tattered t-shirt and a pair of pajama pants.[20]

"Are you able to keep yourself stable on these stairs?" I asked him as he let me in the door.

"Uh huh, I got them good enough," he said softly, glaring at me as if I might be responsible for whatever happened to him.

We made our way back up the stairs and I followed him into his studio apartment. He had covered up the windows with tin foil. Light peered in enough so that I could see a mattress laying in the middle of the room while dishes and trash sat all over the place. It basically looked like a murder scene, sans the murder.

"Close the door behind you," he ordered, as he gasped for air.

Now I realized my mistake. You would think that, after what happened in the last chapter, I would know better than to enter the dark quarters of the mentally unstable. I closed the door behind me anyway.

"What's wrong, Reggie? Are you hurt?"

"Scott," he said, as he bent over out of breath. "Scott, thank God you is here. Scott, I need your help."

"Tell me what happened," I scanned him over to see any signs of self-harm.

"They got to me. Them rich, white, faggot, punks got to me. They came down from the clouds and I thought I was safe, but they came down and they got to me."

---

20. Or "jammie pants" as I prefer to call them.

"Reggie," I tried to get him to focus. "What happened? What did they do to you?"

He stopped panting, stood upright, and blurted out, "THEY ATE MY NUTS!"

"Wait. What?" I didn't understand what the hell he said.

Reggie got a second wind. He yelled louder, "WHAT ARE YOU DEAF, BOY?! THEM RICH, WHITE, FAGGOT, PUNKS ATE MY NUTS! THEY ATE MY NUTS! LOOK!" He grabbed his pajama pants and pulled them straight down, exposing himself to me.

"Oh, God! Reggie! Stop!" I turned away *and* closed my *eyes* and covered them to give myself triple protection from this man's genitals. But it was too late. My eyes had adjusted to the dark and I, to some extent, saw a glimpse of his junk. "Pull your pants back up!"

"No!" He said. "I ain't pullin' my pants up until you look at my nuts! Look at it. They came down from the clouds and they ate it and now it's huge. That ain't right."

I continued to plead with him to pull up his pajamas while he continued to plead with me to seriously take a look at his balls. For a slight moment, I wished I *had* told him I was gay in hopes that he wouldn't have ever exposed himself to me like that. I guess I wanted this man to ask me for help. Now, I got it.

Describing his testicles as both "eaten" and "huge" didn't add up. His initial genital whip-out was too fast for me to actually see what he was talking about. If I were to have any chance at a successful, professional relationship with him, if he was ever going to trust me, I would have to look at this daunting man's testicles.

"Okay, fine. I am gonna open my eyes. Are you ready?" I said as if I was going to charge at him in some kind of sports game. I peeped out from one hand long enough to see that one of his nuts was indeed abnormally large - double or triple the size of its next-door neighbor.

Once I got an eye full, I turned back away.

"Alright, I see what you're talking about. Your testicle does look swollen. Now pull your pants back up."

"Swollen my ass. They ate my nuts. It was them rich, white, faggot, punks. They always trying to pull this shit on me and now they done it." He pulled up his pajamas. "What am I gonna do?!"

I was too busy wishing someone had invented alcohol wipes for our brains to get a grasp on any of it. Although no actual harm happened to the retina of my eye, any remaining shred of my sex drive had vanished.

I didn't know what to do for a man that had a swollen testicle eaten by the auditory hallucinations in his head. *What would I do if I had a swollen testicle? I would likely go see a doctor.*

"Okay, Reggie. Let's make an appointment with your doctor so we can get it checked out."

"What in the hell is a doctor gonna do?"

"I don't know. Maybe nothing." What I really didn't know was how to reason with him. "But I think it is a good first step. It is what I would do if voices, umm, ate my nuts."

I couldn't quite see the connection between auditory hallucinations eating one's testicle and the testicle being so large afterward. But logic did not have its place here. Reggie dug up a business card for his physician and we called to make an appointment. I, at long last, found out that *this* was what case managers did.

A week later, I picked up Reggie in my car to take him to the doctor. He smelled terrible and, while I didn't have a nice car, I hoped the stank wouldn't set into my seats. The doctor's office was all the way on the south side of town and it would take forever to get there.

I tried making conversation, except Reggie wouldn't have it. He answered with a word or two or sometimes in total silence. I wanted so badly to turn on my CD player, but the only albums I had were punk music. With my luck, they'd set off another crazy hallucination and he would start trying to spastically bite me. *Oh, God. Why do I have to have such awesome taste in music?*

When we got to the medical office, the receptionist welcomed us with a warm friendly smile, asking what had brought us in today.

"Them voices ate my nuts," Reggie said flat out.

The receptionist's face dropped.

"Go sit down, Reggie," I ordered him, trying not to laugh. For once, surprisingly, he did what I asked. I leaned into her window and discretely told her that he had a swollen testicle. She handed me some paperwork to fill out and didn't ask us any further questions.

Like Open Hearts, it appeared that this medical office had a high turnover rate. The doctor had never met Reggie before. Since he and I were evidently not related, she wanted to know who I was and why I was there. I seemed to have a pattern with getting such responses from doctors.

I informed her that I was his case manager. Like everyone else, the doctor acted suspicious of me. She asked Reggie if he wanted me there or not. He turned towards me wanting the answer. I nodded that it would be okay, and he confirmed with the doctor that he felt comfortable with me in the room.

"So, what seems to be the problem?" the doctor asked.

"I already told that lady outside. Why do I need to tell you?"

"That lady outside is just the receptionist. I am the doctor and I would like to hear why you came in to see me."

"Then I is here cuz them rich, white, faggot, punks ate my nuts."

The doctor must not have paid attention to Reggie's chart. Like the receptionist (whose title she belittled), her face went blank. I kind of enjoyed this by now. The fact that it no longer shocked me made me feel more professional (and superior) than these boreholes.

"I see," the doctor said, turning to me and asking, "Exactly what type of case manager are you?"

"Mental health," I muttered.

It all clicked for her now.

When the time came for the actual physical exam, she asked me to leave the room. I was delighted to not have to be in the same room as Reggie's exposed balls again. The doctor, in all her amazing, genius medical-school training, confirmed that the testicle had, in fact, swollen up. She ordered an ultrasound, yet another appointment I would have to schedule and take Reggie to.

We couldn't simply get the results over the phone either. The doctor required us to come all the way back in. By now, I grew tired of awkward, silent car rides with Reggie. I had already racked up double the hours I needed on him for the month.

But Reggie continually found new ways to surprise me. When I succumbed to the silence and chose to turn the radio on, he decided to open up. He told me about his whole life: about the abuse he endured as a child, the drugs that the dealers once got him hooked on, when the voices started rearing their ugly faces inside his head, and how he got clean. He even talked about that time he walked into the middle of traffic.

"Doctors always be tellin' me that them voices ain't real. But they is real, Scott. I'm telling you they is real."

My heart started to break for this guy. Back when my grandparents busted out those old abnormal-psych books, I had a mere curiosity about it all. Now I was here, the closest I could ever get into the mind of a schizophrenic without being one myself (who knows what the future will hold?) and it was terrifying.

"I actually believe you, Reggie. I believe you when you say they are real," I told him.

"You do?" He looked at me with those troll-doll-Don-King-puppy-dog eyes. In that instant, he went from being an entirely frightening schizophrenic man to an entirely friendly one. He was "Schizofriendly." The man, who no other case manager wanted, was now warming up to me, and I to him.

"Yes, I do."

I understood that, as psych professionals, we were supposed to tell these people that their hallucinations didn't exist. But the clients never seemed to appreciate it when any of us, especially the doctors, said this. After listening to Reggie, I wondered if telling them this was the right way of going about it.

Even though it's in their heads, and not in our external world, that doesn't mean they don't exist. They just don't exist for us. The voices and the images very much do exist for people dealing with hallucinations. If telling patients to ignore them had genuinely worked, we would have had this disease licked out ages ago. I wanted to try something different. I wanted to acknowledge that these things were real for him and help shift his perspective to cope.

The doctor read off the results saying that Reggie had some form of infection in his testicles. I can't remember if she said why or how it could have gotten there. If it was sexually transmitted, I presumably blocked it out of my memory. The infection would go away with a round of antibiotics that she already had waiting for us.

On the way back to Reggie's house, he screamed and ranted with rage. "It ain't no infection! It was them rich, white, faggot, punks! Why don't them doctors be listenin' to me?!"

"I know, Reggie. Doctors act like they know everything. They're super annoying. But you have to take these pills anyway."

"I ain't takin no pills cuz I ain't got no infection. They ate my nuts and that's it. It ain't right, Scott. It ain't right."

No matter how much I pretended to agree with him, I couldn't convince him to take the pills. *How can I do this? How can I get Reggie to take his antibiotics?* I needed to manage a way to reason with an unreasonable man. I needed to get on his level somehow. I needed to think like a schizophrenic.

Any bad thing that happened to Reggie always came back to the hallucinations - to the rich, white, faggot, punks who live in the clouds. Nothing could purely be circumstantial or mere bad luck, so of course he couldn't merely have an infection. It had to be a battle with his arch nemeses. *Think. Think. Think.*

I came up with a strategy. "Reggie," I said slowly. "Could it be that… when the rich, white, faggot punks came down from the clouds and ate your nuts, *they* caused the infection to happen. That's what they were trying to do all along."

If I had a nickel for every time someone said this, well, then I would also need to live in subsidized housing, because I'm pretty sure that no person in the entire history of mankind has ever uttered a sentence remotely close to this.

Reggie fell silent. I sat on the edge of my seat, wondering if my new technique had been effective or not.

"Yeah, Scott. Yeah, that make sense. I think you is right. Them rich, white, faggot, punks gave me that infection."

I couldn't believe it. It worked. "Yup, Reggie. And I think if you want to prove to the rich, white, faggot, punks that they can't win, then you *have* to take these antibiotics. You can get rid of the infection and show them that eating your nuts won't work!"

Reggie agreed to take the antibiotics.

Word made its way around the office that I had gotten through to him - most likely due to my incessant bragging about it. But who wouldn't? Sure, I didn't get him to increase his psych meds like Katie wanted, but I did get him to take a whole other medication which he refused. And that was huge.

Open Hearts had Friday afternoon meetings in which we'd gather to review the week and give out meaningless awards. The case managers had all convinced each other that it was management's bogus way of not letting anyone leave early for the weekend (even if they worked over forty hours in the days before and deserved it).

"And the award for 'case manager of the week' goes to..." the supervisor made a drum roll sound on the community desk. "Scott!!"

Despite the fact that I had been bragging about my success, this still shocked me. I almost had to stop to think about what I could have done to warrant this award.

"This is for getting Reggie into medical treatment and figuring out how to get him to take his medications. I don't know how you did it, but we are all amazed."

Everyone clapped. Even Dr. Amazonianowitz shot over some kudos.

"I am not sure how I did it either," I told everyone in my "thank you" speech.

"Well, I have never seen anyone get through to Reggie like that, much less as quickly as you did," the supervisor couldn't stop grinning as if I had turned the office coffee into wine or... just better coffee. "I knew you could do it."

"Yeah," I said. "And all it took was him making me look at his balls."

The supervisor stopped smiling. "What?!"

The room fell silent. Dr. Amazonianowitz looked at me like *WTF, Scott?*

"Did I not mention that?" I asked nervously.

The supervisor was clearly not happy. "No, you didn't."

I tried to explain myself. "When Reggie was initially freaking out, he wouldn't let me help him unless I looked at his..."

"STOP! Just stop, Scott." She didn't want to hear it. "Meeting is dismissed. Everyone have a good weekend. Scott, come see me in my office."

The supervisor grilled me on protocol that I should have already known. As it turned out, if a client showed you their genitals, it was considered "inappropriate," and needed to be reported immediately. The client would typically get transferred to someone else and then is monitored for repeat behavior. But, since I failed to report it, I was now the one in hot water.

Because of my success with Reggie, the supervisor let me off with a warning and allowed him to stay on my caseload. This light punishment still made my little award feel meaningless. The moment I thought I knew what I was doing, I went right back to being that fumbling kid out of college.

ALCOHOLICS SYNONYMOUS

I think I've always had a funny relationship with alcohol. As I'm writing this, I'm going on my tenth month of being sober. Two years earlier though, when I wrote the first part of this chapter, I was sitting alone in a bar on a Monday afternoon. I was technically the bartender at the time, but I'd still be getting drunk once the customers came in.

And yes, I have written this book twice. That means if you have bought this book, then you also need to buy it twice. Or if you have borrowed it, then please borrow it twice. That's how it works. It's called "math."

The first time I ever *really* drank came when I was sixteen years old. While spending the night at a high school friend's house, her mom handed the five of us a bottle of tequila and told us to "have a good time" while she went out for the night. I currently don't know if I admire or condemn this style of parenting.

The moment I drank that horrible tequila, I immediately fell in love. Actually, I immediately almost lost my cookies. And I mean that literally because the mom had left us a bunch of cookies. But once I could hold those cookies back, I was in love.

My body became so relaxed and my brain giggly. My face felt numb, which was somehow awesome. And even the spins were a blast. It was like being on an amusement park ride that both tilted *and* whirled! To this day, if I get super drunk, my favorite thing to do is stop moving so that the room can do the moving for me.

My next stint with alcohol came when I dated Roberto. I turned nineteen shortly after we met, and he turned twenty-two. We hated the fact that I couldn't go to the bars with him. A friend of his, a guy by the name of Jorge Martìnez, gave me his Mexican ID to use as a fake (he would arrive at the bar later using his American ID).

Each time I handed this fake ID over to the doorman, I knew I was going to get caught. I would end up getting arrested and going to prison and then I'd have to get one of those teardrop tattoos on the corner of my eye. Yet, each time, the doorman somehow accepted it.

Jorge was more fair-skinned for being Latino, and he had a long face like I did. But there is no way in hell I should have ever been considered a "Jorge Martìnez." The doorman would have to be blind, deaf, and possibly missing his left foot to consider me a "Jorge Martìnez."

My love of drinking didn't ramp up until Rey and I had met Eddie. It was during this time that alcohol became to me what spinach was to Popeye. It didn't give me giant biceps with a super neato anchor tattoo. But, it gave me the courage to be a more incredible version of myself. And by "incredible version," I mean "incredibly fun."

The flip side to discovering my beyond fun drunk side was that I was young and stupid. At the end of the night, I would drive myself home. Sometimes Eddie would ride with me. This did not help. If we made a pit stop at Taco Bell, he would occasionally smear his burrito on the window of my car as a joke. I found it hilarious. What was not hilarious was the idea of the people I could have killed while driving under the influence.

After deciding to stay with Brent, my shenanigans with Eddie and Rey needed to slow down. As Brent lived up to his promise of not drinking and going into therapy, he became a very fragile man. In my desire to support him in his recovery, it only seemed fair that I cut back too.

My job at Open Hearts Mental Health had also become fragile. After my short-lived success with getting through to Reggie, the work slowly got more miserable. A few months into it, my two supervisors set up a special meeting with me.

When they came into the room, they sat down with lots of papers and pens falling everywhere, asking me how many clients I currently had on my caseload. I knew where this conversation was headed so I wanted to lie. But like the good boy (aka timid boy) my mother raised me to be, I told them the truth: twenty-two. They informed me that I would be receiving seven new clients.

"Seven?!" I said, in shock. "That means I will have twenty-nine clients. I was told that we had a maximum of twenty-five."

The meaner supervisor laughed. "Oh, Scott. Did you think you were special? Everyone gets a caseload like that here."

The way this woman talked down to me ate at my soul, as did her bad perm, her flat, wide face and the fact that she talked like she was chewing on bacon. I desired ever so badly to reach across the table, take my dirty index finger, and rub it in her eyeball.

"Fine, tell me about my new clients," I grabbed the pen to take notes.

One by one, they went down the list of people who I had no clue how to help. A fifty-year-old African American male here. A thirty-one-year-old Caucasian male there. One liked to paint (which really meant he liked huffing paint) and another enjoyed cats (which meant he kept trying to smoke catnip). All of them had problems with alcohol and marijuana.

"I just don't know how to get hours for these clients," I told them. "I'm already working over forty hours a week with twenty-two. There's no time. How can I possibly do this?"

The meaner supervisor proceeded to answer my question with a question. "Did we not ask you in the interview if you were good at multitasking?"

"Yeah," I said.

"And what did you say?"

"I said I was good at it."

"Then there's your answer." The supervisors got up from the table.

"But I thought you meant like regular office stuff," I protested. "You know? Like answering your phone while working on the computer and drinking two cups of coffee all at the same time."

She peered down at me through her glasses. "Welcome to Open Hearts. Did you think it would be easy?"

Fuck. I needed a drink.

In place of that drink, I spent the evening with Brent.

"How was your day?" He asked.

"Oh, God. I hate working at Open Hearts!" I proceeded to tell him about the meeting.

After my story ended, he paused. "Umm, you didn't ask me how my day was."

"Oh, I'm sorry, babe! How was your day?" I asked

Except he didn't talk about his day. "You also didn't tell me how nice I looked today."

This threw me off. "Wait. Is today a special occasion? Did you dress up?"

"No," he said. "But you haven't told me that I've looked nice all week."

"I don't get it," I said.

"My therapist says that the people in my life should be reminding me that I am good enough for them on a regular basis."

His therapist was driving me crazy. I wasn't living up to his one-hundred-dollar-an-hour-expectations. The therapy didn't even seem to be helping Brent. He had become a sad, mopey mess who acted needy all the time.

I really, *really* needed that drink. Open Hearts was draining me. Brent was draining me. I had become so drained at this point that my cocktail could use a splash of Drano just to get me moving. That'd be cheaper than a splash of Red Bull anyway.

My going out with Eddie and Rey slowly began to pick back up. This happened so gradually that Brent hardly noticed, or at least he didn't say anything about it. It might have also helped that he lived two blocks away. Each night I drank, I stumbled my way to his place to wake him up for drunk sex. Perhaps this kept him from feeling neglected.

Not only did the frequency of nights out increase, but so did the drinks themselves. Instead of ordering one at a time (like a normal human being), we'd order three or four and down them as quickly as possible so that we could go back for more. My drinking and driving worsened. On a few occasions, I didn't remember getting home.

Every so often, I woke up still very drunk and went to work anyway. This happened once before when I worked at Target during my last semester. I tossed on my red and khaki outfit and stumbled my way into the store, trying to punch in my employee code on the time clock.

Being drunk when cashiering was surprisingly fun. I'd be laughing. The customer would be laughing. I'd forget to scan some items. They'd get free stuff. We all knew it was better this way.

Now, being hungover when cashiering was a different story. I had to hold myself up on the counter, giving it my best shot to not barf on the register. With my exhaustion and pounding headache, the customers still managed to get free shit, though they were the ones that didn't deserve it. When my shift ended, I went out to find my car parked completely crooked - not even remotely in the lines.

Starting my day off drunk at Open Hearts at least made the morning meetings far more bearable. When the hangover kicked in at this job, it proved especially difficult not to at least dry-heave as the severely mentally ill don't always shower. The smell of schizophrenia matched with crack-cocaine could be along the lines of finding a diaper in a sewage-filled river and then microwaving it for ninety-two minutes.

One day, Brent sat me down to say the one thing that every drinker loves to hear.

"I think you have a problem," he said

Uh oh. Apparently, he did notice my drinking.

Like any drinker, I denied the hell out of it. I put the blame back on him, saying that *he* misinterpreted my having a good time as a "problem" so he wouldn't be the only one in the relationship with an *actual* drinking problem. I didn't have the problem. He had the problem. I was just having fun.

"I'm worried about you," he said. "I don't want you to end up in the same place I did, making the biggest mistake of your life which you can't ever take back."

I was offended. "I would never do something like what you did to me."

My judgmental words cut through him like a knife. He somehow responded kindly. "That's not what I meant. I know you wouldn't ever do anything like that. But our rock bottoms can look different. I guess you'll know it if it's meant to happen." Maybe his therapy was working.

It should have been a wakeup call that Brent said this when, in reality, he didn't know the half of it. My bad boozy behavior sometimes led to my doing things behind his back. Sometimes it'd be a flirt. Sometimes it'd be a kiss. Other times it'd be in the bed. And every so often, it'd be in an alleyway.

My low point should have come the night I met a homeless man during my late-night stumble on over to Brent's. No, I didn't go into a back-alley way with the homeless man. I was at least classier than that. When he asked me for a dollar, I told him I'd give him one if he showed me his junk.

Honestly, the homeless guy wasn't that unattractive. I mean, he still definitely looked homeless, but in the way that Denzel Washington would look homeless in a movie - wearing dirty clothes with gorgeous teeth, a decent beanie, and a swagger that you knew meant he was well-endowed. Who wouldn't want a peek?

The homeless guy agreed that if I gave him a dollar, he would show me his penis. The only problem was that I didn't have any cash on me (well, clearly that wasn't the *only* problem). I assumed he didn't take credit cards, so I told him to "hold on" while I ran back to my place to get some money. When I returned, the homeless guy was gone. This was for the best.

I know now that I didn't do these things for the sake of being an inconsiderate asshole of a party boy. Although, I was that too. I realize I never properly coped with what Brent had done to me that night we all went out. He had been proactive by getting a therapist. I had been passive by pretending like it never happened.

When one tries to shove such a painful experience under a rug, crazy rabid dust bunnies can rear their heads. I didn't know it at the time, but I had an underbelly of anger lurking around. The booze would numb me with the underbelly lashing out. I wasn't putting Humpty Dumpty back together. I was destroying myself.

If I went out drinking on the weekends, Brent would wait up for me so he could spend the night at my place. This helped prevent me from cheating on him. This also helped prevent me from dying in case I accidentally threw up in my sleep.

Brent never did have to save me from my own vomit. But on one particular night, he saved me from a very strange dream. I will go over the dream very briefly because I know that there is nothing more annoying than listening to someone drone on about something that never actually happened.

In this dream, I was rushing around to find a toilet to pee in. Each time I'd find a restroom, it'd be taken over by killer spider monkeys. I'd have to get away from them as quickly as possible and rush to find another bathroom.

I finally found a toilet that had no spider monkeys surrounding it. As I started relieving myself, I looked down to see that the toilet had turned into my computer. Brent's voice was calling in the distance telling me to stop. I had to zip up and rush off to find the next non-spider monkey toilet.

I woke up the next morning with a pounding headache. When telling Brent about the dream, he responded, "Yeah, that wasn't a dream."

"THERE WERE KILLER SPIDER MONKEYS IN THE APARTMENT?!" I said.

"No," he rolled his eyes. "You pissed all over your computer."

For a split second, I wished it had been killer spider monkeys - at least one of them waiting outside of my front door. That would have been much better than what Brent said.

When I graduated from college, my parents bought me a new computer. And since Apple hadn't yet invented "geniuses" to transfer everything for us, we had to manually transfer everything over ourselves - not unlike the way the conquistadors did with their computers in 1542.

I put the new computer on my desk and moved the old computer on to the foot-locker that sat at the end of my bed. There it stayed, waiting for me to load its files onto discs. The process had taken a little longer than it should have.

I slowly scooted over to the end of my bed, praying that Brent was messing with my head. The whole surface of the footlocker was indeed wet. I had drunkenly given my old computer a golden shower.

None of it got on the tower itself, which sat next to the foot-locker (it was a PC computer, not a Mac). The screen had seen some splashes, but it was the keyboard that had received the brunt of my drunken watersports. When I picked it up, it was heavy and sloshing. If there's one thing a computer keyboard should never do, it's slosh.

Brent laughed, "Gross."

"Shut up. I need you to help me," I said. I dreaded the notion that he'd use this as another example of me having a "drinking problem."

I unplugged my keyboard and took it over to the kitchen sink. When tilting it over, pools of once steamy (but still very yellow) liquid poured out. FACT: Old school computer keyboards can hold *a lot* of urine - 36 ounces at least.

Brent watched, scrunching up his face at how disgusting this was.

"Don't laugh!" I yelled. "What am I gonna do?"

He shrugged as he got dressed to go home.

I began running water into the keyboard and dumping it out repeatedly wanting to "give it a wash."

"What are you doing?" Brent asked. "Do you seriously think you can save that?!"

"Yeah. I have to try!"

He came over and grabbed the keyboard from me. "No. There is no way this thing works anymore. Even if it does, that's disgusting. You cannot use a keyboard that you drowned in piss. You have to draw the line somewhere, Scott."

He walked out the door with it. I ran over to my second story window to watch as he threw the keyboard in the dumpster before heading home. The moment Brent faded out of sight, I threw my clothes on to go down to fetch it out.

The keyboard, of course, landed beyond my reach. The only way to get it was by jumping inside. I trotted carefully among people's trash, hoping I didn't get stuck by a crack needle or an ecstasy needle, or a marijuana needle, or whatever drugs people used needles for.[21]

I successfully grabbed the keyboard and, as I crawled back out of the dumpster, I saw that several people on the sidewalk had stopped to look at me. I closed my eyes, turned my head away, and wished that *this* had been the weird dream I had that night. But it was real life. It was my life.

Between the blackout driving, showing up to work drunk, senselessly cheating on Brent, soliciting a homeless guy, pissing on my computer, and now crawling out of a dumpster in front of the general public, I wondered if this might be what Brent had talked about - how I'd know it if it's meant to happen - that moment I hit rock bottom.

When I got back up to my apartment, I washed the keyboard more thoroughly with some dish soap this time. It truly didn't sound plausible that this thing could ever work again. But if one doesn't try, how will they know?

I set it by the window to dry out and sat there thinking about my drinking. Things admittedly did look out of control. At last, I understood what Forrest Gump's mother had talked about. Life was totally like a box of chocolates. If you piss all over it, it's gonna make a mess (I think that was her lesson).

I decided to attempt another deal with God. If this keyboard worked, I would admit that I had a problem and stop drinking altogether. If it didn't work, I could at least go get a cocktail to temporarily recoup my self-esteem.

After an hour, my impatience got the best of me. I grabbed the keyboard and put it back on the (now cleaned) foot-locker, plugging it in and hitting the power button. I punched in a few keys. The damn thing still worked. I officially had a drinking problem.

The thing was that I didn't completely feel like an alcoholic. I never

---

21. Had I already mentioned that I was supposed to be a drug counselor?

drank at home or by myself. I didn't exactly try to hide my drinking (I just hid the things I did under the influence). And I never physically craved the stuff.

But what I was doing certainly felt synonymous with alcoholism. I used it as a drug to numb myself from reality. It was causing damage to my love life and my work life. I continued to put others (and myself) in danger. I had buckled myself in on a runaway train that wouldn't stop.

Going to Alcoholics Anonymous didn't seem quite right and there wasn't any such thing as "Alcoholics Synonymous." I'd have to do this on my own - cold turkey - lots of cold turkey, because I loved sandwiches. Sandwiches actually could be a great alternative to drinking.

To this day, I still don't identify as an alcoholic. Part of this is due to the fact that I still go on and off the wagon, knowing that I can drink appropriately when my mind is healthy. The other part is that I have a deep admiration for those who are brave enough to accept the label "alcoholic" and seek treatment.

I was merely some jerk who liked to party and couldn't control himself. Putting myself on par with alcoholism felt disrespectful to those whose broken roads ran far deeper than my shenanigans.

When I told Brent my decision to be sober, he let out a big sigh of relief. I didn't want to give up going out with Eddie and Rey though. They were my friends and I liked being with them. I could still hit the bars with them and strictly drink water. Even though it tasted like nothing, it was still delicious.

Eddie and Rey did not let out sighs of relief when I told them the news. They said the decision was entirely unnecessary. On our first night out with my newfound sobriety, they pressured me into drinking again, saying that it would be fine. The more I resisted, the more they offered to buy my drinks. The more they offered, the more I caved. The more I caved, the more I had another blackout.

I decided to give this one more shot. I knew I could do it. I knew I could successfully tell them "no" while having fun with them at the same time. To cut to the chase (and not the chaser), I did successfully not drink. But, sitting there, watching my friends drink, things didn't appear so fun anymore. What I saw was a reflection of the things I no longer wanted to do.

They say when God closes a door, he opens a window, which seems kind of like a dick move when you think about it. A door you can just walk out of. With a window, you have to crawl out. Then you accidentally land in some rose bushes and cut yourself, which means you have to use the iodine and this burns like a mother.

Here's the thing: even if God did accidentally leave the door open, with something like sobriety, we still have to flop around in those rose bushes. We have to get some cuts and we have to let those cuts burn. It's the surest way to learn how to better crawl out windows for when God does remember to shut the door.

I was solely responsible for my bad drinking behavior. It was no one else's fault. But I also had enough cuts from these enabling roses that I called "friends." The time had come to ghost Eddie and Rey. I stopped returning their calls and didn't step foot in any of our usual bars. It would be at least two years before I would see either of them again. When that time came, their hurt and confusion would be apparent. I never did explain to them why I did it.

By cutting them out, my sobriety became a success. In addition to staying sober, I successfully stopped cheating on Brent. Without alcohol, I didn't lash out in such gruesome ways anymore and I dealt with my emotions regarding his violent outburst.

Not long after that, my time at Open Hearts came to an end as well. I lasted there for about eight months, which was slightly longer than their average turnover rate of about six months. One-by-one, five other employees and I got jobs at a government agency. They became my new social circle and, when we did happy hours, not a single one of them would encourage me to drink.

While Brent and I continued to support each other in not drinking, our relationship did not grow healthier. He didn't want to join me in hanging out with these new friends as he now had social anxiety. On the other hand, he didn't like it if I went out with them solo as it made him lonely.

When I convinced him to join us at a happy hour, an hour into it he had a meltdown and demanded I walk him home. It turned into another embarrassing argument. I knew I couldn't spend my life with a man filled so with such ingrained insecurities - that was my job.

That evening, after two years, I broke things off with Brent. We stood outside of my apartment in the rain as he begged me not to go, but the relationship had come to a dead-end. I could no longer help Humpty Dumpty. I had to start helping myself.

I cut things off completely - more cold turkey - without attempting to remain friends. It was already too chaotic. Over the coming years, I'd run into Brent a handful times. We talked amicably, but I could see the yolk on his face from a mile away. Humpty never put himself back together. Not that I was much better. I still had no clue who I was or what I was doing, but I wanted to see this whole sobriety thing through.

But what happened to the keyboard, you ask?

I will tell you *only* if you promise not to judge me more than you are legally required to at this point. I did the thing that a most upstanding citizen could do: I sold it in a friend's garage sale for two dollars.

I sold it to this young gentleman who was my weakness of weaknesses: the cute nerdy type. He had wispy blond hair and wore glasses and could read binary (I assumed). Thankfully, he seemed straight. Otherwise, I wouldn't have sold him that keyboard for fear of ruining our chances of dating.

A month later, I walked into a gay bar and saw that loveable geek of a keyboard buyer sitting at the other end of the bar, by himself, reading a book. He had been a 'mo after all. I wanted so badly to walk up to this sexy, blond, binary nerd and ask him out. But I couldn't look him in the eye knowing the secret of his pissy purchase.

This eligible man read books and, therefore, must have been a nice guy. No bad men ever read books.[22] Though now I would never know. If drinking ruined the chances of me dating a nice nerd, I'd be damned if I'd touch another drop. While a lot of bad choices pointed me in the direction of sobriety, this was the last of the wake-up calls.

---

22. Did you know Joseph Stalin was illiterate?

JOHNNY BADASS

Starting a new job always seems to renovate our stomachs into a butterfly pavilion. But on my first day working at Longterm Care Options, it was love at first file folder. I thought so highly of this place that I am even comfortable using their real name in this book.[23] It also helps that they no longer exist.

In place of small, shared asbestos offices, we had bright, spacious cubicles with little chalkboards in front so we could write our names in fun, silly ways. I could confidently put my lunch in a clean fridge without worrying what might crawl over my hand. No doctors made me stick my head in their drawer to see if it smelled funny (true story).

And the supplies... oh, Lord, we were up to our elbows in office supplies! At Open Hearts, they locked up the supplies. We had to ask permission if we so much as needed another pen. At Longterm Care Options, a massive supply room existed that remained unlocked and fully stocked. I fantasized about going in there, throwing it all on the floor, and rolling around naked in an endless amount of paper clips, highlighters, and rubber bands.

All this existed thanks to the most efficient office manager who had the strangest hyphenated last name: Anne Swizzle-Swanson. I did change

---

23. I would like to point out that I am aware that "longterm" is an incorrect spelling. For some reason, the company spelled their name this way.

her name for this story, but, I assure you, the original had a very similar ridiculous tone to it. If she ruled that office with an iron fist, that iron fist had sunshine and rainbow stickers all over it.

The CEO, or the president, or whatever those are called, was a man I actually admired. He worked his way up from being a case manager himself, which meant he made decisions based on real job experience. Best of all, he legitimately cared about the well-being of his employees.

With this job being in the line of social work, we didn't make big annual salaries. He made up for this by giving a bunch of other perks. Once a month, each team got treated to lunch at a restaurant of their choice (within reason). Employees got oodles of paid time off. We also got to work four 10-hour days, *and* we got to work from home one day a week.

Our favorite part was that our superiors didn't micromanage us. We could come and go as we pleased. As long as we got our work done, they didn't question how many hours we worked or what schedules we made for ourselves. If I focused (which was not easy for me), I could always clock in at about twenty to thirty hours a week while still getting paid a full salary.

With this extra time on my hands, I discovered a new hobby: fitness. This interest came when looking in a mirror after getting sober. My arms were rail thin with a gut that was pillar thick. A major part of my drinking was to numb how self-conscious I felt about my body. Then the drinking made my body worse and so I drank more.

Now that I couldn't use alcohol to numb myself, it got tough to ignore the fact that I kind of resembled E.T. I know that this Steven Spielberg creation was intended to be cute. But, really, that alien looked like a drunk. I wanted to look healthier and now I had the time to pursue that.

The work itself at Longterm Care Options (or what we called "LTCO"

- pronounced "Lit-Co") was rather mundane. Our job was to manage in-home care services on an ongoing basis, as funded by Medicaid, for disabled and elderly people, ensuring that they can remain in their homes and avoid nursing home placement. Have you fallen asleep yet?

The bulk of this job was really about navigating the bureaucracy and all of its many, many acronyms. If it hadn't been for the acronyms, I probably wouldn't have been employed. It was like sticking your head in a giant bowl of alphabet soup and drowning. A typical phone call would have gone something like this:

"Thank you for calling LTCO, this is Scott. Oh, I am sorry, you're calling the wrong number. I work for the HCBS-MI waiver. You want the HCBS-EBD waiver. You aren't on HCBS-EBD? Are you on HCA? Oh, you are with the PACE program! That one is managed over at TLC. Here, I'll get the number for you!"

This was another reason I decided not to change the company name in this chapter. If I had to try to think of new acronyms too, my brain would have exploded all over the screen. That means I would have soiled yet another perfectly good computer.

Just know that I worked at a boring job in a wonderful environment that required a decent amount of professionalism - a sense of professionalism that I had a tendency to shoot in the foot. Anytime the word "professionalism" is used in conjunction with me, it's most likely hobbling around on crutches. Professionalism was *my* disability.

A couple of months into my time there, I walked in the mailroom to find the Swizzle-Swanson and the President/CEO/Whatever laughing it up. I smiled and they politely let me in on their giggle-fest.

"Hey, Scott," the President/CEO/Whatever said. "If you could have any other name in the world, like a pseudonym, what would it be?"

"Johnny Badass," I said at the drop of a hat. No one had ever asked me this question before, but I had already given it plenty of thought.

But the second the words popped out of my mouth, I knew I made a mistake. You can't say the word "ass" to your superiors in a corporate-style job. And my gut instincts proved correct. They looked at me as if I had said Paris Hilton.

I tried explaining myself. "Because it's like a combination of a silly name and a tough guy name. It's a hilarious dichotomy."

"Ooookay," the Swizzle-Swanson said. Maybe she didn't find dichotomies interesting like I did.

"Well, anyway," the President/CEO/Whatever said trying to change the subject.

Johnny Badass was the personification of how I saw myself, or at least the person I wanted to be - a renegade with a heart of gold. I wanted people to think of me as the nicest guy ever, but I also wanted them to know that if they ever crossed me, I'd cut a bitch. Was that too much to ask?

I was just glad that, when my co-workers asked me their silly question, I didn't accidentally blurt out the name "Johnny Jizzfest" - the pseudonym I use for when people ask what my porn name would be.

Now that I mention this, I should go trademark the name "Johnny Jizzfest" in case I fail as a writer and need to do porn. Not many people know that writing and pornography parlay easily into one another. Stephen King did some wild stuff before his novels took off.[24]

As the holidays approached, our parent company, Total Longterm Care (TLC), announced that they would host a company-wide holiday party in late January. Why January, you ask? Because venue prices drop after the holidays and non-profits always have to do everything on a dime.

This year's party would be held at one of those enormous restaurants with various arcade games that are supposed to entertain adults and kids alike. Instead of using cash to play the games, you have to purchase

---

24. My lawyer has advised me to clarify that this is a joke. I told him that Mr. King has a great sense of humor and would probably be fine with it. My lawyer told me I had to put it in here anyway and then charged me $375 for this conversation.

"gaming cards" that use a point system. And TLC would give every employee a $10 gaming card.

"Did you see they announced the holiday party?" I asked my co-worker/friend, Andrea.

"Yeah, it's gonna suck," she said.

With olive skin and long black hair, Andrea and I met working at Open Hearts. She needed a second case manager to help her run the "Activities Group." We had to work together to think of different outings to take our clients on as an alternative to doing drugs.

Andrea was the first to leave Open Hearts in order to come to LTCO. When she confirmed that the job was far easier, and the company treated their employees way better, the rest of us followed suit. We functioned like veterans who had come back from some pointless war. Except our PTSD was filled with getting bed bugs (true for another guy) and clients puking in our cars (another true one for me).

I found Andrea to be delightfully grouchy and bitchily witty. We had built our friendship on hating all the same things. We hated the same music. We hated the same clothing. We hated the same soups (I never did let go of that Cream of Mushroom crap). It was love at first hate.

"Why is it gonna suck?" I asked her.

"That place is dumb," she said. "And the employees who work in the other divisions of TLC are ghetto. I don't wanna spend my Saturday night with them."

Andrea and I tended to talk a lot of smack. Thinking about this, I bet the reason they call this "talking smack" is because if you do it, you should likely *be* smacked.

"Yeah, you're right," I agreed. "That will suck."

In truth, it had been my boyhood dream to go to an office holiday party ever since my parents would watch the uber kid-friendly movie *Die Hard* on a bi-monthly basis. I became obsessed with the opening scenes from the Christmas party - employees dressed to the nines drinking cocktails, handsome douchey executives doing cocaine, co-workers having sex in offices - the whole thing seemed so fun. I didn't care for all those terrorists ruining it though.

I realized that now, being sober, I wouldn't have the nerve to solicit some Christmas sex from any co-workers. But hopefully I would get to "accidentally" walk in on other co-workers doing this very thing. We *had* to go to this event!

After the company-wide email about the party, the President/CEO/Whomever of LTCO announced that our division (which consisted of 120 case managers) would be doing a holiday cubicle decorating contest. The Swizzle-Swanson would organize a team of judges who would award prizes for first, second, and third place.

Andrea and I both dubbed this as lame too. However, once I saw the other employees hanging plastic snowflakes from the tiled ceiling using paper clips and string, I wanted in on the creativity. I also wanted to win a prize. I never won prizes, which made me only want to win them more.

I bought the same plastic snowflakes and gave them my own twist via some black spray paint. Black would be my holiday cubicle theme. Coincidentally, while shopping, I stumbled upon a three-foot-tall black Christmas tree. I'm not quite sure why a company would manufacture this, but I bought it nonetheless.

After propping the tree up on a black box inside my cubicle, some co-workers got curious and/or concerned. But wait, it got better. The tree got ornaments consisting of black roses, broken hearts, and skull-n-crossbones. I drew some additional inspiration from the movie *The Nightmare Before Christmas,* placing several framed photos of the characters (that I illegally printed up) around my desk.

I bought a few toys, broke them, and scattered their remains under the black tree. If that wasn't enough, I painted the phrase "Kidnapped

Mr. Sandy Claws" (again from *The Nightmare Before Christmas*) in creepy letters on the black box with some whiteout, as if the broken toys were the result of a terrible incident.

To finalize the whole thing, I had to put something clever for that chalkboard that sat on the outside of my cubicle. I erased my name and wrote, "X-mas is not white for everyone." The concept was to symbolize the fact that the holidays are a dark time for some people out there. See how I had to intellectualize the whole thing? I couldn't just let it be weird and fun. Andrea appreciated my dark creation.

For all my efforts, I won first place. My prize consisted of a pair of Smartwool socks which couldn't have cost more than fifteen dollars. I chose to ignore the fact that my cubicle decorations rang in at over one hundred dollars. In any case, my real prize was that now my office mates would see my tough guy ways.[25]

After New Year's passed, and our company holiday party grew closer, I slowly tried convincing Andrea that we should go.

"Absolutely not," she said. "Didn't you see that follow up email that said they wouldn't be serving any alcohol? They want it to be 'family-friendly.' I know you don't drink, but how am I going to tolerate those people while sober?"

While it didn't make a difference for me, this news bummed me out too. Without any booze around, how would I accidentally walk in on any co-workers totally doin' each other in a broom closet? Furthermore, why would I be randomly walking into restaurant broom closets?

Sidenote: I've never understood the idea of making events "family-friendly" by removing the alcohol. Doesn't alcohol help us better tolerate our families? Under that logic, shouldn't family-friendly events have *more* alcohol?

"I know. It's gonna be dumb," I told Andrea. "But the rest of our crew is going. Plus, there will be free food and free game cards."

---

25. And, to this day, I still wear that pair of Smartwool socks.

She sighed. "Ugh. Are we really going to do this?"

"Yes," I said. "And we will potentially hate it. But at least we can hate it together."

"Fiiiiine. But I am making Chris come with us," she said, referring to her fiancé.

When the evening of the holiday party rolled around, I spent the afternoon picking out the perfect outfit. As much as I didn't care about fashion anymore, I intended to blow everyone's minds with something that fashionably expressed the tough guy who resided within me. Think punk rock chic.

I gathered some high-end items that I acquired from my first relationship and paired them in a way that expressed the bleakness of my second relationship. It all started with skin-tight, black jeans. I won't mention the brand since they charge $600 for a tank-top and therefore should be put in jail immediately. These jeans didn't cost anywhere near that as they were acquired on eBay.

Next came a jet-black dress shirt that had a certain sheen to it when compared to the dull mat of the black denim. The wrist cuffs flared outward instead of the typical, polite overlapping on a regular dress shirt.

I slapped on the expected black leather belt with the dress shoes to match and, much like my temperamental holiday cubicle, I was black from head to toe. For a final touch, I attached a keychain to one of my belt loops. It didn't look like a keychain. It looked like a three-inch strap of red leather with a hook on the end. Clearly, it wasn't literally meant to be for keys.

Like so much in fashion, it was completely unnecessary yet utterly necessary. I stepped in front of the full-length mirror and, indeed, Johnny Badass was staring straight back at me. I was officially ready to hate my first office party; or, by the looks of it, do some heroin.

When Andrea and I, along with her fiancé Chris, got to the entrance, we discovered a long line to get in.

"Are you kidding me?!" Andrea shouted. "We have to wait in a stupid line?!"

"Don't worry. It'll move fast," I said.

Waiting in line meant I had more time to think about my badass outfit. I loved the idea of wearing all black to a holiday party with the tiniest pop of red. If I could form a gang, black and red would be my gang colors. Though, I think "The Bloods" already have that. And then I would have to have some kind of legal arbitration meeting with The Bloods on whether or not I could use black and red or not. It wouldn't be worth it.

"We're here," Andrea snapped me out of my gang member fantasies to let me know we had already made it to the front.

"See? I told you it would be fast."

Once inside, we hardly recognized anyone. Most of these people must have been from the other departments in TLC and not from LTCO. I forgot how big the company was. We found the rest of our friends who I had, perhaps, also bullied into coming. The waiters attentively took our drink orders, to which these friends reminded me how they didn't include any beer or liquor. But we had our game cards - GAME CARDS FOR EVERYONE!

The food appeared a bit lackluster too. It was a buffet mostly filled with Tex-Mex style appetizers. This particularly disappointed Andrea and me as we shared the same passion for fitness. I didn't mind the tortillas so much as taking our rage out on gluten hadn't come in style yet, it was the congealed fats that freaked me out.

My weightlifting had begun to pay off by my diving into a high protein diet. And now, I couldn't find much protein in any of these things. It would be a long night of chicken taquitos ahead of me. I still ate the queso because what else was I going to dip my taquitos in? Salad?

Our group played a few rounds of Skee-Ball, which I lost. We then played that basketball game where the hoops move back-and-forth. That I definitely lost. If this place had a Whack-A-Mole machine, I would have crushed it. But, they didn't, so I had to find something else to do other than sipping on club sodas and losing.

I figured it couldn't hurt to go mingle with some of the other coworkers that I didn't know too well. Even though Andrea assured me that we had the best jobs in TLC, it could be good to get to know some folks in the other departments (just in case).

I walked over and began to awkwardly linger, asking people which departments they worked in and whether or not they liked it.

After a while, Karen from HR leaned over and said, "Hey, would you do me a favor?"

"Sure," I said. This was fantastic. Of all people to be in cahoots with, it would be the head of HR.

"Would you go get me some more tortilla chips?" she asked.

"Oh, um, yeah. Okay," I said.

This was not what I expected to come out of her mouth - for me to go get something to put in her mouth. Why would she ask somebody to get her some chips? The chips were not even twenty feet away. Was she the most slothiest person ever? Sloths *do* hate getting their own chips. Or had all those years of working in HR made her accustomed to bossing people around?

I decided to chalk it up to friendly office camaraderie. It must have meant that she was comfortable enough to ask me. Besides, I already agreed to do her the favor before she said what it was. If I told her to get her own damn chips now, it wouldn't make for a great impression. I took Karen's basket and got the woman some chips. It only felt slightly demeaning.

After I dropped off Karen's second or possibly ninth serving of chips, I decided that Andrea might be right. The other TLC employees were, in fact, a tad strange. I figured it best to not return to my conversations with the HR ladies and go back over to my own kind.

I mentioned Karen's chip request to Andrea.

"That's weird," Andrea said. "I'm sure she just likes bossing people around."

"Yeah, that's what I thought!"

"I told you they were whacko. Why'd you go talk to them?"

"Um, because we aren't in high school," I said.

I decided not to overthink it and keep playing games. A short bit later, one of my LTCO specific co-workers, Gladys, came over. I didn't know much about Gladys. She had quite a few years on me and our small talk in the break room always remained minimal.

"Hey, there," she said with a big smile on her face.

"Oh, hey," I said, kind of excited that someone other than my friends wanted to talk to me. I bet she wanted to come tell me how much she liked my slick outfit or that she thoroughly enjoyed my miserable cubicle decorations.

"I was hoping you could go fetch me some more iced tea," Gladys said.

What? This made less sense than Karen asking me for some chips.

"Gladys," I said. "I don't have access to iced tea. You have to ask a waiter for..." I stopped mid-sentence. I realized what happened. Gladys had mistaken me for a waiter.

Karen from HR popped into my head. She didn't ask me to fetch her more chips out of some sort of friendly camaraderie. She must have thought I was a waiter too! But why would she ask a waiter to get her more self-serve food from a buffet? That came off even bossier and slothier than before. It didn't matter. I had to figure out what was happening.

"Gladys, I'm not a waiter. We work together."

"Oh, dear," she said as if *she* were the one to feel embarrassed. "I am so sorry. You're Steven, yes?"

"NO! I'm Scott. I'm the one with *The Nightmare Before Christmas* Cubicle!"

"Tha whaaat?!" She scrunched up her nose.

"Oh, forget it. I've gotta go."

I broke away from that old bag, scanning the room and trying to catch glimpses of the waiters who suddenly seemed to be nowhere. No wonder people were asking me for things. Once I found one, the whole thing made sense. They wore black pants with a black dress shirt.

In my defense, the waiters donned a white apron around their waist, whereas I had a red leather strap hanging from my belt loop. Couldn't everyone see the red leather strap?! The outfits were completely different!

I tried not to stress about it. I wanted to look on the bright side. If people had been drunk and having sex in broom closets, being dressed as a waiter would have made it easier to keep randomly walking into broom closets. But since everyone was unfortunately keeping their dignity tonight, this didn't make me feel any better. I scurried around to find Andrea.

"I'm leaving!" I said as soon as I found her.

"What?! Why?!"

"Because everyone here thinks I'm a freakin' waiter. That's why!"

Now let me clarify. I do not think there is anything wrong with being a waiter, especially after having done a stint in bartending. If I had a choice, I would actually rather be a waiter than a social worker. The idea of a person's roasted chicken weighing down on my shoulders sounds way more manageable than their housing. Not to mention, I would presumably make more money as a waiter.

The problem, for me, lies in the fact that I was *not* a waiter. I was their co-worker and I had met both of these women prior to this night. I tried to be as visible as I could, to all of my co-workers, with my unique, dark personality. Now, not only did they have no clue as to who I was, but these co-workers were asking me to serve them.

"What are you talking about?" Andrea was confused. "No one here thinks you're a waiter."

"It's why Karen from HR asked me to get her some chips!"

"For the last time," she said. "Those people are weird!"

"Then what about Gladys? She just asked me to get her an iced tea and she even works in the same department as us."

"Gladys is like a billion years old. She probably mistakes her cat for her grandson." Andrea paused and scanned me over. "Wait. What's up with your outfit?"

"It's my punk version of holiday party attire," I told her.

"Okay. You kind of look like a waiter, but..."

"Yup! I'm leaving!" I cut Andrea short before she could finish her "but."

"Wait! You can't leave me here with these *freaks!* The whole reason I came to this stupid thing is for you!"

"Uh, you have Chris here with you!" I reminded her.

"Oh, he doesn't count!"

Although none of us ever admitted it, we all said a secret prayer for the man who chose to marry Andrea.

"I'm not going to stay here with people asking me to bring them things. It's humiliating."

Andrea avoided eye contact with a pissy grimace on her face. "Fine. Go. Whatever." She said with that classic, passive-aggressive offer which gave me permission to leave, but, if I did, she wouldn't forgive me.

"Thank you. I love you. I will see you on Monday!" I told her.

I made a beeline for the door. Before I could escape, three people asked me to refill the taquito station, two people asked me if alcohol would at least be served after 10 p.m., and one person asked if they could have the recipe for the guacamole. Okay, none of that happened. But I could sense such things nipping at the back of my heels with each step on the way out.

By the time I got home, it had become painstakingly clear that I was no Johnny Badass. In all actuality, I was nothing more than a Johnny Rainbow - a pushover who would unquestionably go fetch other people's chips.

Back in middle school, when the bullying had gotten bad, I started bringing a small kitchen knife with me to school. I decided that if anyone got too crazy with me, I would take that knife and plunge it into their outer thigh. The outer thigh seemed more rational as their neck would constitute as murder. I just wanted to severely wound - not kill anyone.

Deep down, I knew I wouldn't ever be plunging anything into anybody's thighs. Really, I just wanted someone to see it, whether it was a bully who would think, *okay we shouldn't mess with this kid* or a teacher who would think, *this kid is seriously troubled and needs help.* A girl (who I had a crush on) eventually did see it to which she rolled her eyes. We all knew that Scott would never cut a bitch. Even to this day, I have never thrown a punch at somebody; except maybe when they have asked politely during sex. I don't count this.

Anyway, that night at the holiday party, it was obvious that those other people weren't the freaks. I had been the one to take on that role. I was the one trying too hard to stand out - so hard that I somehow became invisible. They were just normal people having a fun time being themselves while I got lost in trying to be someone else.

THE LONELY HIPSTER

James tried his best to teach me how to use chopsticks, but it was no use. Each time he let go of my fingers so I could do it on my own, my hand automatically converted to a claw. He'd bust out laughing and this made me happy because I knew he found me endearing.

I met James on a social networking site. Let's call it FaceBlorg. FaceBlorg never reached international success like MySpace (may it rest in peace) or Facebook (may it soon rest in peace), but it remained popular in my home city of Denver for years.

James had friended me online and we started casually talking. He was a lean guy with thin blond hair, big ears, and a big nose. It all added up to a charmingly semi-gawky handsomeness. This would be my initial descent into dating in the digital world - not only through social networking sites, but in texting as well.

FaceBlorg wasn't a dating site. It just provided a way to date. James and I could see that we shared a lot of the same interests. I can't remember what any of those interests were, per se, but the one I do remember was that of music. We loved all the same bands.

Are you starting to see a pattern here with me? If you do, then congrats. It would take me *years* and a Hubble telescope before I could see it. Dating guys based on their taste in music means *nothing!* For all we know, Hitler could have had amazing taste in music.

James had been the one to initiate that first sushi date. I admitted that I had never had sushi before (true), but always wanted to try it (false). I swore that I'd never eat raw disgusting sea creatures just because they looked beautiful rolled up in rice. When it comes to a cute guy, though, one can toss their limits to the side.

In the following weeks, we hung out regularly and texted about our days. We'd cuddle on the couch, watch TV and make each other laugh. This came a little soon after the split of my last relationship. But, hey, when someone great falls into our laps, who are we to bounce them off? I liked this guy.

Before I knew it, he was having me meet his roommate and lending me his season one DVDs of the show *Weeds*. This obviously meant things were getting serious. I went on FaceBlorg to change my status from "single" to "seeing someone."

After that, things got busy for James. He had a lot of work going on and his texts slowed down. It got difficult to schedule some hang out time or even a dinner together. A day finally came where we could at least have lunch. He suggested a fast-casual style Japanese bowl joint.

Something about this lunch felt off, like a brand new, shiny car that already had engine troubles. Our conversation kept stalling regardless of how many times I yanked the gear stick and pounded the clutch.[26] Whichever gear I shifted to, it seemed like no topic kept James's attention.

"What are you up to tonight?" I asked, now resorting to small chit-chat, which absolutely sucks when it's with someone you really like and could make conversation flow so freely with before.

"Oh, I'm just hanging out with a..." he paused with a smirk. "A friend."

I knew what this meant. He would be seeing someone else that night. We never talked about being exclusive, so he had every right. But the

---

26. Millennials may not get this analogy.

thought of it immediately knocked on my jealousy bone (which is not a euphemism, by the way). I had to play it cool.

"Oh, well I hope you have a good time with this... friend," I also smirked to let him know that I knew that he knew that I knew what he was up to and that I was totally cool with it. I even decided to not hit him up for a couple of days to give him some space. That's how totally cool I was with it.

A couple of horribly uncool, long days later, I texted him to touch base. He wrote back that we should go ahead and stop seeing each other. This blindsided me. *But we liked the same bands. But he introduced me to his roommate. But he lent me DVDs. Where did this come from?*

I texted back, "I think this is a conversation we need to be having in person."

James agreed, "You're right. I should grab my DVDs anyway."

In the ten minutes that it took for him to walk from his place to mine, I went from being confused to being hurt to being enraged. As we sat down, he explained that he wasn't ready for something like this.

If someone you've dated has told you this before, I'm sure you could understand my desire to set his groin on fire.[27] It feels like a cop-out. If someone isn't ready to find a relationship, why are they going on dates? "Not being ready for something like this" translates to "I'm not ready for something like this with *you*" or "I'm holding out for something better than *you*."

I called him out on this. He apologized and surprisingly acknowledged that he was fucked up for it, but I didn't want to let him off the hook so easily. I've always been one of those people who, when someone apologizes, automatically says "It's okay." This wasn't okay. He led me on. I got stern telling him that he needed to figure his shit out, so he didn't do this to someone else. I gave him his dumb DVDs and made him leave. *Screw you and your Japanese restaurants!*

---

27. Hold still while I light these matches.

Or at least that's the story I would tell people. I most likely made this up because I wanted to feel like I had some control in the matter - something we all want when our hearts get a smidge broke. In all honesty, I had acted very sympathetic to his "not being ready."

What I had essentially done with James was what I had done back at that holiday office party in the last chapter. I had brought him a basket of tortilla chips, or in this case, I had brought him a quesadilla with a side of guacamole.

This should be a new code language for how much of a doormat we can be. The more substantial the Mexican food, the more of a doormat. If you brought them some tacos, you need to rethink your game plan. If you brought them a chile relleno, you need to take a long hard look at yourself in the mirror. And if you brought them a combo platter #12, then sign up for some therapy right ASAP. If you need a recommendation, I've got a great one.

It's weird to say, but I had never *really* been dumped before. I needed to go on FaceBlorg and change my status back to "single." Of course, I had to stay friends with James on there so that I didn't come across as hurt.

Dating was excruciating. You clip your nails, trim your pubic hair, and whiten your teeth. And, for what? All to find out that they still didn't like you? Who in the hell did they want? Charles Manson?

To make matters worse, I thought about how Charles Manson had way more friends than I'd ever had. My social pools were somewhat on the shallow side at the time. Yes, I had my work friends, but we rarely saw each other outside of our cubicles. When we did hang out, it kind of felt like we were still at work.

The only real non-work-related company I had was the extremely overweight cat I adopted and named Bankhead.[28] While her heavy body gave some good cuddles, she didn't make much in the way of conversation. I was lonely.

---

28. Bonus points for you if you know where I got this name without Googling it.

Then, one day, the social gods shined down upon me. As I pulled up to a stop light, the car next to me honked excessively. I got ready to raise my middle finger in their direction before I realized it was an old friend, Tom.

Tom and I met during my time of being an honorary Mexican. He dated one of their crew (the cousin who introduced me to my ex) and, on occasion, we relied on each other for a little Caucasian camaraderie. We were the only two white guys in a sea of hard Rs and thuddy Ds.

With a pair of glasses and a consistently half-grown beard, Tom was a brilliant, edgy, artsy, weirdo photographer and who found himself stuck being a scrappy camera store salesman. He had the most oddball sense of humor. If I had surgery, I would have steered clear of Tom so I wouldn't bust my stitches and bleed to death from laughter.

We screamed pleasantries through our car windows and as the light turned green, he shouted that we should have dinner sometime. I found him on FaceBlorg and we did just that, catching up on our lives since our Latino pasts.

We discovered that neither of us relied on undocumented workers to fulfill the hefty jobs that no one wanted anymore: dating us. The ever-adaptable Tom had a whole new world of friends. With my being low in inventory, he invited me to join them on their evenings out. I jumped on this opportunity.

Tom's friends were unlike any I had ever met. Their looks were so plain and ordinary like mine (sometimes ugly). They dressed in thrift store clothing like I did (oftentimes sloppy). And they liked the most obscure bands as me (and the more obscure, the better). I had discovered the hipsters.

How does one describe a hipster? It was as if they took the things that made us losers in high school and flipped them on their head to be so utterly goddamn cool. They were all non-conformist with big beards, unconventional art, plaid flannel, individualistic thinking, knitted beanies, and independent music. And the tattoos. Oh, the tattoos! They were anything but normal. *These* were my people.

I met a guy who had a double handle-bar mustache (each side looped twice). There was a girl who played the theremin and another who would *only* type on a typewriter. And then came the guy who had tattoos of bacon strips on his forearms *just* to do it. Hardly any of them used any kind of gas-emitting vehicle. How cool is that?!

My first real dive into hipsterdom came when we attended a secret daytime opening of an exhibit at the contemporary art museum. At the reception party, they were serving free martinis that had swanky names. For me, this was a trap. I struggled to turn down free anything, especially alcohol.

I hadn't quite proved myself to the hipsters yet. Perhaps it was the fact that I had a bit of muscle by now. Hipsters don't have muscles. Muscles are mainstream. So, I needed something to help me relax. One drink couldn't hurt. I ordered a "Buzz Aldrin," which was just vodka and Tang. This quickly turned into three Buzz Aldrins and, with that, I officially broke my sobriety.

Out of nowhere, a strange man in a rabbit costume appeared and ordered us to follow him. It was so random and avant-garde that, naturally, we had to do what he said. With so much Buzz Aldrin down my throat, I didn't care if we were headed to our doom. I was laughing it up with my new friends. We found ourselves in a field where a tall Asian man stood with a bunch of paper flowers on the ground. Or maybe they were bows, like the kind you get during Christmas. I can't remember. I was drunk. All I knew was that this wasn't a dream.

The Asian man told everyone to take a flower or a bow or whatever and, on the bottom of it, write down either their best or worst memory. We were then to release the bow into the wind. This was to let go of the memory and someone else would find it. I'm pretty sure that was it. On top of being drunk, I don't get art.

Sometimes, I like to imagine the random person walking down the street that sees a Christmas bow in the middle of spring. They pick it up and see the words "After my dad found out I kissed the stable boy, he shot him right in front of the kittens."

The hipsters invited me to continue the night with them and, the next morning, I woke up to my head pounding. I also woke up to a bunch of posts on my FaceBlorg wall saying how fun I was while drunk. I hated that I broke my sobriety, but I was happy that the hipsters accepted me.

To stay sober and pull this off, I had to think of something else to make me stand out other than that of being a fun drunk. An idea instantly came to me: a kickass haircut. I ran to my hairdresser and, like a stressed-out starlet, demanded the weirdest, most ridiculous thing I could think of.[29]

It's difficult to describe this haircut. I told her to shave the sides of my head, leaving length in the middle for a mohawk. To give it a twist, I asked her to keep the sideburns, attaching them to the mohawk, and having them run down the side of my face and on to my jawline to form a narrow mutton-chop-like effect. The style stayed true to hipster form: something so bonkers that it came back full circle to cool. It was my forearm-bacon-tattoos.

The weird haircut did work. The hipsters wouldn't ever actually comment on how hip it was because it's unhip to tell someone they're hip. But I didn't need to get drunk to keep their attention. That was good enough for me. On the flip side, I got written up at work for the haircut, which made it even cooler.

In the summer, the hipsters initiated their annual kickball league. I hadn't ever really played kickball before, excluding a couple of times as a child. How hard could it be? The name said it all: kick a ball. I signed up

---

29. I still go to this hairdresser and she is one of my longest running relationships. I thank her for indulging me in this ridiculous style and for later making me go with something more flattering. Hi, Thuy!

for it right away. The teams had already formed among friends, so the rest of us had to stand on a stage as the teams' captains would select who they wanted.

This was like elementary school all over again, where the kids would never pick me. In all fairness, I was the boy who stood on the sidelines practicing the moves to "Grease Lightning." But those half-circle hand-twirls and slightly-suggestive hip pops weren't gonna twirl and pop themselves, were they?

Even today, I am the guy who still misses when throwing some trash in the bin from three feet away. Except the hipsters didn't know that. My hair fooled them all and I was one of the firsts-of-the-lasts to get selected.

Our team name was "Hannah and the Palindromes" and our player names had to be palindromes. The team jerseys had a drawing of a pinup girl sitting on roller skates doing the shocker for no reason at all. So fucking cool!

While on the subject, if you don't know what a "palindrome" is, don't worry. I didn't either. When I got selected for the team, I couldn't understand what they were talking about. I had to look it up online when I got home. A palindrome is a word or a phrase that is spelled the same backwards as it is forwards: like "poop" or "a slut nixes sex in Tulsa."

My teammates chose names like "Dr. Awkward," and "Lonely Tylenol." I selected "Ojo Rojo" which translates to "red eye" in Spanish. I chose this as a nod to the fact that I was still kinda bilingual and as a throwback to the time I got a terribly disgusting eye infection while working at Target.

Meanwhile, back at FaceBlorg, I received a message from a new man. He was not a hipster. He was a masculine, twenty-one-year-old, ripped kickboxer with a buzzed head and a jawline so strong you could break a tooth on it (which would be a great lesson to get you to stop nibbling on all those jawlines).

His name was Lyle, and the moment I saw his photo, my eyes exploded out of my head, similarly to Wile E. Coyote when he sees a lady coyote made of dynamite. I appreciated the fact that he had the name of an old man while simultaneously being the hottest guy my pants had ever seen.

It seemed preposterous that this kid hit me up out of nowhere. I say "kid" but I was only three years older than him and he technically didn't come out of nowhere. Lyle was roommates with the guy Tom was dating and now he was interested in me. It had to be because of my incredible haircut.

Lyle and I kept our dates simple. With him still being in college and me being a low-level social worker, we didn't have a ton of money. We did things like sit in my apartment while I played vinyl records (which blew his mind). The next day, I'd swoon about him to my co-workers and pull up his FaceBlorg profile to force them to look at this Hollywood man face that I was dating.

When Lyle asked to come to one of my kickball games, I knew things with him were going well. But this made me nervous. The game had more rules than I remembered, and the hipsters kept getting in kickball kerfuffles over every tiny thing. With my kickball skills not living up to my haircut, I didn't want to get called out in front of him.

As Lyle sat and watched from the rafters (while doing homework), I managed to kick a perfect ball. As it flew past the other team, I bolted all the way to second base. More kerfuffling happened, but the ref upheld my kick.

When Yo Banana Boy kicked, I made it to third base. It was up to Senile Felines to make it happen. Once she booted the ball, I ran like hell. The ball headed back my way fast. I slid to home base just before the umpire caught it and my team erupted in cheers.

Lyle jumped to his feet, fist-punching the air and letting out a very manly "fuck yeah!" I followed suit, letting out my own "fuck yeah." I had officially done the coolest thing in front of my hottest new gentleman-suitor. This could not have gone better. After the game, he let me know how much it impressed him. This didn't mean we had sex. We just made out. Strangely, at this point, we hadn't done the sex.

I wanted to remedy this. Conveniently, my work had a special training on the west side of town, near where Lyle lived. I asked him if I could spend the night at his place (purely for work reasons). He seemed thrown off by this request at first, but he agreed to it.

I packed my stuff and headed to his place. We ordered Chinese food and took his dog for a walk. When bedtime came, and he took his shirt off, I quickly got self-conscious. His freakin' abs had abs.

When he took off his pants, things got worse. And by "worse," I mean amazing. Lyle had a perfect everything. He was just handsome from head-to-toe. Handsome face. Handsome chest. He even had handsome balls. Do you know how many balls I've seen that I can describe as handsome? Like twenty-eight! That doesn't sound too rare, but trust me, that's like 0.1% of the balls I've seen.

When we laid on his bed to kiss, his handsome balls brushed against my leg and I got more self-conscious. For the first time in my life, I started to lose my erection. I ended up pulling through and making it to the end. But, it was a close call, just like my other home run.

A few days later, Lyle and I met up for coffee in my neighborhood. On this date, a very strange thing happened. As we went on to the patio, we witnessed a seriously ugly parallel parking accident. The driver of a large pickup truck misjudged the distance of a spot and the bumper of his truck scraped onto the hood of the sports car behind him.

The patrons on the patio screamed at the truck driver to stop. The sports car's alarm was crying desperately for help. The driver somehow didn't hear it and kept on backing up. By the time he realized it and pulled off, the hood of the sports car was garbled. The patio patrons whispered to each other as they gawked at the whole thing.

Lyle had a different reaction. "Whoa, did you see that?!" He yelled. "The guy in the truck is going to get his ass kicked!"

This was the odd thing - not the car accident. Lyle didn't say this in some kind of apprehensive way. He was thrilled about it - energized by the idea that a fight could break out between a truck driver and a sports car driver. This had me wondering, *Could Lyle be an over-the-top aggressive nutbag?*

The truck driver got out of his car and sheepishly waited for the sports car driver to arrive so that he could exchange information. As I was about to mention how I hoped they could work it out in a civilized manner, Lyle struck a kickboxing pose.

"IF I WAS THAT GUY," he gestured to the truck driver loud enough so everyone could hear. "I WOULD HAVE DRIVEN OFF!"

Lyle began leaping around and acting real proud, throwing punches into the air. The patio patrons stopped staring at the car accident and started staring at us. I just stood there - not knowing what to do.

Lyle continued, "AND IF I WAS THE DRIVER," throwing some kicks in the air. "I WOULD HAVE COME BEAT HIS ASS BY NOW!"

This was so disconcerting. Normally I cherished the idea of being seen in public with Lyle. Now, I awkwardly stood next to him as he let all this out of his system while everyone watched.

After he went home that afternoon, I couldn't stop getting the taste of his aggression out of my mouth. Had I been so hooked on Lyle's good looks that I hadn't noticed this side of him? Could I really go out with a guy like this? I had already been with an aggressive bag of nuts. I couldn't do that again. I *shouldn't* do that again. I decided, on the spot, that I had to break things off. It didn't matter how gorgeous his face, abs, or balls were.

I logged on to FaceBlorg to send him a break-up message (not entirely unlike the cowardly way James did with me) and saw that he had changed his relationship status from "single" to "seeing someone." It wasn't me who did it first this time. It was him. *He likes me!* I thought. *He really, really likes me!*

My hand suddenly lost control. Rather than moving the mouse to send him the message, it guided itself over to *my* relationship status. I told it to stop, but the stupid thing wouldn't listen. Next thing I knew, my own relationship status had been changed to "seeing someone."

On FaceBlorg, when you both had the same relationship status, it gave you the option to link yourself to the person you were dating. It put a smaller version of your profile photo below their profile photo and vice-versa on their page. Everyone would see that Lyle and I were dating, especially James. He could take his "I'm not ready for this yet" and go shove it in a bento box.

The next afternoon, while wondering what our wedding colors would be in 2.5 years, Lyle called. "So, umm, I wanted to talk to you about something," he said.

Has he already decided which wedding colors he wants?

Lyle continued, "Recently I've developed feelings for this girl in my kickboxing class. I didn't expect this. I didn't think I was attracted to women. It has me pretty confused and I kind of need some time to explore this. I'm sorry. I hope you understand."

What had I just done? It didn't take a super-genius to figure it out: Lyle hadn't changed his dating status for me. He did it for someone else. And here I had made an ass-bucket out of myself in front of anyone who saw me link our profiles together.

As much as I wanted to believe Lyle, my jealousy bones (I had plenty more than one) told me he made this story up about the girl. But what else could I do? I told him that I did understand and was so sorry to hear about his confusion.

I logged onto FaceBlorg and disconnected our profiles, once again returning my status back to "single." Then, I went over to the bed, crawled under the covers and prayed that the baby Jesus would strike me with lightning. Just like that, I had fallen flat on my face, not once, but twice in my first attempts at really dating - perhaps three times if you count the fact that I had been kind of dating the hipsters too.

At the next kickball game, we had to face one of the most difficult teams in the entire hipster league: the team of guys who wore singlets with nothing underneath. No wonder they won every match. You could clearly see their pork swords winking at you from every base.

Normally, I'd very much be into this. Instead, I couldn't stop feeling stupid and sad from what I had done. I felt frustrated at the singlet guys for doing more kerfuffling than any other team. They complained to the referee about every damn thing. It's hard to admire a guy's visible penis line when he is whining about petty things.

It was around this time that I noticed the hipsters, in general, complained a lot. They complained if their craft brews weren't crafty enough. They complained if their kimchi burrito didn't have enough smokey tempeh. And, I swear, one of the singlet guys complained to the ref that, when I kicked the ball, it looked too unhappy.

I didn't catch on to this at first because I also tended to complain about everything. This helped me fit right in. It wasn't until after I picked up on it that I wondered, *Are they complaining about me?* After all, my haircut had failed to satisfy its kickball potential.

I thought it would be so easy to fit in with people that didn't want to fit in. It somehow proved to be way harder. That's the thing about counterculture: it takes just as much energy, maybe more, to prove how not mainstream you are. By the time you finish this sentence, the current hipster trends will probably be out of date. I was exhausted with trying to keep up.

Hipsters didn't necessarily come off as the nicest folks either. When people try excessively hard to prove how alternatively cool they are, they have a tendency not to smile or introduce themselves.

Not even my cool t-shirts by obscure bands would help me strike up conversations with or keep me connected to these people. I would tell you which bands, but I wouldn't want you to feel inferior for not knowing them. That's the kind of shit hipsters would say!!! Or at least they said it with their facial expressions.

With all these extremely cool friends I had, I still felt as lonely as before, if not more. This was how I learned that feeling lonely when you are around people is far lonelier than if you were actually alone. It was awful. Every time I was around my "friends," I had this need to prove myself worthy of their presence.

After that last kickball game, I decided not to return to the league or the hipster bars in general. I basically ghosted friends again. That's how I apparently dealt with things. If I couldn't figure it out, I'd just run away.

Except for this time, I don't think it would have been considered ghosting because no one would notice I left. None of my teammates or bar peeps called to make sure, at the very least, I wasn't lying in a ditch somewhere or, worse, going to a Britney Spears concert.

My time in these new social circles and dating these new guys had officially ended. I went back to being alone. Still, I would keep Tom, the friend who connected me to all of this, as one of my closest friends.

Ten years later, I would end up running into both James and Lyle, one month apart from each other, while completely naked. This initially happened during my attempts to write the first draft of this book. I had taken a break and found myself road tripping throughout the western states, ending up in Las Vegas. Not being much of a gambler, I treated myself to a day of pampering at the spa in Caesar's Palace. In the dry sauna, a big-nosed, big-eared face asked if my name was Scott.

It was James. He looked the same but different, like a teacher who had lost his will to teach. James had a towel around his waist. I did not. Mine was tossed to the side as I sat like those guys who do a "man spread" on the subway.

James had long since moved to New Jersey (although he would consistently tell people that it was New York), so running into him in a spa in Las Vegas was beyond bizarre. He seemed kind and was genuinely interested in hearing about my life.

A month later, I ran into Lyle in the locker room at one of my local gyms, again, sans towel. Now bearded, hairy, and gloriously tattooed himself, I hardly recognized him. He was with his new husband whom I had already met separately years prior. They both ate apples as we made pleasantries at our lockers. They were friendly and we kept in touch on Facebook (FaceBlorg had closed down by this time).

Neither of these naked run-ins were in the least bit bothersome. Partly because, in a dry sauna, my balls look a bit handsome themselves. And partly because, by this decade later, I would learn to like the person that I would eventually become.

HIGH SOCIETY

While dozens of people chatted amongst each other at the party, I somehow managed to wedge myself in a corner next to a tall houseplant. Since houseplants aren't known for making great conversation (regardless of how tall they are), standing by myself made for a really awkward scenario.

I blamed this occurrence on two things. First, the alcohol – or, in my case, the lack of it. As my stability with sobriety increased, my ability to mingle decreased. Without a good buzz, my socialization powers had been rendered useless. Second, the friend I had come with abandoned me the moment we arrived.

When you end up wedged in a corner at a party, you will find any excuse to pry yourself out so that you can move across the room in hopes of slipping into an unsuspecting conversation. I'd either go get more funny-tasting, lukewarm tap water or I would go to the bathroom.

All the water coincidentally made my bathroom trips somewhat legitimate. By the first hour, I went to the bathroom so many times that people potentially thought I had IBS. I could only be so lucky. IBS would be a *great* conversation starter at a party! Who doesn't love talking about IBS? But the only IBS I had was "Intimidated Boy Syndrome."

This party was mostly comprised of gay men, which had been the big draw for me. I figured if I floundered as a hipster, then I should give "sticking to my own kind" a try. The only problem was that these guys all looked like they stepped out of a Sears catalog - all pretty with their first-hand pants, tanned skin, dandruff-free hair, and talented white teeth.

I, on the other hand, had buzzed all my hair off, was very pale, and came wearing a rock concert t-shirt with cut off sleeves. If anything, I looked like a skinhead. And these people probably didn't know how to strike up conversations about "white power." I couldn't blame them. I wouldn't either.

I had gone into this party excited to show how boldly different I was. Being different would make me stand out and, so people would find me interesting and want to talk, right? The glitch here was that this is the social algorithm for hipsters - not these people. While I did stand out, I did so as a sore thumb.

But here's the thing I really need to admit: I *wanted* to be like these people. When I said the thing about the Sears catalog, I didn't mean that as an insult. Secretly, I envied this clean-cut, put-together look where your clothes matched your car. I just didn't know how to do it, much less be able to afford it.

The plant-corner started to become painful. Without smartphones being invented yet, I couldn't even pass the time by crushing candy, turning my face into a zombie, or watching other people have more interesting lives than my own.

When you check your watch and it is the exact same time as when you checked it twice before, the time has officially come to leave. I said goodbye to the plant, thanked him for his company, and went in search of my friend so that we could go.

I found him knee-deep in a conversation of his own. Being unsure of how to interrupt them, I lingered behind him like some lingering lingerer. When I went to tap on his shoulder to get his attention, someone else tapped on mine.

"Heeeeey, you're cuuuute," a voice cooed out before I could fully turn around.

I came face-to-face with a Middle Eastern man, somewhere between the ages of 40 and 100. I couldn't quite tell, most likely a result of some plastic surgery. He wore the blingiest, flashiest outfit of the bunch - something Sears would never carry. How did I not see this guy before?

"What's your name?" he asked.

We made small chit-chat, mostly involving questions about myself, which was nice for someone who felt ignored most of the night.

"Well, hey," the gentleman leaned in to talk quietly. "I am having a pool party next weekend and you should come."

He handed me a business card with the details. "It's a secret. But feel free to bring some of your other hot friends," he added. "Just don't bring any women. This party is strictly for us boys."

With a wink and a smile, the mystery man bounced out as quickly as he bounced in. I didn't even have time to get his name.

My friend grabbed me. "DO YOU KNOW WHO THAT WAS?!" He whispered out a scream. Now he had apparently been paying attention.

Because of not having stuck to my own kind, I didn't have a clue who it was.

"THAT WAS ALEC AMARI!" He said.

My social-dunce-savvy still couldn't decipher it and the friend had to fill me in on the details. Amari was a prominent, powerful lawyer for the oil and gas industry. I had evidently come face-to-face with one of the city's wealthiest bachelors and he had dubbed me hot enough to come to his pool party. I think. I wasn't sure. What exactly did he mean by "bring some of your other hot friends?" Did that mean I was hot? Or did I just come off like the type of guy who would have hot friends?

It was all so vague, but if I had been invited to a secret gay pool party, maybe I had misjudged myself. Maybe I wasn't as trashy, gangly, and off-putting as I imagined. Maybe that night's IBS actually stood for "imitation boy stud."

In my life so far, I tried being rock-n-roll. That ended up making me insecure about my masculinity. I tried being Mexican. That gave me diarrhea. Then I tried being a hipster and that made me aware of my inability to fit into a pair of skinny-jeans (in addition to everything else). Perhaps I could try being a "hot guy."

I couldn't fathom this idea. It went against everything I believed to be true. Although, lately I had received more compliments about my progress in working out. My teeth had also remained fairly straight after years of braces and dedicated retainer-wearage. Maybe they had become talented too. But that was about all I had going for me. Still, it was worth a shot.

If a rich guy called me attractive, it could possibly be true. Because rich people like Alec Amari certainly *never* lie. That's *obviously* how they get rich: by always being honest and forthcoming about everything.

"I can't believe you got invited to his pool party," my friend shook me as if the business card in my hand had been a lottery ticket. "We *have* to go."

Yes, we did. But that "we" could not include this friend now that he had a track record of leaving me behind. I needed someone who I could rely on to help make me look impressive and fun all while staying sober. Basically, this wallflower needed a wingman to help him become a social butterfly.

I knew the perfect person; Tom, the friend with whom I rekindled the old friendship through the car window in the last chapter. Over the last several months, he had slowly been becoming a close friend. I could always rely on him.

Tom was a bit like me in that he didn't really fit in with any specific type of social group. Unlike me, he used his attribute of being different as an advantage rather than a handicap. The guy could easily float in and out of all kinds of social groups. Tom did this with the help of two superpowers; the first one being that he didn't give a shit and the second one being that he had an incredibly distinctive sense of humor.

When you can do a stellar job of making people laugh, you can socialize with *anyone!* Sure, I can also make people laugh, but my shyness and unparalleled ability to get inside my own head often prevent me from doing it well. That's why I have a tendency to be funnier in my writing than in person (as several people have so kindly pointed out).

Landing this invite to Amari's party was a *huge* deal. With Tom there, I could relax and not feel so much pressure to perform. Since he did this so effortlessly, I could sit back, relax, and be funny by association. When things went pleasantly enough, I'd get the confidence I needed to take flight on my own.

This would open the door for Amari's guests to see past my awkwardness and discover whatever "hot guy" he saw. And by getting to be a hot guy, I would hopefully get a one-way ticket to Rubbing-Shoulders-With-The-Wealthy-Town (Population: 1%).

That's what a lot of this actually came down to: a yearning for a more affluent life. Being broke in college was one thing, but being broke after college during the height of my career was another thing, and it totally sucked. Having money had been ingrained in my blood, and social work was not cutting it.

I wanted a big beautiful house like the one we had growing up. I wanted to be able to buy brand new Ethan Allen furniture like my mom did (and then get anxious every time the cat got near it). I wanted to take vacations on cruise ships like my parents - nice ones that don't break out in listeria.

After college, I still struggled to afford any kind of vacation, and my living situations left little to be desired. The 420 sq. ft. studio wasn't so bad, but it overlooked a dumpster and smelled of decaying wood. This was also the place where I drunkenly urinated on my keyboard, which tainted it a bit.

I tried upgrading to a 650 sq. ft., one-bedroom apartment, which seemed decent at first. Then, I discovered the six people living in the unit above me loved blasting their music at all hours of the night, and the couple next door would take their drunken fights into the hallway right in front of my door. I'd gladly call the cops on all of them. This somehow failed to stop them from doing it.

Around this time, I had the good fortune of meeting a nice young man who was moving to town to go to college. He wanted a roommate to keep things affordable, and I wanted a roommate to pool our money together to get something posh. It was a perfect match.

When we checked out an incredible 1,200 sq. ft., two-bed, two-bath apartment in a luxury high rise next to one of the most expensive country clubs, I knew we couldn't afford it. It had large closets and all the rooms connected to a massive balcony. The master bedroom overlooked the pool where I could spend my summer days indoors watching sexy tenants enjoying the outdoors.

When the leasing-lady told us the price, I nearly made a Boston Cream Pie in my pants. It was only slightly out of our price range as opposed to being entirely out of our price range. My new roomie was nervous. He already didn't want to be at the top of his budget, much less over it.

But this had to happen. I had to get back into the bougie lifestyle. I told him if he was willing to pay his max budget, I would pay for everything after that (not including utilities). This at least gave me dibs on the master bedroom. We signed the lease and moved in immediately.

Being in a luxury high rise tasted amazing. I mean that literally! The building had fresh baked cookies along with coffee and tea for the residents in the morning. When we returned in the afternoon, there'd be a doorman to welcome us home and a musician fingering the keys of a grand piano in the lobby.

This was my first step back into affluent living. Sadly, that was the last step. I stretched my funds so far that I didn't have the money to do much of anything. I was like a princess stuck alone in an ivory tower. I'm betting that was Rapunzel's real problem. The witch's actual curse was the outrageous cost of luxurious living. The only thing she could afford to do was hang out at home and watch her hair grow.

Worse than my bad budget was all my hand-me-down furniture. The 1980s beige, braided couch that my parents gave me (which was *not* Ethan Allen) didn't quite match the 1960s round kitchen table that my grandparents gave me. Anything that wasn't hand-me-down - my desk, the tv stand, and the coffee table - were made out of particle board.

I know it shouldn't have, but these things all ate at me. I just wanted to be comfortable like I was growing up. And by "comfortable" I mean living in nice homes, having nice things, traveling to nice places, eating nice food, and other nice things that are really nice. Was that too much to ask?

This explains why I so badly needed to make a kick-ass impression at Amari's party. I could get wealthy friends. They probably wouldn't buy me new furniture, but I could at least be high society by association. And, surely, if I milked it enough, they would pay my way to go on vacation with them.

The day the party arrived, I called Tom to find out what time we should go, what swimsuits we should bring, and how much we should whiten our teeth. I seemed to care a lot about teeth. But Tom didn't answer. No biggie. I would wait for the allotted amount of sane people time before reaching out again.

A few hours later, I called. He still didn't pick up. Twenty minutes later, I sent a text. No response to that either. I urgently began pacing back-and-forth, freaking out like a sane person (insane people pace in circles).

How could Tom do this?! He knew how much this party meant to me. He knew I needed his help to make a good impression. Now he ditched me, and I didn't have a social wingman. I couldn't do this on my own.

I spun my brain's Rolodex thinking about who else I could invite. They needed to be attractive, fun, and engaging. The Rolodex landed on Brandon and Brad, a couple that I had somewhat of a regrettable three-way with during a snowstorm the winter before. Brandon was blond, down-to-earth, and freakishly tall. Brad was blond, dashing, and freakishly arrogant. I liked Brandon just enough to stay friends with both of them.

Brad would bring the extreme level of attractiveness and outgoing fun. Brandon's chill, easy-going vibe could provide a route to more casual conversations. The three of us would make the perfect trifecta (if I had much of anything to bring to the table, that is).

I called them up and they were on board. Being the nice guy that he was, Brandon offered to drive. I told him it'd be better for me to drive since I was sober and could be their designated driver. He said it'd be better for them to drive because they were on the other side of town. I lived closer to the party (near the country club, I'd like to remind you) and it'd be easier for them to pick me up. Brandon won.

By the time we arrived, the pool party had already been in full swing. Rich people apparently didn't mess around. Upon letting ourselves in the house, I realized that my concept of wealth had been a little skewed. My mother might have been right all those years ago. We were "upper middle class." *This* was rich.

This was not a house built in a high-end subdivision. It was designed by an architect. These were not the people who bought an Ethan Allen chair for one or two grand. They had their chairs custom made for ten or twenty grand. They did not go on cruise ships for vacations. They took helicopters to private islands.

Practically everything in this house was made of glass - glass walls, glass tables, glass fireplaces, glass sculptures. Thank God I couldn't get drunk. I would have definitely fallen through the glass coffee table and bled all over his endangered polar bear rug.

When we closed the front door, a group of men standing in the kitchen all turned their heads and glanced over at us. None of them cracked a smile and, within a matter of seconds, they simply turned back around as if it had been a gust of wind that had blown the door shut. Something about this didn't feel all that encouraging.

We had to pass them to get to the table with the alcohol. As Brandon and Brad poured their drinks, I noticed one of them had been this guy I hooked up with a couple of months prior. The moment we caught the other's eye, I gave him a smirk that said, "Hey, you. I'll come over to say hi." Before I could even take my first step, he quickly turned around and gave me a shoulder that said, "Please, don't come over here."

Had he just pretended to not know me? Did he not want his friends to know that we had already been slurpin' the gherkins once before? Was he embarrassed to have been with a guy who'd use a phrase like "slurpin' the gherkins?" C'mon, that's hilarious. This brush off was not very encouraging either.

It wasn't until we made our way to the pool that I got the full-blown jimjams. The moment we stepped out there, we were blinded by a sea of young muscular man-torsos. Some were playing chicken while others tossed around a football. I was now definitely discouraged.

I kept staring at their hot abs - not with lust, but with terror. I hadn't reached ab status. Lord knows I had been trying, but my midsection always remained on the softer side. If you could grate cheddar on these guys' stomachs, you could maybe shove a fist-full of brie into mine.

Just then, my eyes locked onto a familiar set of abs. They were handsome. The chest was handsome. Next came the face. It was Lyle, the hot kickboxer with a handsome everything that I had assumed I dated approximately one chapter ago.

Seeing Lyle gave me proof that I was not truly a "hot guy" and that I didn't belong there. It was basic math. One hot guy who rejected me times forty other hot guys equals forty hot guys who would reject me. I once again stuck out like a sore thumb - this time a bland one.

To prove I wasn't being overdramatic, let me tell you that when we found Amari to thank him for the invite, the guy didn't even remember me. He had a look on his face that said, *Are you sure you're at the right party?* Perhaps I fooled him into thinking I had abs by my deceptively big chest (more on that in the next chapter).

The good news was that, when Lyle saw me looking at him, neither of his shoulders swiveled around to tell me I needed to stay at bay. Instead, he cracked a smile. It was a horribly awkward smile, but a smile nonetheless. I made my way over.

"Hey, so random to see you here," I said.

"I know. So random to see you here," he said

"How are you?" I asked him.

"I'm good. How are you?" He asked me.

"I'm good."

That was about the extent of our conversation. I really wanted to be like *How's that girl you're crushing on?! Clearly that's a thing!* I wish he had told me the truth. I could have handled it. Although, that's a bigger lie. Studies show that ultimately, we would prefer to be lied to when getting dumped.

Anyway, Brandon, Brad, and I found a couple of poolside recliners to set up shop. The moment we sat down, Brad popped back up, slipping his shirt over his head.

"I'm ready to get in the pool," he said. "Who's with me?"

"Umm, I am gonna chill out here for a sec," I said.

"Yeah, I'll hang back too," Brandon decided to keep me company. I'm guessing he could sense the anxiety seeping out of my every pore.

Brad couldn't care less about my nervous pores. He shrugged and ran off, doing a cannonball in the middle of the pool. Everyone would know that he had a giant penis in no time. He could never stop talking about it (hence: regrettable three-way). I like my giant penises the way I like my deities: humble.

I knew my problem. All this anxiety had made me tense. I needed to loosen up so I could show everyone that, while my looks might be second-rate, I can make up for it with my decent personality.

As I stared out across the pool, I noticed a strange group of older men who were leering at the young guys the same way seafood lovers would leer at a lobster tank. Except in this situation, it was the seafood lovers who should have rubber bands binding their hands shut.

"I don't get it," I told Brandon. "What is up with all these creepy guys?"

"You don't get it?" he sounded surprised. "They're the rich guys. They're the Sugar Daddies. Some of these young guys are their 'kept' boys. They give them money and free drugs and shit."

I wasn't so naive that I didn't understand the concept of Sugar Daddy. Hell, I technically had one before he tried blackmailing me out of the closet as a teenager. But I was naive enough to not know there could be drugs involved. I still had a hard time with drug culture - perhaps a result of the D.A.R.E. program having been a little too effective on me as a child. That, and I happened to have tried a few drugs and the experiences weren't great.

The time I did cocaine, my teeth couldn't stop rubbing together and my eyelids refused to close for the entire night. At one point, a guy turned to me and said, "Are you coked out of your mind?" Getting called out on doing coke does not go over well with someone who is already paranoid about doing coke.

After that, I tried ecstasy. I rather enjoyed ecstasy, what with all the generous shoulder rubs and the electronic dance music sounding like Mozart. Even the birds sounded amazing when I got home as the incredible sun came up and lit brilliant colors in the sky.

But then came the come-down. The coming of the come-down was the worst. When the come-down comes, your whole world comes down. I must have cried for like one or two days straight, though, I couldn't figure out how long I had been crying because I was so busy crying. It jumbled with my well-being badly.

The fact of the matter is that not a lot of happy stories begin with the phrase "When Johnny first got into drugs…" The idea of these older men using chemical addiction on top of their money made me genuinely worry for these boys. Why couldn't it be like the good old days when Sugar Daddies would pay their counterparts in nice meals and diamonds?

Brandon interrupted my apprehensive inner dialogue. "Hey, there goes Dave. He always has the best weed. Let's go talk to him."

Before the streets of Denver were flowing freely with legalized marijuana, our people still had to get their weed the old-timey way: through semi-sexy-stoner-retailers named Dave. I had seen Dave many times out in the city and had no clue that he had the best weed. It made sense. He was always squinty-eyed.

"Yes. Let's definitely go talk to Dave," I said.

I know I just got done touting on drugs. But again, being from

Denver, I am one of those hippie-crunchy-granola types who doesn't believe that weed is a hardcore drug - no more so than alcohol. It comes from the earth and it's natural.[30]

Plus, no one smokes too much weed and then beats someone up. Getting high doesn't make you hallucinate or want to sink into a hole in the middle of the earth. And stoners' teeth don't all fall out over time (unless they eat too much candy-corn), so marijuana felt reasonably harmless.

I had already tried it a few times and didn't have a particular affinity towards it. The worst thing that ever happened while on it was when I missed the countdown at a New Year's Eve party. I had become so laser-focused on trying various kinds of chips with various kinds of dip, I didn't notice everyone left the room to go watch the ball drop on TV. And I didn't care because I was stoned.

That's what I needed now, not to be stoned, but to not care. I was caring *way* too much. I was caring all over the place. It had to stop. And while I had been sober from alcohol, weed was still an option for me. So getting stoned it would be.

A bunch of us piled into Dave's car and passed around the pipe. When it got to me, I lit up, I sucked in, I held my breath, and I proceeded to cough my guts out. Tears rolled down my face, making me look like the total novice I was. When the pipe came around a second time, I did one more hit to make sure I could get extra mellowed out.

By the time we got back to our lounge chairs, I could sense my chemistry starting to change. A numbing-relaxation-cloud began to billow its way through my body and mind. At last, I could take a deep breath in and a deep breath out. This was exactly what the doctor ordered (and I mean that literally considering that doctors prescribe marijuana to treat anxiety all the time).

So what if I wasn't wealthy? So what if I wasn't a real "hot guy?" So

---

30. On that note, I would like to admit that the "it's natural and comes from the earth" argument doesn't hold a lot of clout as poison ivy is also natural and comes from the earth.

what if Sugar Daddies provide free drugs to their kept boys? So what if that numbing-relaxation-cloud was starting to put pressure on all my organs? *Wait. No. That's not right.*

"Okay, that's good," I told the cloud. "You can stop billowing now."

As I am sure many of you already know, you can't boss around a numbing-relaxation-cloud. It will do whatever the hell it wants and mine decided it wanted to make the insides of my body so thick that they could all touch each other.

Brandon said something.

"Wait! What did you say?!" I asked him with my own set of squinty eyes. I missed his words due to the fact that time was now simultaneously moving slow and fast.

"I asked if you were ready to get in the pool," he said.

My brain fired off like a racehorse out of a gate. *I don't know. Am I ready to get in the pool? Am I ready to let all these people see me with my shirt off? Maybe I could keep my shirt on. But then I would be that weird guy in the pool wearing a wet shirt. Where did I even get this shirt? Did I buy it from Target? Do any of these people know I worked at Target? They can't judge me for that! I was in college!!!*

"Wait! What did you say?!" I asked Brandon again.

He laughed. "Oh my god. You are so stoned, aren't you?"

Yes, Brandon. Yes, I was. But I couldn't figure out how to tell him that. By the time I heard his words, my racehorse brain had run off again. When I caught up with the damn horse, I had forgotten what Brandon asked me. What in the hell was happening?

"Hold on a sec," I told him. I tried tuning everything out so that I could focus and give him a normal human response. The more I tried, the more I could feel the earth spinning on its axis. No joke. The more I held still, the more the ground moved at a 23.5-degree tilt. This was horrible. I needed it to stop.

At that instant, it hit me. Ginger Spice, from the Spice Girls, was named Ginger Spice, because she had red hair. This had *never* occurred to me! I always assumed they meant actual ginger - the spice itself! What the hell? How could this have happened?!

"I NEED TO GO TO THE BATHROOM!" I blurted out.

Brandon found this odd. "Oh, umm, sure. You have the freedom to go do that."

I hurried into the house, finding myself back in the kitchen with that group of guys from when we arrived. The moment I ran into them, I completely forgot why I had come inside. I just stood there hoping one of them could tell me.

One kitchen guy noticed. "Uh, can we help you?" he said. He said it in that way that does not literally ask if I needed help. It was more like he was asking, "What's your problem, weirdo?"

It fortunately came back to me quickly. "Bathroom?" I said. "Do you know where... that... be?" I could unfortunately barely get the words out of my mouth.

They pointed down the hall and I ran off hoping I didn't crash into a piece of glass. I slammed the door shut and locked it. Each time I locked it, I forgot whether I locked it or not. I had to repeat this step approximately five or six times before making my way over to the sink.

"Ginger Spice was named after her red hair this whole time," I murmured to myself as I splashed water on my face. "It wasn't about the spice at all. They were play-on-words. Or was this a pun? Or was it a metaphor? Or was it a double entendre? None of the other girl's names were double entendres. There's no such thing as a 'posh spice.' Why would they do this?"

A loud clicking sound broke my spice-thoughts. "Oh fuck! Someone tried unlocking the door! What do I do?"

I responded by standing very, very still. Maybe if I stood still, they would think no one was in there and go away. That didn't work. They knocked some more. The running water had blown my cover.

Even though I knew someone stood on the other side of the door, I was *still* startled by them when I came out. It was two of the hot guys, presumably going into the bathroom to have some hot sex or snort some hot cocaine or do anything else hot that I wouldn't be good enough for. As they went in, I could hear them laughing behind me.

"What's up with that guy?" one of them said.

That did it. Everyone knew something was up with me. No splash of water on the face or coming to terms with the Spice Girls' nicknames could fix it. If I thought I stood out before by being mediocre or bland, I now stood out for being a total freak. I had gotten too high in high society and I was making a fool of myself. I had to get out of there ASAP.

I ran back to the pool to find Brandon and Brad. But I couldn't see anything beyond a bunch of sexy thrashing man bodies in the water. All I could do was stand there, breathing at all of them. Even though no one was looking at me, I could tell everyone was looking at me. I had now become the poolside creeper. I turned around and very slowly toddled my way towards the exit - a little too slowly. So slowly that everyone could tell I was one paranoid bastard.

The walk home was about three miles. By the time I made it 0.3 miles, I called Tom in a frenzy.

"Hello?" he answered as if he had been lying under a tranquilized gorilla.

"WHERE HAVE YOU BEEN?!" I screamed. "I WENT TO THAT PARTY WITHOUT YOU AND IT WAS HORRIBLE!!"

Tom groaned. "What time is it? I laid down for a small nap earlier. I must have been out this whole time. Are you okay?"

"No," I said. "I got too anxious at the party. Then I smoked too much weed and I got too stoned, and Ginger Spice was named after her red hair.

And I freaked out in front of everyone and now I'm walking home. And it's kind of hard to walk since I keep feeling the earth spinning on its axis."

"Shit, Scott. I'm sorry. Where are you? I'll come pick you up."

I told him not to worry about it, but Tom insisted that he come get me. We met at a nearby street corner and he took me to a diner where we could get some food while I tried sobering up. Tom had been a good friend all along.

When I got back to my ritzy apartment, I laid on my braided beige couch commiserating with myself. My experience in being a hot guy had been so short lived. I had blown my chance at being a part of a wealthy world that I wasn't even sure I liked. It all felt shitty which made me feel even shittier about not fitting in with the shittiness.

When I reconnected with Lyle years later, I told him about writing this book and his being in it. When I asked him if he remembered our awkward dating disjuncture, he promptly apologized.

"I'm sorry," he said. "I was a stupid kid back then."

"No, don't apologize!" I told him. "It was *me* who made the assumption about us dating. It was *my* fault."

We wound up talking about the night of Amari's party. He had no recollection of my marijuana freak-out presumably because, in reality, no one really noticed. But he did recall feeling super insecure about the whole thing too.

This couldn't be possible. He honestly was/is a beautiful man. He also happens to be one hell of a nice guy that I was fortunate to reconnect with. How could a guy like him experience the same self-doubt as a guy like me? Still to this day I don't understand it.

But what this did help me understand is that, when all we think about is how we were the sore thumb of the evening, we don't stop to think that there could be other fingers that hurt just as bad. It doesn't matter if we get manicures, pretty-up our cuticles, and paint on a nice color. Slapping on silly labels like "hot guy" won't help us feel more confident when the bones on the inside are already so very bruised.

FREE MEAT

One early afternoon, Tom called me up and asked if I'd like to go to a BBQ. It wasn't unlike him to hit me up with some random last-minute invite to the most random thing. More often than not, I accepted these invites as I didn't have anything better to do. I also fully appreciated his sense of adventure.

I should have been suspicious about this one though. BBQs don't typically have a huge reputation for being adventurous and Tom was never quite the type to "throw a steak on the grill." His diet consisted mostly of pizza rolls and off-brand sodas like RC Cola, which wasn't even good enough to be Royal Crown Cola. It stood for something like Rickety Conrad's Cola. I'm fairly certain it contained sugar that was banned in 73 countries, including Zimbabwe.

All that said, my workouts had really ramped up and, in hopes of gaining another inch around my arms, I had become a total meatatarian. What kind of carnivore would I be if were to say "no" to a BBQ? Free meat is free meat.[31]

I fully acknowledge that free meat *does* come with a cost: you need to bring something with you to not look like a total stump-muncher for showing up empty-handed. Tom covered this part as he said he would

---

31. I would like to take a moment to apologize to my vegetarian and vegan readers. You are welcome to rename this chapter "Free Tofu."

grab some beers on our way over. Not drinking often worked as a "get out of jail free" card for this kind of thing. Otherwise, I told people I had a phobia of potato salad and coleslaw.

As we pulled up to the house, I could tell that Tom was nervous. Tom never got nervous about anything except who won American Idol (I swear to God if I had to hear about Kelly Clarkson one more time...). Right when I opened the car door, he stopped me.

"Wait. Before we go in, there's something I have to tell you," he said.

These are words that you typically don't want to hear, like before going into a mortuary filled with clowns or that your safari tour will be guided by clowns. Basically, anytime clowns are involved and you're not going to a circus, you will hear these words. Also, I am trying stall to keep you on the edge of your seat as to what Tom had to say.

"Oh, God. What is it?" I asked him.

"So, this is... umm... a naked BBQ?"

"IT'S A WHAT?" I screamed.

"A naked BBQ," he said. "All the guests will be naked."

"WHY ARE THEY GOING TO BE NAKED?!"

My brain seriously could not register what Tom was saying. No joke. How could the words "naked" and "BBQ" even make their way into the same sentence? This must be what happens when the dictionary gets stoned. Words stumble on to the wrong pages and become straight-up nonsensical.

Tom explained that he had encountered this nudist group online and, when talking to them about participating, they invited him to this BBQ. Of course Tom would try nudism. And when they said he could bring a friend, that friend would apparently be me. There was evidently a cost to the free meat after all: for my own meat to be free.

How could he dupe me like this? Didn't he read Chapter 10? Didn't he know how terrified I was when I landed myself in a gaggle of Mexican men who dubbed it "okay" for swimsuits to be "optional?" Didn't he know that I almost considered taking my swimsuit off for a microsecond, and then I didn't because the cold water gave me an angry dick?

It's doubtful seeing as how he would have to jump in a time machine to travel many years later to now-times and read this damn book. But, by this time in our friendship, Tom should have known me better than that. I wasn't a naked guy. This kind of thing would never be *my* kind of thing.

"I can't believe you tricked me into going to a nudist BBQ," I said.

"I didn't 'trick' you," he said. "I just didn't tell you right away. C'mon. You had to have known that's what this was going to be. I already told you that I'd been chatting with some nudists."

"Yeah, and I told you that you were crazy. I can't do something like this. I'm gonna drop you off and go home."

"Noooo," he whined. "Do this with me, pleeeeaase! It'll be fun! I promise!"

He promises it'll be fun? Had he sprung this on me while bobbing for apples at a county fair, I'd have held his face under water. I would have rather gone to that clown mortuary than to a naked BBQ. That's how "fun" I thought this would be.

Ever since I was old enough to start thinking about my body, I hated it. Not just disliked it. Hated it. This came about for a few reasons, the biggest one of which was being raised in a household of women. Saying that may come off as a little sexist, but my dad never ran around saying things like "I wish I didn't have a beer belly."

My mom and my sisters, on the other hand, practically made it a competition as to who had it worse. Stacey wished she had Sara's ample butt. Sara and Mom wished they had Stacey's bigger boobs. Mom wished she had Sara's thick hair. Sara wished her hair laid flat like Stacey's. Stacey wished she had Sara's full lips. Sara wished she had Stacey's narrow waist. The girls wished they had Mom's height. Mom wished she had the girl's youthful skin.

The scary thing is that my family members were not vain, vapid tartlets. These were intelligent, strong women, and they were normal. That's the thing: this is normal for women. And I admired them. Their mentality burrowed its way deep into my soul, laid eggs in my psyche, and gave birth to thousands of self-criticizing babies for years to come.

But, guess what? Physical self-loathing ain't just for the ladies. In college, I took a "Sociology of Gender Roles" course where we learned that men can also join in on some of the fun. While women get more self-conscious about being overweight, guys tend to get self-conscious about being underweight.

Society expects men to be big - to take up space. It's like the literal version of our figurative take on gender roles. Men are supposed to be large and in-charge, preferably with muscle, which represents strength and agility (even if the giant, muscular guys can't fully put their arms down).

If a guy doesn't have muscle, then being overweight will suffice too. That's why, in old sitcoms, you often see an overweight husband with a petite wife.[32] Society doesn't want their men to be skinny. Although guys can get self-conscious about being overweight (especially gay men), this is more socially acceptable than looking like a stick figure.

While writing this chapter, I had been driving for Uber and, one afternoon, I picked up this girl and guy who were friends; both a bit overweight, and both attractive. During the ride, the girl complained that the two guys she was dating were too skinny.

"I just want, like, a real man," she said. "A guy who can just take me."

She then proceeded to say the word "like" five more times and talked about how, if a guy ever cheated on her, she could absolutely never forgive him. This coming from the girl who dated two men that didn't know about each other. She obviously had the intelligence of a biscuit. But

---

32. One exception being Roseanne who can go eat a bag of dicks as far as I'm concerned.

there's plenty of women out there who have better IQs than baked goods that share this same sentiment.

When you take all this man-sociology into account, being a guy with space rocket metabolism was more of a curse than a blessing. Between the likes of that Uber passenger, those old sitcoms, and *all* superhero movies, I continued to receive the same message: I was not a "real man."

To some people, I hardly even looked human. Because underneath my scrawny frame laid another problem: a large sternum (aka the breastbone). It stuck out so far forward that it brought my rib cage along with it, giving my torso the overall appearance of a creature who is very interested in beaming you up for a good, old-fashioned probing.

At swim practice, the other kids would point to my chest and asked why it was so weird. I lied, telling them it was called a "swimmer's chest" and that it made me a better swimmer. None of them caught on to the fact that, when it came to swimming, I had only ever gotten blue ribbons. I used this excuse all the way through high school.

All this uncomfortable attention continued on into adulthood. My translucently pale skin somehow made it more obvious. On more than one (or five) occasion(s), when stripping down with a guy for some hot "doin' it," he'd ask, "What's wrong with your chest?"

The swimmer's chest excuse no longer cut it.

I'd shamefully mumble, "I have an extended sternum."

None of these guys would ever tell me I disgusted them, put their clothes back on and leave. But the "doin' it" was no longer hot after making me talk about it out loud. It was about as sexy as having to tell them, "I have a burning sensation when I pee."

My scrawny, bony frame became my main motivation for working out and putting on some muscle. Regardless, body-dysmorphia doesn't typically go away. It didn't matter that I put on 30 pounds of lean mass. Each time I stepped in front of the mirror naked, all I could see was that alien prober staring back at me.

Also, there was the thing that most men worry about: the size of their penis. My penis tends to fluctuate between a mid-size sedan and a two-door coupe. Unless I am coming out of the ocean, in which case it is very much a Smart Car.

I truly wanted my penis to be more of an SUV. I didn't care if it got good gas mileage. I wanted people to stare at it with wide glossy eyes and think, *Damn, how is it gonna fit in that parking spot?!* Nobody has ever told me my wang wasn't enough, yet somehow, I still worried about this. Sometimes, I still do.

Sitting here, writing about the anguish I had whenever I thought about my own body sounds so stupidly self-indulgent. I picture many of you rolling your eyes, telling your cat, *Who hasn't been here? What makes this guy special?* Then, your cat agrees and tells you to go re-read Harry Potter instead. His favorite character is Hermione.

These were the things that went through my head as I now faced the reality of going to a naked BBQ (my body, not your talking cat). Working out had given me *some* confidence, but the idea of being naked in front of a room full of people made that same confidence slip away like chicken nuggets off a nonstick pan. And, like a nonstick pan, it all felt very toxic.

I had to ask Tom a legitimate question. "Is this like… an orgy sort of thing?"

"It's definitely *not* an orgy," Tom said. "This is legit nudism. If anyone tries to do anything sexual, they'll get booted out."

Strangely enough, this was not the answer I had hoped for. Not that I wanted it to be an orgy. But if it had been some type of crazed-sex-BBQ, I could at least make some sense of it. Getting naked to have sex made sense to me. Getting naked to talk about the capitalistic approach to healthcare in America while standing next to some hummus dip - did not.

Tom's clarification also stirred up a new fear in me. At first, I worried that I wouldn't have a very impressive car for this whole automobile show. Now I worried that it's surprisingly powerful engine would get revved up without even turning on the ignition.[33]

The thought of getting an erection in front of legit nudists became the fear at hand (so to speak). I never got over my teenage problem of boning out too easily. This might sound less like a problem for a grown man and more of a benefit. But when you have to try to think of Betsy Ross sewing flags to not pop wood when your doctor tells you to turn your head and cough, trust me, it's a problem.

"I can't go to a nudist event," I told Tom. "I'll get hard."

"You *won't* get hard!" He supposedly knew more about my organs than I did. "C'mon! I can't do this without you. Please. I promise. It'll be fun!"

"This is easy for *you* to say," I told him. "You can drink. I can't!"

"You don't need to drink. You've been doing fine with your sobriety. Trust me, you can do this!"

"I'm sorry," I told him. "I can't. I will make it up to you. I'll come get you later when you need a ride home."

"Scott," Tom's tone changed. He stopped pleading like an eight-year-old wanting some candy and started pleading like an eighty-year-old wanting to change his will. "This is something I have to try and I need you here with me. Why do you think I called *you* up today? You're the only friend I feel comfortable enough with to do this."

Stupid Tom knew my weakness - that flattery gets you everywhere with me. And making me out to be a close and trusted friend shot a cannon full of warm fuzzies into my belly. Tom was not the most sentimental person. Saying it like this said a lot about what this meant to him.

"Oh, Jesus. Fine," I caved. "I can't believe I'm gonna do this. But

---

33. On a separate note: I am very impressed with myself for all these car terms I've been using in the last couple chapters.

alright. What other choice do I have?"

Tom instantly turned back into that eight-year-old who received his candy. He jumped so much out of excitement that the seat belt yanked him back.

"But you owe me big time!" I yelled at him.

"Yes, anything you want."

I threw up my hands. "Okay. Fine. Let's go get this over with."

As we made our way from the car to the house, the warm tummy fuzzies that had gotten me to agree to this had all been gassed and left for dead. All that remained were some hammers and chisels hacking away my insides. I couldn't do this because being naked at a party was obviously a set up for failure.

I mean, I couldn't even take my shirt off at the high society party, and look what happened there. Now, I had to get completely nude?! Everything that made me self-conscious would be on display in front of everyone. If I could barely hang on by a thread with my clothes on, how could this go well? This was, without a doubt, going to be the most embarrassing event of my life.

The moment we stepped onto the stoop, I became faint. Tom rang the doorbell, and I genuinely had to lean against the siding of the house. I had to stay strong. I couldn't pass out. I'd ruin the afternoon before it began.

The doorknob turned from the other side. *Oh, God,* I thought. A *naked person is about to answer the door. I can't do this.* The door opened, and there we saw it: a group of people standing around totally freaking nake... wait... no... they were all dressed. What the hell? I got so worked up that I nearly fainted just so that they could have their fucking clothes on?! This was bullshit!

Right as we walked inside, their heads all rotated to check us out exactly like at that last party (or like in The Exorcist). But, rather than simply turning away (or spewing split pea soup), they smiled. It was weird. They even had the audacity to reach out to shake hands and say "hello." Weirdos.

We got settled in, which meant that Tom got his cocktail and I got my water. Actually, screw it; I got club soda this time. I earned it. My eyes darted back-and-forth as I didn't know where to go or who to talk to. But I didn't have to worry about it for long as some folks made an effort to invite me into their conversation. Phonies.

This overt friendliness was entirely foreign. They were probably just trying to size me up for when the time came to strip down. Couldn't these filthy animals wait? They would have plenty of time to get an eye-full whenever we all got naked. Pervs.

Another thing that seemed unusual was the diversity in this crowd. As more people arrived, the room filled up with different races, ages (over 21), and different sexual orientations. Guests didn't have to be naked yet to tell that we had a wide array of body types. Nobody bothered with sticking to their "own kind" like at the other parties I'd been to.

These weird mind tricks started to work on me. I could feel myself getting more comfortable with everyone. After a while, I noticed that no one had actually talked about nudity at all. The topic didn't come up once. I wondered if Tom had mixed up his BBQs. Perhaps the naked one was scheduled for Sunday and this was the BBQ where we would all have to eat while blindfolded.

I ventured outside to meet the grill-master - a slightly overweight, middle-aged Hispanic man. I peered over his shoulder to get a peek at his meat, and he got thoroughly excited to show me. From burgers to brats to chicken, as well as tofu, black bean burger patties, and vegetable skewers (you're welcome, vegans), even the food was diverse.

By the time I was finished stuffing my face, I was certain that Tom had this all wrong. We were at a nice, normal BBQ where the only exposed wieners were the ones going into people's mouths. Wait. That sounded sexual. You know what I mean.

Then it happened. Someone shouted, "Alright, is everyone ready?"

The guests all got up and made their way to one of the bedrooms.

"What are we doing?" I asked, hoping they'd say this was a surprise dog adoption BBQ and there would be puppies back there waiting for us.

"We are *finally* going to take our clothes off," one guy said. "I was beginning to think it would never happen."

So, no puppies.

"I don't get it," I told him. "Why now? Why has everyone been waiting?"

He explained. "This is a new group. We all found each other on a nudist website, but none of us have hung out before today. We're seeing how it goes, and I guess someone needed to get the ball rolling."

In the bedroom, everyone started taking their clothes off and sticking them into trash bags. They'd take a marker, write their name on it, and stash it somewhere in the room. With each layer of clothing, I became increasingly horrified. I couldn't believe I was going to see all their daylights in broad daylight.

I hung back in the hallway, waiting to go last. Dozens of naked people walked past me while talking and laughing with one another. I kept my eyes up towards the ceiling and thought about how it was a very lovely ceiling. *Why couldn't my ceiling be this nice? Nice ceilings are nice. The world needs more nice ceilings.*

When the last of them had finished, Tom and I made our way into the room.

"Are you ready to do this?" he said, as we wrote our names in big letters on trash bags.

"No," I said. "And I plan to murder you as soon as we leave this place."

He laughed and slipped off his shirt a little *too* casually.

"You're already drunk, aren't you?" I asked him.

He belched. "Yup. Just a little bit."

"I hate you."

I took off my socks and stuffed them in the bag, thinking about how so *not* fair this all was. Next, came my shirt. Then, I stripped off my pants. Tom had waited for me so that we could take our underwear down together. I grabbed on to the elastic, but my hands froze.

"You're not taking your underwear off?" he asked.

"I'm sorry. I don't know if I can," I said. "Maybe in a bit. I just can't right now."

Tom shrugged, yanked down his briefs, and stuffed them in his bag. There he was - one of my closest friends now fully naked in front of me. That scrappy bastard had the audacity to have an SUV. No wonder he wanted to do this. Again, so not fair.

When we walked out of the room, someone immediately noticed that I hadn't gone full monty. They weren't rude about it. They were just surprised. I apologized, telling him how this was all new to me, and I didn't know if I could do it, and that I should put my clothes on and go home. He smiled and said I should do whatever made me comfortable. How dare he.

I remained in my briefs for a good while. No one gave me any flack for it, but the more I stood there, the more aware I became of another increasing conflict: I was damned if I did and damned if I didn't.

On the one hand, it would be embarrassing to get fully naked and be exposed in front of everyone. On the other, it would be embarrassing to keep my undies on and be the one person there who didn't do go through with it. And given that I was the rebel who always wanted to fit in, I needed to push through.

With the dining table being a few feet away, I broke from my conversation and took a seat. I took a deep breath. I took ahold of my briefs and I took them down past my knees (this process involved a lot of "tooking"), kicking them off with my feet.

My heart was racing. I was now naked in front of everyone. Kind of. Not really. No one could see as I had pulled myself all the way up against the table. But I still felt more exposed than I ever had in my life. The sudden shift in my energy must have been noticeable as one of the gentlemen came over to sit down beside me.

"You took your underwear off, didn't you?" He asked, knowing the answer.

"Uh huh," I said. I couldn't look at him and kept staring straight ahead.

"How does it feel?" he said.

"Umm, really fucking weird."

He laughed. I laughed. My soul didn't explode.

The next step would be to push the chair away from the table. I did as such and closed my eyes to give my nerves a moment to calm down. I stood up. Nope! Too soon! I promptly sat back down. The nerves won that round.

Thirty deep breaths later, I not only stood up, I also stepped two feet away from the table. I scurried back as quickly as possible, but was still proud of myself. Next, came four feet, and then six feet. Before I knew it, I was back at the group I had been chatting with moments before.

They all cheered for me with hollers and hand-claps like I had just juggled a bunch of rabbits without dropping a single one. But I had dropped trou, and while I didn't want that to necessarily be a huge deal, it was a *massive* deal. I was officially doing nudism!

I can only describe this sensation as that first time you ride a bike without any help. There are no training wheels to keep you balanced and no dad to hold on (which suddenly made this analogy sound very creepy). You're screaming, *I'm doing it, I'm doing it,* yet you're still convinced you're going to crash and die (and now it's morbid).

When the organizer/pseudo-leader of this group came our way, and saw that I had gone full monty, he beamed with pride. "LOOK AT YOU!!!" He said with a gigantic smile.

Leader-man was an extremely muscled black guy and, true to stereotypes, he didn't have a penis so much as he had a stretch limousine. It was literally one of the biggest penises I have ever seen. If someone revealed that sucker to me, I'd smack it and run away. He reached up for a high-five, so the only thing I smacked was his hand.

That high-five unfortunately sent a shockwave of physical contact through my whole body. I could sense the inevitable stirring right in my Charles Dickens. *Oh, no. Please, don't get a boner. Please, don't get* a boner. Please, *don't get a boner. Betsy Ross. Betsy Ross. Betsy Ross.* It was no use.

"Oh, Jesus," I apologized as it went full mast. "I'm so sorry!"

"Dude, it's okay," Leader-man said. "We are here to celebrate the human body. Erections are a part of that, and they happen sometimes. Don't be ashamed about it. Celebrate it. We just ask that you don't stick it inside anything. Here, give me another high-five."

I couldn't believe how understanding everyone was being. They didn't mind me leaving my underwear on. They had no qualms about my getting an erection. What would be next? They'd be all chill if I accidentally sat on the bundt cake? It was as if they weren't judging me at all.

Conversing with a naked person while you are also naked is an incredibly strange sensation. Not knowing exactly where to look ended up making me look them directly in the face. Having no clothing to separate our bodies created a physical hyper-awareness that I couldn't ignore. I couldn't remember any social situation where I had been *this* engaged.

The longer I did this, the more I was like a walking bag of

contradictions. My instinct was to be self-conscious, yet I got oddly comfortable. And even though I got oddly comfortable, none of it ever felt normal. And the abnormality of it started to make it exciting. The whole thing slowly shifted from terrifying to terrifyingly fun.

It reminded me of a roller coaster. Waiting for it to start skyrockets your anxiety. Then being dragged up that first hill, you think, *Oh, God. What have I done?* In that initial drop, you want to throw up everywhere. In each loop and drop after that, you start to realize how incredible it feels as you let out various laugh-screams.

Also, this is a very ironic analogy seeing as how I hate roller coasters. That's why I wrote it in the second person. *You* can ride the roller coaster. I'll sit on a bench and watch while I eat funnel cake.

At one point, the grill-master asked me about my tattoos. I didn't have nearly as many at the time, but I had enough to warrant some advice. Yes, it's expensive. Yes, it hurts. Yes, it hurts more in some places than others.

When I asked him what he wanted to get done, his answer surprised me. He wanted a large-scale piece to cover up a massive scar on his lower back. This didn't seem right. Why would anyone want to cover up a scar? Scars aren't ugly and most of the time they come with an incredible story that tells what a person has been through. That's badass!

Grill-master told me that he hated it. It made him self-conscious. As much as I wanted to tell him it shouldn't, I stopped myself. I was all too familiar with what he meant. And him talking about this body part he didn't like while letting it all hang out there for everyone to see, felt lovely and generous.

I decided to call attention to my big sternum, talking about how I struggled with that and that I wanted reconstructive surgery. This is a real surgery where they go in to break the sternum and reassemble it. I begged my mom for this as a child. She refused to let me have it as it would have, interestingly enough, left a giant scar.

He peered down at my big breastbone. "Oh yeah," he said as if he *just* noticed. "I see what you mean. I thought maybe your chest was muscular." I told him not to get his scar covered up with a tattoo. He told me not to get reconstructive surgery. It was at this moment that I realized I wasn't just engaged with the people at this party, I was feeling connected with them.

With each passing minute, I continued to become more and more into this bizarre experience. As I got more relaxed, my conversations began to play out more authentically. Before I knew it, I was playing games and laughing with total abandon, like the kid who finally understood that his bike wouldn't crash.

Out of nowhere, the clock hands hit midnight. This shindig had been going for eight hours - six of which were naked. I was so caught up in it that I forgot to eat my protein bar. That's a huge deal. If you've seen me out at a bar, chances are you've seen me alone, in a corner (or on a dancefloor), eating a protein bar. Next time, be my guest to come say hello and I will give you a taste.

The gentlemen who owned the house wanted to retire for the night. This nudist BBQ had to officially wrap up. How was this thing already over? Weren't we just getting started?

I couldn't believe I made it through the entire evening completely unscathed. Nobody was judgmental. They weren't weirdos, phonies, or pervs. In fact, it was I who had been judging them. I gave them all those labels before getting to know them or giving nudism a try. It was me who cut myself down to size, not them.

Putting my clothes back on now felt somewhat disappointing, like I had to come back down to earth after traveling to a different planet (insert Uranus joke here). Tom had already left with someone else, which was fine by me. A part of me needed to be alone to try and digest what I had just inadvertently experienced.

Somewhere during the evening, I lost my body dysmorphia. I would say it could have fallen out of my pocket, but I didn't have any pockets. I only had me. And this whole gathering wound up being less about free meat, and more about meat freedom - a freedom from worrying about my physical self.

In due time, the struggles would find their way back. But, for this one night, I successfully let them go. This had been the complete opposite of what I predicted would happen, and it left me totally baffled.

How could taking all my clothes off in front of people do such a thing for me? It just didn't add up. In any case, the roller coaster had officially come to an end. I had to exit the ride and go back into the real world. Now all I could think about was how badly I wanted to ride it again.

GLASS BALLOONS

As I sat in the waiting room, with my friend Sarah by my side, my left leg kept shaking up and down. I bit my nails which I *never* do, and I could hardly say a word (which I also never do). My life was either about to stay the same or turn itself inside-out.

Sarah (not to be confused with my sister Sara) always said that if I wrote about her in a book, she wanted me to change her name to Olivia. But she is another person who I refuse to give a pseudonym as she was (and still is) too good of a person to not mention her real name. I don't think she will try to sue me.

She had become another close work friend. I chose to have her come with me since she had spent the last few years taking care of her mother who was in hospice. If anyone could help me deal with the potential bad news, it would be her.

This all started the week before when I stopped in to get your average, run-of-the-mill, no-big-deal STD screening - ya know, a Tuesday. The standard "every six-month check" had probably gone too long, especially because the new norm had been three months by that time.[34]

None of it had me worried as I lived a low-risk lifestyle. I didn't do drugs, I always had safe sex, and I had successfully gotten this far without

---

34. For those concerned that I am not using the term "STI" (sexually transmitted infections), this did not come out until many years later. During the time of this story, "STD" was still the norm.

ever contracting an STI (if you don't count those teenage crabs, which I don't since I got them from a toilet seat… A TOILET SEAT, I TELLS YA!).

My tester was a guy named Aaron. He wore glasses, had a lean body, and had long hair pulled back into a ponytail. Aaron happened to have done my previous STD testing the six or so months prior.

I automatically liked him when we met before. His endearingly high levels of nerdiness helped me get comfortable in the testing room. He had a laid-back vibe which helped me to shoot the shit easily over an otherwise nerve-wracking subject. So, when I saw him again, I was able to unclench my butt cheeks right away.

Another thing I liked about Aaron was that, when all my tests came back clear last time, he said, "Thank you for helping to keep our community safe!" It was the sexually-active-adult-equivalent of getting a lollipop from your doctor.

Like before, Aaron welcomed me into the small room and had me take a seat.

"You did my testing last time," I told him.

"Oh, yeah?" he perked up. "How long ago was that?"

I didn't know if this was some kind of Jedi mind-trick to inquire how often I got tested. He also clearly did not remember me. This was for the best. You don't necessarily want the local STD-tester to be like "Oh, you again! Did you remember to bring that punch card this time?"

He went over the whole process ahead of time which, in all honesty, I wanted to skip. I remembered most of it from the last time. It all seemed fairly straight forward and nothing had changed. But hinting at that didn't move things along any faster.

The first item on the list was the HIV rapid test. The rapid test functioned a bit like a pregnancy test. But instead of splooshing lady urine all over a stick, you just use a non-gender specific drop of blood to drip in the stick's tiny hole. If a line appears in the window, some kind of antibody has been detected.

Aaron covered up the rapid test. It would take twenty minutes to reveal its answer. In the meantime, he went over a questionnaire about my sexual practices. *What gender do you have sex with?* Men. *During the last 90 days, how many people have you had sex with?* I dunno. A million? What was I? A calculator?

Out of those people, how many were anonymous? Purple. What kind of questions were these? *Out of those people, how many did you use condoms with?* All of them. That I knew. I was always extremely adamant about using condoms, even when my long-term relationships were monogamous. That's why I never worried about getting tested.

After the questionnaire came the real fun: peeing in a cup. I went to the restroom, filled it up to medium-high (like I was instructed to), and brought it back to Aaron. He dipped his toes in it, or swished it around in his mouth, or did whatever he needed to do to determine that I did not have gonorrhea or chlamydia. I think he just stuck a testing strip in it.

Once those were cleared, Aaron went back to the rapid test to see the results.

"Hmmm," he said in a way that implied he wouldn't throw any confetti in my face just yet (as is the typical practice when it comes up negative).

"What is it?" I asked.

"Well, there is a faint line here."

This didn't sound good. "Wait, what does that mean?"

"The line is very faint which may not mean anything, so don't stress," he said. "There can be a number of antibodies that can trigger a false positive."

"This means it could be positive?!" I started getting worked up.

"Not necessarily," Aaron said. "I've already had three false positives this week. Really, this can be normal. Have you been sick at all recently?"

YES! Yes, I had! A month before, I had come down with some weird-ass random summer flu. Remembering this helped calm me down. It obviously meant that whatever antibodies remained from that unseasonal sickness most likely triggered the results. I relayed this info to Aaron.

"Oh, well," he did not seem quite as optimistic. "Sometimes, when a person contracts HIV, they can get a flu. It could be a sign of an early HIV infection or it could just be the flu."

My antibody assumption had proven somewhat incorrect. Whatever calm it had given me quickly made its way through the emergency exit. All sirens and alarms had been set off.

"This doesn't make sense!" I said. "I *always* use condoms! How can this be happening?"

"Then it may not be anything," Aaron continued to try to keep things calm. "But we have to be sure. I need to draw more blood and send it in for testing."

He slid a needle in my vein as I placed my head in the palm of my other hand. The blood sucked its way through the narrow tube. My whole body, especially my face, clenched up in both pain and fear. Even though he took only about two or three vials worth, it felt like gallons.

"Regardless of what happens," Aaron said while pulling out the needle. "You are going to be okay. I promise you."

He wrapped a cotton ball over my new pin-hole sized wound and got some paperwork in order. "Okay. It'll be about a week before we get the results back. Hang tight. I'll be in touch."

With that, Aaron sent me on my way. There would be no lollipop this time.

A week?! I thought. *I might have contracted one of the world's most deadly diseases, and I had to wait a whole week to find out?!* That was absurd! After waiting one day, it already felt unbearable.

I knew my primary doc could get the results within four days. I called her office the next morning and told them that I needed to come in for an HIV test as soon as possible. The receptionist said they could get me in some time the following week. I told her what happened and, magically, a new appointment was available that same day.

My doctor was a kind, motherly woman who probably shouldn't have ever been my doctor. I randomly picked her from a list when I got my new health insurance at that first job out of college. She had an interesting last name and practiced in a great location. But it was clear from the start that she dealt more with families as the waiting room looked like a daycare facility.

"You're in here for an HIV test?" she asked, as she came into the exam room. She seemed confused as to why this had been a rushed visit.

"Yeah," I told her. "And I need it to be a 'viral load' test."

"But, Scott, those are for people who already have HIV."

The viral load test measures how much or how little of the virus is in a person's system. Doctors primarily use it as a tool to see how a patient is responding to treatment. A friend had told me to ask for it since it tests for the actual virus as opposed to the antibodies. But doctors don't hand it out like candy as it's far more expensive than the antibody test.

I told my doctor about what had happened while testing with Aaron.

Her face grew slightly concerned in the same way his did. "Oh, Scott. When you came in here last month sick, I didn't think it could be from something like this."

Her comment confirmed Aaron's same suspicions. *This can't be happening. THIS CAN'T BE HAPPENING!* She authorized the viral load test and said they wouldn't get the results back before the weekend. I'd have to call in on Monday to get the results. I met with another nurse who took more of my blood.

By the time the weekend came, my patience had run out. Waiting became excruciating. Every minute felt like an hour. I couldn't sit still. I confided in a few people - Sarah and Andrea (my co-worker from the "Johnny Badass" story), and a guy that I chatted with online who was the only positive man I had ever talked to. They all told me the same thing: not to worry and that it'll turn out fine.

When Monday came, I hopped out of bed with so much anticipation as if it were the darkest, most jacked up Christmas you could ever think of. I called the doctor's office. The receptionist said the results were in and scheduled me for a time slot.

Since I worked four ten-hour days, I had Mondays off. Sarah had the same schedule. When I asked her to come with me, she graciously said she would. Then there we were, sitting in the waiting room, twenty-feet away from children pretending to cook in a plastic kitchen. A receptionist, or a nurse, or some lady walked out to hand me back my $15 co-pay.

"You don't need this copay today," she said with a smile that had "compassion" written all over it.

"Oh, no," I whispered to Sarah. "Doctors don't give you back your co-pay. This can't be good."

"You don't know that, Scottie," she said as she rubbed my back. I liked that she called me Scottie. Only my family ever called me that. At this moment, I needed to feel like I had family there with me.

When the doctor's assistant came out to call my name, we stood up and followed her down the hall. I was a dead man walking. Each footstep brought me closer to my execution. With every breath, I prayed that I would get a last-minute pardon.

Sarah and I sat in the medical exam room in dead silence. We could hear the tick of the clock and, with each second, my stomach tied in tighter knots. The door opened, my doctor walked in, and, before the door shut behind her, she said the viral load test came back positive.

I clasped my hands over my face as I let out a yell of pure emotional shock - a noise I had never made before and will hopefully never make again. I cried faster than I could breathe. I was now HIV positive.

Sarah and my doctor held on with me as I crumbled in front of them. This is exactly what to do when someone is in crisis. Don't tell them it'll be okay. Their whole world is falling apart and they need you to let them freak out, at least for the first part.

The moment my doctor found a break in my hysteria, she stoically explained the next steps. "Scott, the kind of care you need is out of my range of practice. We can't work together anymore."

My own doctor couldn't work with me anymore? If you are a doctor and you are reading this, this is exactly what *not* to say when someone is in crisis. My terrifying disease just came off as ten times more terrifying.

"I'm writing down the name of a specialist you can see," she continued. "He will take good care of you."

She skimmed her way through a booklet and found a name and number - not unlike the way I found her. I couldn't tell if my doctor knew who she was referring me to or if she picked some specialist at random. She wrote the name down on a sticky note and handed it over.

"I need to see my next patient," she stood up to go. "Take as long as you need to in this room. I'm sorry, Scott. You will be in good hands."

I don't know if doctors aren't allowed to give their patients hugs, but I needed something more than that. And, as I'd come to find out, this didn't mean she couldn't work with me anymore. A specialist wouldn't replace my primary care doc. I would still need both. So, yeah, I had chosen the wrong doctor.

I needed more time to collect myself so that I wouldn't be an utter disaster in the hallways in front of perfectly good strangers. At the same time, I couldn't stay in there for very long as I could feel the walls getting ready to close in on me.

As we walked out of the building, the air felt thick. I became hard to move. Sarah kept her arm around me as I had become too frail to walk on my own. My legs began to buckle. Sarah grabbed onto me tighter.

"C'mon, Scottie," she said. "You can do this. We're almost to the car. Just keep walking with me."

I gave her my keys. She slumped me against the car as she opened the passenger door to help me inside. It may sound dramatic, but when your mind, body, and soul have been annihilated, it can become so damn difficult to move.

By the time we got to my apartment building, the air thinned out a bit. I could breathe a little easier and walk a little steadier. She asked me if I needed help getting out. I told her I didn't, and we successfully made it to my apartment without me collapsing.

Andrea joined us. We all sat around awkwardly figuring out what to say and how to process this. Sarah talked about hope. Andrea cracked jokes. I had no idea if her approach was helpful or hurtful. Probably both. They eventually had to get back to their own lives. Being solo in the apartment wasn't going to work for me. The empty space felt like a telltale sign of my future: empty.

I had arrived at the ultimate embarrassment. I somehow contracted the most undignified, controversial disease. This was my scarlet letter. Nobody would want to be with me now that I had become hazardous material. This was the last stop. My life was done. Game over.

I flipped on the TV in hopes of finding some kind of escape. *The Simpsons* had come on for their usual two-episode syndicated time slot. Surely, one of my favorite shows could help me step out of my own reality. But, each time I came close to forgetting the situation, terrible thoughts came flooding back into my brain.

So many memories, including stories from this book, pounded at my mind's eye. These stories - they weren't just about someone who once forgot a birthday or accidentally spilled spaghetti in their lap (although there are plenty of those kinds here too). There was so much more to them than the simple idea of embarrassment.

I always considered them a random series of unfortunate events. Now, things didn't seem so random anymore. Fate had come into the picture. A stronger connection existed. I had to ask myself that fundamental question when faced with my mortality: if I died tomorrow, would I have lived a "life well-lived?"

Each beat of my heart gave me the answer. No. No. No. I would not have lived a life well-lived. If I were to die, I would die feeling lonely, feeling empty, and feeling lost. As that answer sank deep into my throat, it became painfully clear. The *one* thing all these stories had in common... was me. The problem had always been me.

This whole time, I had been living in a world filled with the "wanting of things." I had been running off a combustion engine fueled by desire. In Buddhism, they say that desire (often referred to as "attachment") is the root of human suffering. We aren't Buddhist monks, though, who can find refuge in an East Asian monastery. We are people plugged into a modern culture that makes desire not only inevitable, but also a tricky and alluring bastard.

I think desire can begin innocently enough with our basic human needs - love, shelter, security, etc. But, without noticing it, outside factors can so easily turn such needs into something a bit more precarious. It becomes about something more artificial - wealth, power, appearance, popularity, sexual currency, etc.

Now that I had a virus below my veins slowly killing me, chasing artificial desire felt like playing with glass balloons. They required so much of my energy - all my breath. Sure, they would have looked beautiful, as glass often does. The problem is that no matter how much air we put into glass balloons, they can't ever take flight.

Even if I had obtained such seemingly glorious things, the satisfaction would have only been temporary. Because, when it comes to chasing the more artificial side of life, "enough" is rarely ever enough. Instead of flying into the air (as balloons should), glass balloons remain heavy and fragile. They weighed me down.

And the more we play with glass balloons, the more I think we set ourselves up to trip over rocks on the path, holes in the ground, and, more often than not, our own two feet. Glass balloons are supposed to look gorgeous and perfect. It is when we crack or break them that people see our imperfections, our flaws, and our insecurities. And it's when we see ourselves as imperfect, flawed, and insecure that we feel so horribly embarrassed. In the wake of this HIV diagnosis, I realized I had been playing with glass balloons my entire fucking life. With my shoes untied. While wearing a blindfold.

Philosopher George Santayana once said that we are doomed to repeat the same mistake until we actually learn the lesson. No wonder stories like these continued to happen over and over again. I never stopped to understand that I had been the one perpetuating most of them.

I was just as much the perpetrator as I was the victim. Because of this, I couldn't recognize the biggest lesson of them all: that, in the end, none of it ever mattered. Everything I chased and all the ways I felt or looked like an idiot, none of it ever really mattered.

Laying on the couch that afternoon of my diagnosis, I found myself no longer caring about money, beauty, wealth, or popularity. All I wanted was to be healthy. I wanted to be okay. Imagine that: simply wanting to be okay - a balloon not made of glass.

I wasn't okay. The biggest balloon of them all hadn't just merely cracked, it completely shattered in my face. I laid there with cuts so severe, I was convinced I would never stop bleeding. I had nothing left but shame - shame at the person I had been and shame about the disease

I now had.

The second episode of *The Simpsons* began to wrap up and I panicked. Next up would be the news. God knows I didn't need to see that. The moment my cartoon ended, I had to fully exist back in my own reality.

I turned off the TV. Even though the sun was still out, the apartment grew dark. The walls began closing in on me like they tried to do in the exam room. I couldn't do this alone. My heart picked up the pace while my breath started to run out. I scrambled to grab my phone to call someone - anyone.

Not knowing who, I dialed the number of a man I had met earlier that summer. His name was Luke. We had gone on one date and I had written him off as a potential partner. He wasn't edgy enough. We remained friends though, which included the occasional "friends with benefits" moments.

Luke wasn't like other people. He had a sense of optimism that felt warm and flavorful every time we hung out. He appeared content in his life - acting genuinely humble and kind - hardly ever saying a bad thing about anyone. Luke was basically the opposite of who I had been, which made him the obvious front-runner of whom to call.

The phone rang.

Luke answered. "Hello?"

"Hey, it's me." I tried choking back the tears so I could at least get the words out.

"Hey," he said.

"The test came back positive," I told him.

"Oh, fuck," he said. The man didn't have a habit of cursing like I did. When he said it, you knew he meant it.

I had already told Luke about the potential status. When the rapid test showed up reactive, I knew I could confide in him. And, seeing as how we had slept together, giving him the heads up felt like the proper thing to do.

"I don't know what to do," I said, as the crying wouldn't hold back any longer. "I can't be alone tonight."

"Give me twenty minutes. I'll be right over."

The moment Luke arrived, he grabbed me for a hug and I sobbed intensely into his chest. He didn't say a word. He just let me let it out. I can only imagine the amount of facial fluids I got all over his shirt. He didn't seem to mind. Or maybe he did mind and just generously understood the importance of letting all those fluids get out of my face.

Once I gained some composure, we sat down and I immediately lost it again. I launched into the hysteria of all those could-bes and what-ifs. Luke was one of those people who didn't claim to know a lot of things, but somehow still knew *a lot* of things. He didn't know much about HIV, but he knew that everything would be okay.

It sounded like another person telling me what I needed to hear, thus I continued to catastrophize my future. When you're in this dark of a place, it's somehow easier to believe it will always remain dark no matter who is trying to hand you a flashlight.

Luke didn't express any concern for himself during our time together. He was secretly terrified and would go on to get months of testing. For the time being, he selflessly let it be all about me. I thought about how lucky I'd be to end up with a guy like that. How could I have written him off so quickly?

When it came time for him to leave, I struggled to let him go (both physically and emotionally). I asked him to stay the night so I wouldn't have to be alone. He declined. The man knew I couldn't start off this journey on a stepping stone of codependency. That, and he also had a great dog to take care of.

In the days and months that followed my diagnosis, I had to figure out who I wanted to be from here on out. I didn't want to go back to doing the same thing. I didn't want to put all my breath into things that would never take flight. I didnt want to spend all my energy hiding the cracks in my glass. It was all so exhausting.

I got my HIV diagnosis at a very strange time in the evolution of this disease. Medical science had already nailed super effective medications that had lower side effects. With the viral loads being undetectable, patients were expected to live a normal life expectancy.

Yet, because people were no longer dying, the conversations around HIV and AIDS stopped. Nobody talked about it anymore. As a result, people's understanding of this disease walked out the door. And, since it is contracted mostly through sex (and needle use), in walked stigma to replace awareness and compassion.

Getting any kind of diagnosis like this is traumatic as hell. But when stigma is attached, it makes it that much more agonizing. It meant an opportunity for rumors and gossip. Not only had I contracted a deadly disease, I had contracted a social disease as well.

I was clearly the only modern person stupid enough to get HIV. It would be me and the long-term survivors. That's it. And they had an excuse. I didn't. Now, no one would ever love me again. They wouldn't even want to be my friend for the fear that associating with me could risk the way they'd get perceived.

Obviously, none of those things were true. People are not stupid for getting HIV and I was by far not the only person in my city receiving this diagnosis. This was just what the stigma (along with my own ignorance) told me. As these messages echoed around my soul, I knew that the one thing I so desperately needed from everyone would be empathy.

Like desire, empathy is a tricky bastard as you can't really expect to receive it unless you offer it first. That was my problem. I was so extremely guarded that I often resorted to pointing out the cracks in other people's balloons in an effort to hide my own. While I wanted people to take a walk in my shoes, I never could be bothered to take a walk in theirs.

This was how I would begin the process of rebuilding myself. Life had knocked me down and dragged my body to the other side of the fence. Being on this side of the fence made me truly want to know the other folks who were there with me - those who had been damaged by more than first world problems. My heart wanted to speak to their hearts. I could only hope their hearts would speak back to mine.

To grasp this whole empathy thing, I also needed to learn about grace. This was a difficult one for me. I tended to hold on to my anger. And this wasn't just about letting go of my anger towards others, but the chance that others could let go of their anger towards me too.

I hadn't been the kindest person and now I was filled with so much regret for the people I had hurt over the years - some mentioned here in this book, too many to list them all. With some grace, perhaps we could share our broken glass with one another and make amends. Maybe I could find some forgiveness for myself as well.

Gratitude was another component seriously missing from my life. It makes sense though. It's 'Glass Balloons 101.' A person cannot simultaneously be thankful for what they do have while they're focusing on the things they don't.

This really hit me hard as I lay on the couch on the afternoon of my diagnosis. My hand-me-down furniture didn't seem so bad after all. It was given by people who loved me and I had been so ungrateful for it. That was the real lesson I failed to learn from the "High Society" story. Nothing makes you have more gratitude than when your life suddenly has an expiration date.

Above all else, I needed to have some humility. The moment the doctor said the test came back positive, the one thing I knew was that I knew absolutely nothing. This was huge because, with all of my broken glass, I had gotten stuck in a cycle of arrogance perpetuated by self-loathing. When my mind was too busy knowing everything, I couldn't be open to learning anything.

HIV created an opportunity for me to be fallible. To become fallible meant I could become self-critical (rather than self-loathing). I could hold myself accountable and I could own my mistakes. This would help me learn how to accept being wrong in order to feel alright. I was finally learning my lesson and seeing the truth in the wisdom of George Santayana.

And, for fuck's sake, I needed to learn how to laugh at myself like my mother told me to so many years ago. Laughing at one's self isn't the same thing as hating one's self. Trust me, I did a lifetime of the latter. Self-loathing is not the same thing as self-deprecation.

If we don't laugh at ourselves when we fumble, we hold on to that sense of shame deep within our bones. We imagine others laughing harder at us. Our own laughter can be a way to let go of all that. Laughing at one's self is the sound of shame leaving the body.

This is why I choose to tell these honest stories with a sense of humor - not to merely poke fun at myself, but to make it easier to tap into my humility, to ask questions, and to gain new insights. When I do poke fun at myself, I do so in the likelihood that people will relate and not feel so alone. That's the interesting thing about stories of embarrassment. They can be the stories that we don't want to tell anyone, yet they are the stories that can connect us the most.

Gratitude, grace, empathy, and humility are the values we tend to lack when we play with glass balloons. Now that everything changed, they would become the tools - the superglue - I needed to build myself back up into someone new, someone different than before.

However, this wasn't the first time all four of these values made their way into my life. This happened just one chapter ago at the nudist BBQ. But, what on earth could these two things have in common - casually getting naked in front of strangers (an entertaining rush) and getting HIV (a horrifying nightmare)? Can you guess what it is? The answer eventually became clear. The connection was vulnerability.[35]

This might seem confusing given that all of these embarrassing times I've written about also left me feeling totally vulnerable. What was the difference? I knew something incredibly different happened at that naked BBQ. I couldn't put my finger on it at the time, but my diagnosis gave me a new perspective. The difference was that, at the BBQ, I was vulnerable up front and on my own terms.

In lieu of running from this fear of being naked, I ran towards it. Or, at the very least, I tiptoed my way into it. Actually, no. I am going to stick with "ran towards fear" since I didn't use alcohol to numb the experience.

This type of vulnerability kicked in my human instincts of grace, gratitude, empathy, and humility. And gaining those from facing my fear head-on left me feeling alive, connected, fulfilled, and even empowered. Glass balloons did not have their place here (hence no more body dysmorphia for the night).

This was the same case with my HIV diagnosis. Or at least it could be. Having this disease left me more vulnerable than anything else, ever. And I realized I had two ways of going about it. I could either keep the disease a secret like most of us felt we had to, or I could do things differently and live with it in total transparency.

If I did the former, it would require me to keep my guard up, which meant chasing more artificial desires. Grace, gratitude, empathy, and humility would slip from my fingertips. The cycle of my foolish behavior would continue and, when my peers would uncover this secret disease, it'd be humiliating. My HIV status itself would become another glass balloon. It would have been the glassiest of all glass balloons. I couldn't do that again.

With all the stigma behind HIV, taking a naked approach with it

---

35. I wrote this part using voice-to-text on my phone and later, when I checked it, Siri had written "vulnerability" as "boner ability." Apparently, she thought I was going in a different direction. Also, this means we've reached the part of the chapter where we can laugh again.

was beyond terrifying - more so than getting naked in front of a bunch of strangers. People would talk behind my back. They'd call me terrible names or be afraid to be seen talking with me. Could I really afford to do this? More importantly, could I afford not to?

The conclusions didn't come to me overnight. It took months of processing to understand it all. I essentially had no other choice. I couldn't go back to being the person I was. For the sake of having a life well-lived, I had to try this experiment and be completely transparent about my HIV status with anyone and everyone.

The process itself would be a slow one too. I didn't wake up the next day and say, "Hello, World! Check out what's in my bodily fluids!" It would take several more months to put it all into practice.

In due time, I began telling everyone about my diagnosis - my family, my friends, my co-workers (including upper management), my former dates and hookups, and even that one lady at the grocery store who always holds up the line by writing a check (if it came up naturally, otherwise that would be weird). The process was scary as hell, but that was the point. Rarely can we change our lives by staying in our comfort zones.

Long story short, my HIV transparency did, in fact, spread quickly in the community. It garnered the big attention that had me so afraid, though, it looked different than I had suspected. I feared that people would dislike me and stop talking to me. I worried this attention would result in them calling me names like "whore" or "unclean." Instead, they gave me their hugs, their hearts, and sometimes their tears. They ended up calling me names I had never heard before, like "brave" and "hero."

It's true that some people struggled with my openness. I'm also sure there were others who called me terrible names behind my back, but who cares when so many people are calling you such wonderful names to your face? My newfound empathy would help me understand why people did such things anyway. I had done it myself, kicking back against what I didn't understand - what scared me.

When I opened up and lived in exposure, amazing things happened. I got my first paid writing gig at a local newspaper. My column became one of their most successful. I came to be a prominent, celebrated public figure in my city - speaking to youth, joining boards of organizations, and being a mentor to those going through their own diagnosis. I became a warrior battling the stigma. And, best of all, I became the kind of person I never knew I wanted to be.

When it comes down to it, we can't connect with each other when our guards are up or when we are presenting a false image. It's when we are honestly objective about ourselves that it gives people the opportunity to identify in a more legitimate way. For at least a moment, if not more, they can forget about their own glass balloons. This is raw human connection at its finest.

People often mistake choosing to be vulnerable as being weak. In the wake of this whole ordeal, I discovered it's the opposite. It is actually strength. When people are brave, it's not that they don't have fear, it's that they feel the fear and do it anyway.[36] It doesn't take guts to try to fit in (like I had always been doing). It takes guts to stand out. *That* is the beauty of preemptive vulnerability.

I loved the results of this transparency and vulnerability so much that, to this day, I still try to live in exposure and be more forthcoming about the real me - my thoughts, my mistakes, my fears, my hopes, my feelings, or any of it in the most objective and honest way that I possibly can. I also still get naked... *a lot.*

This doesn't mean I always do it perfectly. When living as an open book, my pages can't be pristine. They are tattered, torn, and a little muddy. But the whole thing continues to revolutionize my world. The more honest I can be, the more authentic connections I get to make.

---

36. I can't own that one because Oprah, John Wayne, TJ Hoisington, Gloria Steinem, and many more have said some version of this.

What Luke had predicted on the night of my diagnosis was correct: everything really did turn out okay. He didn't just tell me what I wanted to hear. He genuinely believed that I had the strength to do things differently and overcome this. This goes to show that, when someone genuinely believes in you, it gives you that much more courage to continue.

What even Luke couldn't have predicted was that, together, he and I would embark on a different kind of journey. It turned out that he needed me as much as I needed him. Because of Luke, I learned to live more humbly, laugh more freely, and love more deeply. Because of me, Luke learned how to get out of his comfort zone and try new things (which doesn't sound as impressive, but trust me, it was significant).

During my darkest time, we somehow found love. Four years later, we stood up in front of our friends and family - who all loved us despite my HIV status and despite his love of *Judge Judy* and country music - and declared one another as our chosen partner for life. I was indeed getting to live a life well-lived.

This didn't mean I wouldn't ever get embarrassed again. Let's face it, I'm a ditzy goofball mouth-breather who tends to constantly trip over nothing ("Oh, snap!" Goes my self-deprecation). While these things would never change, my reaction to them and acceptance of them would. I'd learn how to play with other kinds of balloons - ones that would never be perfect, but are less fragile and more flexible.

Of course, glass balloons roll their way back into my life from time-to-time. But, after having gone through what I did, rather than hide the cracks that I create, I show them off. Then I figure out how to throw them in the trash. That is until I dig them out later to simply tell another story for anyone who wants to hear.

EPILOGUE

When you tell people you are writing a book, the third most popular question they will ask is "What's the title?" This comes after "What's it about?" and "Are you insane?" The answer to that last one is yes, anyone who chooses to write a book is, at a bare minimum, slightly insane. More on that in a later book.

When I told people the title "Breaking Glass Balloons," I got a wide mix of responses. Some people squealed at how awesome it sounded (I know a lot of squealers). Others would look at me sideways and talk about how they "didn't get it." Then there were those who just flat out said they didn't like it. This all made me very anxious.

In truth, "Breaking Glass Balloons" was not the first title or even the fifth. And, although the book has come to an end, I thought it'd make for a good epilogue to tell you some of the other terrible titles I had come up with. If you're like me, you love a good epilogue. They're like awesome bonus content for books.

The first title that came to me was the ever so eloquent, but ever so boring, "Random Frantic Actions." I stole this title from a lyric in a song by Amanda Palmer: "Can you see the means without the ends, in the random frantic actions that we take?"

I'd like to point out that Ms. Palmer admittedly stole it from author Bill Bryson who used the phrase to describe how electrons work. I *loved* how she used this description of electrons to describe human behavior. But, while it made for a phenomenal lyric, it made for a snoozeable book title.

Then came a title during a period in which I used marijuana edibles to help deal with my god-forsaken insomnia. One night, while super stoned and trying to sleep, I came up with the title "Salty Crackers." It was brilliant. I got out of bed and ran to my office (naked, of course) to write it on a sticky note.

The next morning, when I woke up, I found said sticky note on my computer and thought, *what the fuck?!* When I realized I intended it to be the book title, I actually tossed the idea around for bit. I decided it was *so* brilliant that it actually didn't make any sense.

After that, I came up with "Dog Returns to Vomit." Catchy, huh? Plot twist! I got this one from the bible. I bet you didn't think I would ever be referencing the Bible in this book. It came from Proverbs 26:11 which states, "As a dog returns to his vomit, so a fool repeats his folly."

The moment I heard that passage (shortly after my HIV diagnosis) I saw myself in that dog! It reminded me of my tendency to repeat my mistakes because I couldn't learn the lesson. Now that you've read the final chapter, you know that's what a lot of this book is about.

But I don't consider myself a particularly religious person, which would make it awkward to have a title based on a religious passage. That, and it also lent itself to some majorly gross imagery. Can you imagine picking up a book with that title?

For the next idea, I went for another one of the book's more common themes: my being a total dipshit. I figured I would call it "The Dipshit Diaries." It was a perfect fit. And books with the word "diary" in the title often sell really well. "Diary" insinuates someone's juiciest stories, and I feel I have provided an overwhelming amount of juice here.

While using "diary" in the title may sell it well, though, it also felt predictable and unoriginal - an overused concept in the literary world. Also, pairing the word "shit" next to the word "diary" had the potential for some gross imagery yet again.[37]

Finally, I landed on "The Dipshit Theorem." But I thought This was ironic seeing as how I struggled to even spell the word "theorem." It fit my writing well as it showed my wonky combo of an offbeat, slightly vulgar sense of humor paired with some deep, reflective thought. However, this title didn't roll off the tongue very well and I already have that problem with the name of my blog.

Using the word "dipshit" would also most likely be too harsh for those who weren't already familiar with my work and/or sense of humor. And the "The Dipshit Theorem" sounded more like a super rad self-help book rather than a memoir of short stories. Still, I loved the idea of embarrassment being its own school of thought.

Other random titles included "Lowest Common Denominator" (because that's how I stooped), "Pants On Fire" (because a lot of stories involved me lying), and "Brink of Disaster" (because that should not need any explanation). None of them felt right. I panicked.

I took that panic and ran with it to spew it all over my friend, Dan. He said the most jarring thing a fresh writer could hear: the title isn't *that* important. How could he say that?! He was *clearly* wrong. A title is one of the most important parts of a book!

Just as I got out my shiv to stab him for saying this, he explained. He said to think of my book like a cake. The icing on top can look all fancy and perfect, but if the cake itself is terrible, no one is going to recommend eating it.

I kindly put my shiv away and decided not to stab Dan after all. This simple analogy put my heart at ease. We sat down, workshopped the title,

---

37. If you didn't make the connection, then I will point out that the word "diary" kind of sounds like "diarrhea."

and "Breaking Glass Balloons" won out. This title truly felt right as this *more complex* analogy meant so much to me.

So, my fellow Epilogians (my new word for people who enjoy epilogues), you may have found the icing to look really good or you may have found it to be total crap. But either way, since you made it this far, I would like to thank you for eating my cake. I hope you found it delicious.

ACKNOWLEDGMENTS

After having written this book, I learned that someone cannot "just write a book." I am also learning that I can't stop writing! What is wrong with me?! Make this stop! Anyway, it takes a team of people to make something like this come together and I couldn't have done this without them. Each name you read, take a moment to send them a mental thank you card.

First and foremost, thank you to my editors: Glen P. Trupp, Michael Putnam, George A. Paraskeva, and Dan Balski. If I didn't have these guys, this book would have ended up being a bunch of word garbage. They worked their assess off, they did it for free, and I can never show enough gratitude.

Thank you to everyone involved in the book cover: cover photo by AshLeePhotog, cover concept by Brad Beasley, and cover design and layout formatting by Creative Madness Studio. You all are such incredibly visually talented people. I am beyond fortunate to work with you.

Big thank yous to everyone who gave me permission to write about them (especially my family). Also, thanks to those who didn't give me permission, but aren't going to give me a hard time because I totally changed their names. Thank you to Mike Cusic and everyone else who helped in *The Bare InkSlinger* blog development. Without you, I wouldn't have been able to build such a cool platform prior to this book. Thank you to Thuy Hau for the affordable haircuts. You helped me look my best when I was at my most broke.

Thank you to Brandon Witt for the advice, guidance, and inspiration. You're the most dedicated writer I know. Thanks to John R. Johnson for helping to create the book's synopsis. You are one of the smartest people I know (and I'm flattered that you'd think I know words like "antecedent"). Extra thanks to Dan Balski (again) for taking on a mentorship role, sitting with me for hours (in-person and on the phone), and not letting me off the hook. You are one of the most committed people I know.

Speaking of smart and committed, the biggest recognition and gratitude goes to my partner, Luke Simington. You sacrificed so much to help me on my writing journey: your finances to keep me afloat, your time to cook my meals and read my work, your patience when I kept fucking it up, your heart when I was depressed, and your hope when I said I wanted to give up. You are my rock for life.

Okay, everybody! That's it! Go home! You have your own life to live! (I love you.)

ACKNOWLEDGMENTS

Throughout the book, the author references certain trademarks held by third parties. All rights to the following marks are held by their respective owners: CARE BEAR is a registered trademark of Those Characters From Cleveland, LLC ; SUBWAY and SANDWICH ARTIST are registered trademarks of Subway IP, LLC; MICKEY MOUSE CLUB is a registered trademark of Disney Enterprises, Inc.; OUIJA is a registered trademark of Hasbro, Inc.; KOOL-AID is a registered trademark of Kraft Foods Group Brands, LLC; VOLKSWAGEN and BEETLE are registered trademarks of Volkswagen Aktiergesellschaft Corporation; LIFETIME is a registered trademark of Lifetime Entertainment Services, LLC; RITALIN is a registered trademark of Novartis Corporation; WALMART is a registered trademark of Walmart Apollo, LLC; TACO BELL is a registered trademark of Taco Bell IP Holder, LLC; GAP is a registered trademark of Gap (apparel), LLC; MY LITTLE PONY is a registered trademark of Hasbro, Inc.; TARGET is a registered trademark of Target Brands, Inc.; TEENAGE MUTANT NINJA TURTLES is a registered trademark of Viacom International, Inc.; KMART is a registered trademark of Sears Brands, LLC; GOOD HOUSEKEEPING MAGAZINE is a registered trademark of Hearst Communications, Inc.; TEDDY RUXPIN is a registered trademark of Alchemy II, Inc.; BARBIE is a registered trademark of Mattel, Inc.; TUMS is a registered trademark of SmithKline Beecham Corporation; HIGHLIGHTS FOR KIDS MAGAZINE is a registered trademark of Highlights for Children Inc.; CHEEZ WIZ is a registered trademark of KRAFT Foods Group Brands LLC; MIRACLE WHIP is a registered trademark of KRAFT Foods Group Brands LLC; NATIONAL GEOGRAPHIC is a registered trademark of National Geographic Society Corporation; ROLODEX is a registered trademark of Berol Corporation Corporation; MTV is a registered trademark of Viacom International, Inc.; HOBBY LOBBY is a registered trademark of Hobby Lobby Stores, Inc.; MCDONALDS is a registered trademark of McDonalds Corporation; SPECIAL K Cereal is a registered trademark of Kellogg North America Company Corporation; SQUIRT SODA is a registered trademark of A&W Concentrate Company Corporation; WHELCH'S GRAPE JUICE is a registered trademark of Welch Foods Inc.; HOME DEPOT is a registered trademark of Home Depot Product Authority, LLC; TROLL DOLLS is a registered trademark of DreamWorks Animation, LLC; DRANO is a registered trademark of Johnson & Son, Inc.; RED BULL is a registered trademark of Red Bull GMBH LLC; GENIUS/GENIUS BAR/SIRI is a registered trademark of Apple, Inc.; SMARTWOOL is a registered trademark of TBL Licensing LLC; FACEBOOK is a registered trademark of Facebook, Inc.; MYSPACE is a registered trademark of MySpace, Inc.; SEARS is a registered trademark of Sears Brands, LLC; ETHAN ALLEN is a registered trademark of Ethan Allen Global, LLC; UBER is a registered trademark of Uber Technologies, Inc.; TABASCO is a registered trademark if the Mcilhenny Company; CHIPOTLE is a registered trademark of Chipotle Mexican Grill; and SMART CAR is a registered trademark of Daimler AG.

CPSIA information can be obtained
at www.ICGtesting.com
Printed in the USA
LVHW091721220519
618749LV00005B/679/P